# QE2

## *Forty Years Famous*

First published in Great Britain by Simon & Schuster UK Ltd. 2007
A CBS Company

Copyright © Carol Thatcher

Simon & Schuster UK Ltd
Africa House
64-78 Kingsway
London
WC2B 6AH

3 5 7 9 10 8 6 4 2

Design: Andy Summers, Planet Creative
Editor: Richard Williams

Printed and bound in China

ISBN 13: 978 1 847370334
ISBN 10: 1847 370330

# QE2

*Forty Years Famous*

By Carol Thatcher

With Eric Flounders and Michael Gallagher

SIMON &
SCHUSTER

LONDON · SYDNEY · NEW YORK · TORONTO

*Fireworks herald QE2's departure from Southampton on her 25th World Cruise, January 2007*

# Acknowledgements

There must have been more books written about *QE2* than any other ship except *Titanic*. Some authors have even contrived to write two!

So what is the point of yet another book; what else can be left to say? I hope the main achievement of this book is a comprehensiveness not seen in any other so far, but it also contains much new material – especially relating to the ship's design and construction. Most importantly, though, the purpose of the book is simply to mark the 40th anniversary of *QE2*'s launch – a very significant anniversary indeed.

I am indebted, naturally, to a number of people as books are rarely the product of the author alone.

First, and above all others, I am indebted to Michael Gallagher and Eric Flounders without whom this book would not exist. I am especially grateful for Michael's vast and meticulously referenced personal archive – it is from this that most of this book's new material is taken. Both have reviewed, revised and rewritten the book at length, and it is the better for their efforts.

I am grateful also to a number of former captains and senior Cunard personnel who willingly gave of their time to 'flesh out' some of the well-known stories about the ship. Captains Arnott, Stanley and Woodall were immensely patient in answering questions, as was John Whitworth who was Cunard's managing director when *QE2* entered service. I also received help directly from Captain Peter Jackson, and indirectly from Commodore Ron Warwick whom I interviewed extensively for an earlier book and whose own book proved invaluable for reference.

Thanks also need to go to a select group of public figures, *QE2* fans who took the time and trouble to supply me with their own personal views and memories of their favourite ship.

And, lastly, I must acknowledge the commitment of four individuals from Simon & Schuster, my publishers: Janet Copleston, who had sufficient faith in the nebulous proposal put to her to ensure it became a reality; Paula Borton, managing editor, who guided the project from beginning to end; and Richard Williams and Andy Summers whose meticulous editing and inspired design have resulted in a fine-looking and readable book.

**Carol Thatcher**

This book is dedicated to the memory of Sir Samuel Cunard
without whom there would be no *QE2*.

# Contents

Introduction     8

**Part 1: Origins**     10

**Chapter 1**
A Matter of Pedigree     12

**Chapter 2**
The Queen That Never Was     26

**Chapter 3**
Drama by Design     36

**Part 2: Construction**     56

**Chapter 4**
Conflict and Construction     58

**Part 3: *QE2* in Service**     106

**Chapter 5**
Making an Impression     108

**Chapter 6**
A Decade for Decision     148

**Chapter 7**
Coming of Age     180

**Chapter 8**
Breaking Records     220

Appendices     248
    General Information
    *QE2* Masters
    Famous Faces on Board
    The Royal Connection
    *QE2* World Cruises and Extended Voyages

Bibliography     252

Index     253

Picture Credits     256

# Introduction

QE2 is the most famous ship in existence: she has been for over 40 years. Rarely has she been far from the news, for good reason or bad. She has become a strikingly potent symbol, recognised around the world, not just of all that is best in Britain, but of the enduring excellence of Scottish engineering. So far she has sailed around 5.5 million nautical miles, more than any other ship ever, has completed 25 full world cruises, and has crossed the Atlantic, surely the world's cruellest sea, over 800 times; yet her hull is as sound today as the day she first slipped into the waters of the Clyde 40 years ago.

QE2 is a magnet for well-wishers wherever she goes; thousands turn out to greet her, not just out of passing curiosity but because they love her. It is impossible to say just why this should be so, but it is so; QE2 is celebrated, acclaimed, revered and respected.

Yet it is a miracle she ever came into being at all. In the early sixties, in a miasma of muddled management and indecision, Cunard began planning replacement tonnage for the ageing *Queen Mary* and *Queen Elizabeth*. With alarming consistency the company made the wrong decisions, and only as late as the last minute was it pushed by external forces into avoiding disaster. But what this relatively conservative company eventually embarked on was a revolutionary replacement, 25 years ahead of her time: *QE2*.

## A Difficult Birth

After a shaky conception, *QE2's* gestation and birth were bedevilled by one potentially fatal drama after another. Building *QE2* was 'hell', said Cunard's company secretary at the time. Strikes, management incompetence, restrictive practices, vandalism, financial crises, business reorganisation and larceny on a grand scale all conspired to make the process of *QE2's* construction one of conflict and recrimination.

Even when she took to sea and could be seen by all to be one of the most beautiful ships ever built, truly

*Above: An aerial view of* QE2 *in the Clyde, immediately after her launch on 20 September 1967*

the pride of the Clyde, she was dismissed by City analysts rather unoriginally as 'a white elephant' that, in another inappropriate metaphor, would be 'mothballed' within six months. The age of the transatlantic liner, they said, was dead.

Well, how wrong they were. *QE2* is still here, still wowing the crowds, still making money and, even at 40, still looking impressively modern. The aforementioned analysts, of course, are not.

*QE2* has spent all her 40 years in the limelight, and her career at sea has been even more eventful than her birth. It has not all been exotic voyages and ecstatic welcomes. It has included sailing 6,000 nautical miles south, partly through an icefield in the dark, without radar, to make her singular contribution to the Falklands War; it has involved various threats, from extortionists, from the IRA and from the Libyan government; it has included rescuing all the passengers from a liner in distress, and having all hers similarly rescued after she hit rocks; it has featured visits from every senior member of the Royal Family, from prime ministers and presidents, rock stars and film stars, and from Nelson Mandela. Not a year has passed without something happening that would have been once-in-a-lifetime for any other ship – and usually hitting the headlines in the process.

*QE2* has been a phenomenon for 40 years, and there is no doubt she will continue to be so for a few more. She is just one of a long line of noble Cunard transatlantic liners, but she has served longer than any other, she has travelled further than any other, she has visited more places around the globe than any other, and arguably she is more loved than any other. Like her predecessors *QE2* has pedigree, but she is the ultimate triumph of a great tradition.

*The distance travelled by* QE2 *in her lifetime equates to 15 return trips to the moon.*

# Origins **1**

# Chapter 1
# A Matter of Pedigree

Samuel Cunard was an austere and conservative man, measured in his judgements and with little tendency to hyperbole or overt displays of emotion. But even he, with all his reserve, might be induced to do a little jig of delight at the end of the pier if he were able now to see his company's newest transatlantic liner, *Queen Mary 2*, surging up Southampton Water at the end of another 3,000-nautical mile journey from New York. Because, fearless and forward-looking though his original concept may have been, nothing in Cunard's most exquisite dreams could have hinted at what his fledgling company would become.

When we think of Cunard Line now, two things immediately spring to mind: Britishness and luxury.

Britishness, partly because at so many crucial periods in this island's history Cunard has been there: Cunard ships took to Crimea all the horses that charged with the Light Brigade; it was a Cunard ship, the little *Carpathia*, that raced through an icefield in the night to rescue the survivors of the *Titanic*; they were Cunard ships that carried over 2.5 million emigrants from the poverty of the Old World to a new life in the New; they were Cunard ships, *Queen Mary* and *Queen Elizabeth*, that – according to Churchill – shortened the Second World War by a year as a result of their unescorted high-speed shuttling across the Atlantic bringing over 15,000 US troops at a time; and they were Cunard ships, along with others, that made victory in the Falklands possible.

And luxury along with Britishness, because the abiding view of Cunard is impeccable white-gloved

*The Canadian founder of a British institution: Samuel Cunard (1787–1865)*

service, the clink of the teacup, potted palms, string quartets and film stars gliding back and forth across the Atlantic.

## Survival Against the Odds

However, the eventual fame of the Cunard name, the degree to which it became synonymous with a sybaritic lifestyle, and its perception as being quintessentially British, would have seemed odd to Samuel Cunard back in 1839 as he contemplated the setting up of the company. Its survival for 168 years would have seemed even odder to observers, including those who rejected the opportunity to join the venture, who thought Cunard had taken on much more than he – or anyone else – could possible manage.

The oddest thing is that the company was ever formed by a man like Cunard at all. The gamble, the challenge, the uncertainty, the sheer modernity of it all would have sat well with a maverick genius like Brunel, but not with Samuel Cunard. To begin with, a Canadian of American parentage does not seem the classic candidate to establish a British icon. A man so unremittingly prudent, conservative, cautious, austere – and, let's face it, old – doesn't seem the man to take such huge economic risks or to push so far the boundaries of known technology.

By the time he came to set up the British and North American Royal Mail Steam Packet Company, as the company was originally known, Samuel Cunard was already a prosperous businessman and significant figure in Nova Scotia. He was a comfortably settled widower, with his children around him, and at an age by which most people in those days were already dead. A gentle retirement in the cosy glow of local esteem seemed to lie ahead rather than the creation of a commercial revolution.

## A Monumental Gamble

Yet in 1839, Cunard gambled everything he had to set up, thousands of miles from home, a highly speculative and enormously risky venture uncomfortably close to the forefront of known technology. To do it, he even uprooted himself from his native Nova Scotia and took up residence in London. It all seems markedly out of character

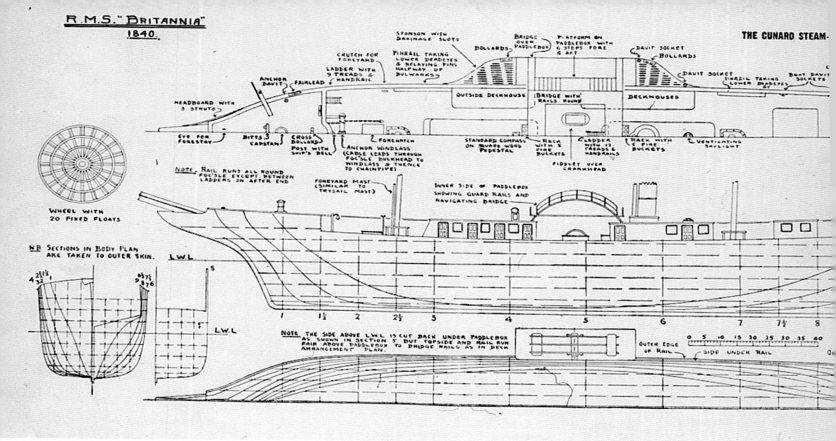

with everything he'd done before, and with everything he did subsequently when the company settled down to be a singularly cautious and conservative one in the mould of the founder.

What stimulated Cunard's interest in establishing an entirely revolutionary transatlantic steamship service a mere two years after the first successful crossing by steam was an advertisement that appeared in *The Times*. The notice, placed by the British Admiralty – at that time responsible for carrying the Royal Mail overseas – invited tenders for the provision of a timetabled steamship service between Britain and North America to carry the Royal Mail. A contract of £55,000 a year was offered. The spur for the Admiralty's apparent generosity was the grotesquely vulnerable service provided for the mail by sailing ships. The journey times were 'flexible', with a transatlantic crossing lasting for six weeks, and with no fixed times of departure or arrival. So it was never known when the mail would arrive – or, since so many sailing ships foundered – whether it would arrive at all. What the Admiralty wanted, in line with the thrusting technology of the Victorian age, was a maritime extension of the brand new timetabled railways on land.

## A Foolhardy Venture?

Unable to find partners in Nova Scotia for what must have seemed a foolhardy venture, Cunard submitted his successful bid beyond the Admiralty's deadline, without sufficient finance,

MPANY LIMITED.

*Deckplan for* Britannia. *This is not an original as it is issued by the Cunard Steam-ship Company Limited rather than the British and North American Royal Mail Steam Packet Company, Cunard's original company name.*

with no steamships and with limited knowledge of what, technically, was required. His bid was successful despite all this because, unlike his competitors who told the Admiralty what they should have, rather than bid on the basis of what was asked for, Cunard's bid – like the man – was straightforward. He offered simply to provide the required service for the sum offered. He then went on to sign a contract with potentially ruinous clauses: £15,000 payable for any cancelled sailing, and £500 for each day a ship was late.

Nonetheless, Cunard found his financial backing in Scotland and Liverpool, and after having ordered four ships – each twice as big as he'd originally intended – renegotiated the contract, from a position of strength, to be marginally more favourable.

---

*Passenger on* Britannia *to officer:*
'There's water pouring down the stairs.'
Officer to passenger: 'We only worry, madam, when it's coming up the stairs.'

---

Cunard's first ship, the 1,156-ton *Britannia*, left Liverpool on 4 July 1840 with Cunard himself on board, and arrived on schedule in Halifax just ten days later. Within a year *Britannia* and her

three sister ships were providing a timetabled weekly steamship service across the Atlantic – the first ever.

Cunard's early ships were far removed from the luxury associated with them now; indeed, Cunard and luxury were total strangers. Like the man, the ships were plain, practical, sturdy and unostentatious. Cabins were small – like a 'profoundly preposterous box', according to Charles Dickens, who travelled on *Britannia* in 1842. Each was divided from the next by a partition, atop which sat a shared candle; there was a wooden bunk with a straw mattress and a small cupboard. Passengers were responsible for washing their own plates and cutlery, though eating was often far from their minds in inclement weather as they paddled about below decks ankle-deep in water. 'There's water pouring down the stairs,' exclaimed one early passenger to an officer. 'We only worry, madam,' he replied, 'when it's coming up the stairs.' Fresh meat ran out early in each voyage, after which salted meat was all that was available, and milk was supplied by a cow slung on the deck in a hammock.

China, *Cunard's first propeller-driven ship*

## Cunard in the First World War

During the four years of carnage that made up the First World War, Cunard ships transported over a million men, served as hospital ships, prisoner-of-war ships, food and munitions carriers, and as armed merchant cruisers. It was in the latter role that the *Carmania* had the distinction of taking the first German casualty of the war when she sank the *Cap Trafalgar* off South America in November 1914. Another Cunard ship, *Campania*, was equipped with a 73m (240ft) long platform and so became the forerunner of today's aircraft carriers.

All in all, over 22 Cunard ships were lost – including the unrequisitioned *Lusitania*, which was torpedoed by *U20* off the Old Head of Kinsale in 1915 with the loss of 1,200 civilian lives.

But uncomfortable and basic though they were, Cunard's steamships had two great advantages over sailing ships: first, they got the agony over more quickly – ten days as opposed to six weeks – and second, they were steadfastly safe and reliable. Cunard himself made safety his priority – and to this day Cunard has never been responsible for the loss of a single passenger or a single mailbag on the Atlantic run.

Cunard's original instruction to his first master, Captain Woodroffe, was simply 'Speed is nothing…safety is all that is required,' and that has been followed religiously by the company ever since – even when, in later years, there was great competition for the Blue Riband. Though Cunard ships held the coveted transatlantic speed record for over 61 years, when a trophy was made in the 1930s as a manifestation of the regularised record, Sir Percy Bates – then chairman of Cunard – refused to accept it despite Cunard's *Queen Mary* being the current holder.

> '*Speed is nothing…safety is all that is required.*' ***Samuel Cunard***

Cunard's safety record – which was such that passengers would refuse to board the ships of other lines but insist on waiting for the next Cunarder – together with the mail contract, made Cunard's profits.

### War Service

The company's first excursion into war, however, produced a serious risk to that prosperity. In 1854, nine Cunard ships – almost the entire fleet – were requisitioned for the Crimean War. While the company's contribution to the war effort was remarkable – including transporting all the horses that charged with the Light Brigade and carrying the injured to Florence Nightingale's hospital in Scutari – almost all Cunard mail services on the

Atlantic stopped. Competition, notably the much-subsidised American Collins Line, won Cunard's lucrative business by default. The Crimean War gave Samuel Cunard a baronetcy – but it gave Collins a virtual monopoly on the Atlantic.

However, over-expansion and a cavalier attitude to safety did for Collins, which, despite being subsidised by the American government to twice the value of Cunard's mail contract on condition that 'its ships could outstrip Cunard', went bankrupt in 1858. Cunard quickly regained its pre-eminence.

Samuel Cunard's innate conservatism, which made the founding of the company so remarkable, flared up again in the late 1850s when he refused to change from paddle wheels to propellers – despite mounting evidence that screw propulsion was more efficient, more powerful and made more space available. He only relented in 1862 with the construction of the *China* – after first having to seek the permission of the Admiralty as the mail contract specified 'paddle steamers'.

next guarantee of prosperity. Between 1860 and 1900, 14 million people emigrated from Europe to the United States and Canada. Of those, 4.5 million passed through Liverpool; and of those, half made the voyage with Cunard.

Cunard's next challenge was the introduction of 'floating hotels', spearheaded by the newly formed White Star's *Oceanic* in 1870. Where *Oceanic* had bathtubs, Cunard offered a basin; where *Oceanic* had central heating, Cunard offered stoves; where *Oceanic* had taps, Cunard offered jugs; where *Oceanic* had lamps, Cunard offered candles; and where *Oceanic* had lavatories, Cunard managed with chamber pots.

Declining revenues forced Cunard to follow suit, and even to innovate. The *Servia* of 1881 was the first steel Cunarder, the first to be built with an electricity supply, the first to have ensuite bathrooms and – interestingly – the first budgeted to rely solely on passenger revenue. The reliance on the mail diminished even more.

## The Business of Emigration

The *China* also hinted at a coming decline in the importance of the mail contract, as it was the first ship specifically to cater for emigrants. And so emigration became Cunard's

*Crew on board* Carpathia *(1903–1918).* Carpathia *achieved worldwide fame when she rescued all the survivors of* Titanic.

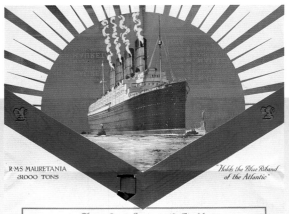

R·M·S MAURETANIA
31000 TONS

"Holds the Blue Riband of the Atlantic"

Fastest Ocean Service in the World
Sailings from SOUTHAMPTON (via Cherbourg) to NEW YORK

| | | | |
|---|---|---|---|
| WED. FEB. 9 | MAURETANIA | SAT. MAY 7 | BERENGARIA |
| WED. FEB. 16 | AQUITANIA | SAT. MAY 14 | MAURETANIA |
| WED. MAR. 2 | BERENGARIA | SAT. MAY 21 | AQUITANIA |
| WED. MAR. 9 | AQUITANIA | SAT. MAY 28 | BERENGARIA |
| SAT. MAR. 26 | BERENGARIA | SAT. JUNE 4 | MAURETANIA |
| SAT. APR. 2 | MAURETANIA | SAT. JUNE 11 | AQUITANIA |
| SAT. APR. 9 | AQUITANIA | SAT. JUNE 18 | BERENGARIA |
| SAT. APR. 16 | BERENGARIA | SAT. JUNE 25 | MAURETANIA |
| SAT. APR. 23 | MAURETANIA | SAT. JULY 2 | AQUITANIA |
| SAT. APR. 30 | AQUITANIA | SAT. JULY 9 | BERENGARIA |
| | SAT. JULY 16 | MAURETANIA | |

CUNARD

*An early 1920s advertisement showing* Mauretania

*Magazine spread about preparing* Aquitania *for her next voyage*

## Carpathia *and* Titanic

The year 1902 saw the virtually unnoticed launch on the Tyne of a minor Cunarder destined for the Mediterranean trade – and also destined to become one of the most famous ships of all time. She was the 13,600-ton *Carpathia* which, in 1912, achieved immortality under the command of Captain Arthur Rostron when she sped through icefields in the night, without the benefit of modern radar and at a speed greater than she was supposedly capable of, to rescue all the survivors of the *Titanic*. Captain Rostron, later commodore of the Cunard fleet, master of the *Queen Mary*, and knighted by the king, remarked that a hand greater than his own guided the little ship that night.

But that was glory yet to come; when *Carpathia* was entering service Cunard was looking none too glorious, battered as the company's ageing transatlantic fleet was by ferocious competition from the Germans and Americans. However, Cunard's fight back led to the introduction of three of the company's most famous ships – *Lusitania, Mauretania* and *Aquitania*. These were the first 'floating palaces' in the Cunard fleet – palaces that moved at unprecedented speed. The *Mauretania* held the Blue Riband for 22 years.

Again the company was ensnared in conflict when its ships were requisitioned for the First World War. During the four years, Cunard ships served as troopships, hospital ships, prisoner-of-war ships, food and munitions carriers, and as armed merchant cruisers. Cunard paid a heavy price for its involvement – 22 of its ships were lost. After the war, the Cunard fleet was bolstered by the addition, as part of war reparations, of the former German vessel *Imperator*, renamed *Berengaria*.

## First World Cruise

The inter-war years were successful and lucrative for Cunard – so much so that the company seemed not to notice the significance of Charles Lindbergh's transatlantic flight in 1927. Nonetheless, the first real move from reliance on transatlantic revenues was made when, in 1922, *Laconia* undertook the first-ever world cruise.

*Captain Arthur Rostron*

Cunard did not set out to create in 1928 what King George V called 'the stateliest ship now in being', nor did it intend to give birth to a ship which her last master, Captain John Treasure Jones, said was 'the nearest ship ever to a living being'.

---

'…the nearest ship ever to a living being'.
*Captain John Treasure Jones on*
**Queen Mary**

---

It was purely by chance that the company produced a ship which more graphically shared the country's triumphs and tribulations, and which was more loved by people who had never even seen her, let alone set foot on her, than any that had gone before.

Cunard's intention in 1928 had been simply to replace its ageing transatlantic fleet with a new pair of steamships that could provide a weekly service in each direction and so meet the growing challenge of German competition on the North Atlantic. When the first of the pair, No. 534, later to be named *Queen Mary*, was revealed to be the largest and most powerful ship ever built, the chairman of Cunard, Sir Percy Bates, diffidently said she was just 'the smallest and slowest ship that could accomplish such a service'.

Work on No. 534 began at the Clydebank yard of John Brown and Co late in 1930. She was being built at an estimated cost of £6.5 million out of Cunard revenue, without the benefit of any state subsidy. Almost alone at the time Cunard operated on the North Atlantic as a commercial concern. Every other major line was subsidised to a significant degree by its national government, but Cunard was expected not only to compete but to ensure Britain remained dominant on the North Atlantic without a penny of state aid.

## The Depression

The company did so until the Depression cut revenues of £9 million in 1928 to under £4 million in 1931, and despite Cunard staff on shore and at sea taking a pay cut, work on the construction of *Queen Mary* stopped just before Christmas 1931.

It was not until April 1934 that Neville Chamberlain, then Chancellor of the Exchequer, made funds available for the work to restart. Only five months later, Queen Mary, wife of George V, launched the ship that bore her name in an emotional ceremony on the Clyde.

## England's Most Illustrious Queen

A popular story has it that Cunard's board had not intended to name the ship *Queen Mary*, but to stick to the traditional 'ia' endings prevalent among the Cunard transatlantic fleet. They despatched one of their members, Lord Royden, to ask his friend the king for permission to name the ship *Queen Victoria*. Allegedly, he didn't ask directly but intimated that Cunard would like to name the ship after 'England's most illustrious queen'. 'My wife will be delighted,' replied King George, 'I will go and tell her now.'

A good story – but not true. Cunard had already decided that since the White Star and Cunard transatlantic fleets had been combined under the new banner, Cunard White Star, neither the traditional White Star 'ic' ending nor the Cunard 'ia' ending was appropriate. The first ship of the new company needed to break with tradition – and *Queen Mary* it was to be.

The maiden voyage began in Southampton on 27 May 1936, and *Queen Mary* left to the sounds of bands and ecstatic crowds. On board were the famous bandleader, Henry Hall, scheduled to give a series of live radio broadcasts during the crossing; the virtuoso harmonica player, Larry

*Australian troops board* Queen Mary *in 1941*

Adler; and a well-known singer of the time, Frances Day, who performed a song written specially for *Queen Mary* by Henry Hall, 'Somewhere at Sea'. Much as she may have liked being at sea, Miss Day did not trust the ship's eggs to be fresh by the end of the voyage so she took along her own hens.

The rapturous welcome in New York on 1 June 1936 marked the completion of the first voyage of four years of glamorous transatlantic service, during which *Queen Mary* gained the Blue Riband twice for the fastest Atlantic crossing.

The sister ship to *Queen Mary, Queen Elizabeth*, had a less glorious start. She was launched in 1938 by Queen Elizabeth, wife of George VI – who could not be present himself because the growing pressures of impending war kept him in London – accompanied by Princess Elizabeth, the present queen, and Princess Margaret.

## A Secret Voyage

As fitting-out work was progressing it was decided that not only was *Queen Elizabeth* a target for German air attacks, but she was also occupying Clydeside shipyard space required for the war effort. She had to move.

The captain put to sea, with workmen still on board, and once out of the Clyde opened his sealed orders, which he expected to instruct him to go to Southampton; instead, he was told to head at full speed to New York. The secret dash was done with the launching gear still affixed to the underside of the ship, and without proper fitments inside. Men who expected to be going home by train from Southampton within days did not get home for months.

After bringing troops from Australia, in 1942 *Queen Mary* and *Queen Elizabeth* began bringing American GIs across to Europe at full speed and unescorted. Not only were they faster than the U-boats whose crews had been offered £100,000 by Hitler to sink either of them, but they were faster even than the torpedoes. In summer, 15,000 soldiers were carried on each voyage – such a huge number that the men had to sleep in shifts, observing a strict one-way system on board. *Queen Mary's* master, Commodore Sir James Bisset, noted that the ship was so difficult to handle under these circumstances that he was concerned for her stability. All told she made 28 such trips, taking soldiers eastbound

*Cunard has never been responsible for the loss of a single passenger or a single mailbag on the Atlantic run.*

Queen Mary *in wartime livery*

and prisoners-of-war westbound, with *Queen Elizabeth* undertaking a similar number. On three occasions *Queen Mary* was the nerve-centre of the Empire as Sir Winston Churchill crossed the Atlantic to see President Roosevelt.

The trooping record of the two *Queens*, together with *Aquitania*, reduced the duration of the war – according to Churchill – by at least a year.

## Film Stars and Royalty

After the war *Queen Mary* and *Queen Elizabeth* had a golden period, doing what they were built to do. This was the era of film stars and royalty being photographed by dozens of press photographers as they stepped ashore in Southampton or New York. But in 1958 the ghost of that Lindbergh flight caught up with Cunard as, for the first time, more people crossed the Atlantic by air than by sea.

Finally, *Queen Mary* left New York for the last time on 22 September 1967 – her 1,001st voyage. This was just two days after the launch by Her Majesty The Queen of *Queen Elizabeth 2*. During the crossing she passed *Queen Elizabeth* for the last time, just a nautical mile distant, at a combined speed of 60 knots.

## The Last Voyage

Having carried 2,114,000 passengers, plus 810,730 military personnel, 19,000 GI brides and 4,000 child evacuees, and having travelled 3,794,017 nautical miles, *Queen Mary* left on her last journey from Southampton on 31 October 1967, bound for her present home in Long Beach, California. On board were two double-decker London buses, and the passengers on board delighted in rounding Cape Horn on a bus.

She arrived to an ecstatic welcome in Long Beach where she remains today – officially now a building, rather than one of the greatest ships ever built.

*Queen Elizabeth* ended her career just a year later in an ignominious fashion, just as she had started it in less triumphant circumstances than *Queen Mary*. Sold by Cunard in 1968, she eventually ended up in Hong Kong, undergoing conversion into a floating university. There, in 1972, a number of mysterious fires broke out simultaneously and, inundated by millions of gallons of water from fire hoses, the ship turned over and sank – her side visible above the water.

The sale of *Queen Mary* and *Queen Elizabeth* was the nadir of Cunard's fortunes. Towards the end the ships had been criss-crossing the Atlantic virtually empty – on one voyage *Queen Elizabeth* had only 200 passengers – and in so doing they were losing the company £4 million a year.

Yet, in what seemed to many an act of lunacy equal only to Samuel Cunard's original madness in establishing the company, the Cunard board was planning to construct another transatlantic liner. Or maybe two.

*Between them, Queen Mary and Queen Elizabeth carried many celebrities and famous Hollywood stars across the Atlantic. Clockwise from top left: Fred Astaire, Cary Grant, Gregory Peck and family, Victor Mature, Tennessee Williams, Marlene Dietrich, Elizabeth Taylor.*

# *Queen Mary* Survives the Depression

When the Depression stopped work on *Queen Mary* just before Christmas in 1931, 3,640 men in Clydebank – a town where half the wages came from that ship – were thrown out of work.

The rusting skeleton of *Queen Mary*, with 80 per cent of the hull rivets in place and £1.5 million already spent, was symbolic of the financial catastrophe that had hit both Britain and America. It was such a potent symbol, and the public was so conscious of it, that people sent thousands of unsolicited donations of money to Cunard in an effort to get the work restarted.

The government was implored to lend Cunard the capital to complete the ship and get so many back to work – but it steadfastly refused. Until 1934, that is, when, in a complex deal that required Cunard to take over the running of White Star's ailing transatlantic fleet, Neville Chamberlain, then the Chancellor of the Exchequer, agreed to lend Cunard sufficient to complete *Queen Mary* and build her sister, *Queen Elizabeth*.

So, on 3 April 1934, the John Brown workforce, led by the Dalmuir Pipe Band, returned to work and began by removing 130 tonnes of rust and dozens of nesting crows.

Just five months later *Queen Mary*, wife of King George V, became the first monarch to launch a merchant ship, a job she accomplished with a bottle of Australian wine rather than the traditional French champagne. As she said the words, broadcast over the radio: 'I name this ship *Queen Mary*; may God bless her and all who sail in her' millions of the king's subjects heard his wife's voice for the very first time.

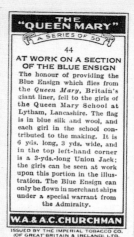

## All Hands on Deck

*A series of cigarette cards celebrated the building of* Queen Mary. *Here, Lancashire schoolgirls are given the task of sewing the Blue Ensign for the massive ship.*

## A National Disaster

*When work stopped on* Queen Mary *the ripples were felt by 10,000 ancillary workers further away. They were felt in Stoke-on-Trent, busy working on 200,000 pieces of crockery; in Sheffield, where 100,000 items of cutlery were being crafted; in Walsall, which was producing 400 tonnes of tubes; in Rugby, manufacturing seven turbo-generators; in Liverpool, producing 300m² (3,200 sq ft) of toughened glass; in Millwall, casting four 6m (20ft) propellers; in Darlington, forging the 190-tonne stern frame; in Belfast, working on the 5.5 tonne gear wheels; in Halifax, weaving 16km (10 miles) of blankets; in St Albans, producing 600 clocks; and in other towns up and down the land making curtains, carpets, anchor chains and furniture. All of them stopped.*

## Propellers From Millwall

*Workmen manhandle one of* Queen Mary's *monster propellers into position.*

THE "QUEEN MARY" COMPARED WITH THE FIRST CUNARDER

### THE "QUEEN MARY"

A SERIES OF 50

47

#### THE "QUEEN MARY" COMPARED WITH THE FIRST CUNARDER

The remarkable progress in shipbuilding is emphasized in this most interesting comparison of the giant liner *Queen Mary* and the *Britannia*—the first Cunarder—which sailed on her maiden voyage from Liverpool on July 4th, 1840. She was driven by paddle-wheels, was barque-rigged, and used her sails in addition to her engines. The passage to Boston took 14 days 8 hours, at a speed of 8½ knots. The *Britannia* was 207 ft. long, and 1,154 tons, while the *Queen Mary* is nearly five times this length, with a tonnage in the region of sixty-three times that of the pioneer ship.

**W.A.& A.C.CHURCHMAN**

ISSUED BY THE IMPERIAL TOBACCO CO. (OF GREAT BRITAIN & IRELAND) LTD.

## Size Matters

*This cigarette card shows the comparative sizes of* Queen Mary *and* Britannia, *highlighting the huge progress in shipbuilding in less than a century.*

'I name this ship *Queen Mary,* may God bless her and all who sail in her.' *Queen Mary launching* **Queen Mary**

## Stepping the Masts

*One of the processes involved in the building of* Queen Mary *that required ground-breaking engineering techniques.*

### THE "QUEEN MARY"

A SERIES OF 50

14

#### MASTS IN POSITION

The difficult and dangerous operation of erecting, or "stepping," the 2 graceful steel masts of the *Queen Mary* in true alignment and rake, is shown completed in this illustration. These masts are steel tubular poles reaching a height of 234 ft. above the keel. The base of each extends downwards through 2 decks before being fastened down, but even below this point substantial local stiffening is introduced to ensure a firm foundation. To-day the masts fulfil many useful functions, such as the carrying of navigating lights and signal yards for flag signals, while one of increasing importance is the carrying of wireless aerials for wireless telegraphy and telephony.

**W.A.& A.C.CHURCHMAN**

ISSUED BY THE IMPERIAL TOBACCO CO. (OF GREAT BRITAIN & IRELAND) LTD.

THE "QUEEN MARY": MASTS IN POSITION

# Chapter 2
# *The* Queen *That Never Was*

Because of the outbreak of the Second World War, *Queen Mary* and *Queen Elizabeth* – launched respectively in 1934 and 1938 – were unable to operate in tandem across the Atlantic as planned until 1946, when peace had returned to Europe, and American GIs (together with their brides) had been returned to the United States.

The succeeding years, certainly to the end of the 1950s, saw not just the realisation of the Cunard company's long-held ambition of a two-ship weekly transatlantic service but also a high point in the company's public image. Cunard was already known for its grand hotel standards, properly established with the introduction of *Mauretania* and *Lusitania* in 1907. However, the rise of Hollywood and its creation of stars desperate to be 'big' on both sides of the Atlantic handed Cunard a continuing publicity opportunity it did not hesitate to exploit. Like everyone else, glamorous film stars had no realistic option but to cross the Atlantic by sea, and for many the shipping line of choice was Cunard – firmly established as a beacon not just of sophistication and luxury, but also of safety. Where there are stars, there are cameras; each arrival in New York or Southampton was met by droves of newspaper photographers and reporters, and the resulting pictures of arriving notables would, much to Cunard's benefit, hit the papers the following day. Of such things are reputations made.

If this golden period were to continue beyond the 1950s, particularly in the face of competition from increasingly attractive jet aeroplanes, Cunard knew it had to replace the ageing *Queen Mary* and *Queen Elizabeth*. These grand old ships were just too grand and too old.

## Two New *Queens*

The company was equally certain it had to replace them with not one, but with two similar large, fast and single-purpose ships; to Cunard executives these were known by the shorthand *Q3*, destined to replace *Queen Mary*, and *Q4*, destined later to replace *Queen Elizabeth*.

*'The Queen That Never Was', a painting of the projected Q3 by Mervyn Pearson (courtesy of David Williams)*

The two-ship plan involved vessels just like the *Queens* but with updated technology. It never entered Cunard's corporate head that some flexibility might be introduced to these ships so that in winter months, when transatlantic travel could be far from pleasant, the ships could stay full by going cruising instead. The company's tunnel-vision deemed the replacement ships to be for the transatlantic trade only.

Originally convinced that it could build these new ships without subsidy or government loan, Cunard soon realised that the estimated cost of £40 million was beyond the means of a company whose revenue in 1957 – the first year the numbers of people crossing the Atlantic by air equalled those crossing by sea – was down by over £6 million on the previous year. Cunard's financial problems were exacerbated by the fact that the move to the jet, which still offered a fairly modest capacity, was greatest among the rich. And the rich were Cunard's people.

## French and US Competition

Further, Cunard was not simply facing competition from the air, but also from heavily subsidised French and American shipping lines. In 1957, the new 66,000-ton *France* was ordered, its construction costs heavily supported by the French government – which also undertook to subsidise its operation once in service. Similarly the US

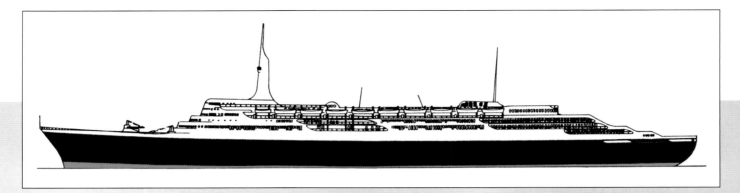

government built the *United States* at a cost of $75 million, and then proceeded to sell it to United States Lines for a mere $34 million.

The argument for Cunard to 'go it alone' was shot to pieces, and if a government loan was required so was the prospect of the company doing just what it wanted. The old adage about paying pipers and calling tunes must have crossed the minds of the Cunard board members.

---

'We cannot justify to our shareholders a larger expenditure on *Q3* than £12 million and nor can we afford anything more than that figure.' *Colonel Denis Bates, chairman of Cunard*

---

Cunard's auditors, Cooper Bros, issued a memorandum on 21 January 1959 that stated: 'If Government aid is not obtained, *Q3* and *Q4* cannot be built.' Colonel Denis Bates, brother of the late Sir Percy Bates and now himself chairman of Cunard, wrote: 'We cannot justify to our shareholders a larger expenditure on *Q3* than £12 million and nor can we afford anything more than that figure.'

In March 1959 Colonel Bates told the Annual Meeting of Cunard shareholders that the entire future of the North Atlantic service had been placed before the government. Bates commented: 'Faced with the overwhelming odds of ever-increasing governmental subsidies to our competitors on the score of national prestige, your Board have decided it is impossible to continue with such unequal and unfair competition to free enterprise.'

What he did not say, however, was that the government did not agree with Cunard's rather outmoded and blinkered view of the replacement ships; and if government money were being used, government opinion was almost certain to prevail.

In April 1959, as discussions concerning the financing of replacement vessels continued between Cunard and the government, John Brown and Co, of Clydebank, builder of both *Queen Mary* and *Queen Elizabeth*, was engaged to draw up preliminary plans and outline specifications for ships of the 'express' type – each of 80,000 gross tonnage (grt) and capable of 30 knots.

Official public notice of plans to replace the *Queens* was given on 8 April 1959 when the House of Commons was told that negotiations were under way with Cunard to try to maintain the North Atlantic service, and that the estimated

*Queen Elizabeth's two-funnel design made her easy to tell apart from her three-funnelled sister, Queen Mary*

*Left: A drawing of the proposed Q3 vessel issued in March 1961*

cost of each of two ships would be in the order of £30 million.

## The Speed and Size Equation

Several issues needed to be taken into account when planning vessels to replace the *Queens*. These included speed, since the distance between Southampton and New York required, on a two-ship basis, a minimum speed of 28.5 knots. Capacity and the space available per passenger was crucial; if overall dimensions became excessive, an increase in the engine power and fuel required for the same speed would be needed, and berthing would become problematical – as to some extent it already was for *Queen Mary* and *Queen Elizabeth*. But additionally, in the more egalitarian post-war age, the question of class exercised the minds of the designers. Most lines had already done away with the old three-class

system in favour of a relatively small First Class and a much bigger Tourist Class. Air travel was still expensive, and if ships were to compete they had to maximise the number that could travel at modest cost.

When the designs were advanced enough, Cunard approached the government for a loan of £40 million. It was not rebuffed.

---

'…as the government is already a shareholder in the Cunard Company, it is therefore natural that it should be interested in plans for replacing the two transatlantic liners.'
*Ministry of Transport spokesman*

---

In diverting criticism of government involvement in the financing of a private company, the Minister of Transport responded to a

questioner in the House of Commons by saying: '…as the government is already a shareholder in the Cunard Company, it is therefore natural that it should be interested in plans for replacing the two transatlantic liners.'

The government went on to allay fears by announcing that Cunard would receive no financial commitment until a government committee had looked at the options and reported back. This was the point at which Cunard's preferred option began to unravel….

## The Chandos Committee

In September 1959, the Government set up the three-man Chandos Committee. These men, Lord Chandos, John Hobhouse and Thomas Robson (with J N Wood as secretary), had the responsibility of evaluating the situation and reporting back by June 1960. The committee began with Cunard's favoured assumption that two liners would ultimately be built to replace the *Queens* and maintain the existing service. After initial investigations, two 75,000-ton ships were considered with speeds of 30 knots and passenger capacities of 2,270. Before long, however, the Chandos Committee was diverging from Cunard's insistence on replacing like-for-like.

Minutes from the seventh meeting of the Chandos Committee held on 31 December 1959 reported Lord Chandos as saying: '…there was no

possibility of the Committee's recommending replacement of the *Queens* by two ships of similar size….' The committee favoured exploring the possibility of a smaller, dual-purpose ship that could offer transatlantic services for part of the year, and warm-weather cruises in the winter months.

The committee also estimated the return on the total investment would be under 2 per cent, while if Cunard were to be assured of a reasonable return on their own capital of £12 million it would be impossible to repay fully any of the remaining £17 million loan. On these grounds alone it would be difficult for the committee to recommend to the government the building of two ships of the size envisaged by Cunard.

---

'…there was no possibility of the Committee's recommending replacement of the *Queens* by two ships of similar size….'
*Minutes of the Chandos Committee*

---

Chandos also believed that such a subsidy would give Cunard an unfair advantage over the competition, and that the main arguments in favour of a subsidy were on the grounds of defence and prestige. The committee had not yet received formal advice on the strategic value of the *Queens'* replacement but it seemed that it would be small.

Whether the committee members would have taken such a view had they been able to see *QE2's* role in the Falklands War just over 20 years later is another matter.

Soon after the formation of the Chandos Committee, on 13 September 1959, Colonel Bates died and Sir John Brocklebank (whose career had hitherto been in cargo ship operations) was appointed his successor. Sir John publicly at least took the Cunard view that it was difficult to design a multi-purpose ship that could be successful on the Atlantic.

The committee remained convinced, however, that with ingenious design, the use of modern materials and flexibility between classes, much could be done to overcome any problems. But Cunard was resolute in its view, citing *Caronia* as an example of a dual-purpose ship that didn't work well as such. The committee was right, of course, and Cunard was wrong – as *QE2* eventually proved to dramatic effect.

*At the same time that the cash-strapped Cunard was seeking a £40 million loan for new shipping from the government, it was investing £8.5 million in a two-plane airline to be called Cunard Eagle Airways.*

The recommendation of the Chandos Committee was finally made on 1 June 1960 and, to the consternation of Sir John Brocklebank, the recommendation was for the government to support one ship not two. The hardening of the committee's view had been brought about by Cunard's contemporaneous excursion into the airline business, which was one of Sir John's first initiatives on becoming chairman. While it may have seemed forward-thinking and bold to take 'if you can't beat 'em, join 'em' to such extremes, the Chandos Committee was frustrated by the notion of a cash-strapped shipping company that was seeking a £40 million loan investing £8.5 million in a two-plane airline to be called Cunard Eagle Airways. As a result, Sir John's continuing

*Sir John Brocklebank, chairman of Cunard*

One of Cunard Eagle Airways' two Boeing 707 airliners, competing on the transatlantic run with BOAC and PanAm

insistence on two 75,000-ton 30-knot ships was ignored and the committee recommended government input of £18 million into just one ship.

## An £18 Million Loan

On 10 October 1960, some five months later, Ernest Marples, by then Minister of Transport, announced the government's acceptance of the recommendations of the Chandos Committee and approval of an £18 million loan at 4.5 per cent interest over 25 years. The replacement proposal sounded reasonable enough; in effect the British taxpayer would lend £18 million with repayment over a 25-year period, the loan being interest-free during the anticipated construction time of four years and thereafter the whole loan would bear interest at 4.5 per cent.

However, reasonable or not, the proposal was met with criticism from every side. There were those who felt that if the government had £18 million to spare there were better projects on which it could be spent. The government's response that Britain needed to sustain a presence on the Atlantic as a matter of prestige for a maritime nation was dismissed as 'nebulous', and Cunard shareholders joined in the criticism by voicing the view that for the company to build a new transatlantic liner as the jet age was gathering momentum was a nostalgic notion.

Probably the only argument that carried real weight was the boost the construction would give to Britain's hard-pushed shipbuilding industry – all of it operational in areas of high unemployment.

## The Tender Process

Undeterred, Cunard continued with its plans. Only a few British yards were capable of handling a contract of this size and six firms were expected to tender – John Brown and Company, Clydebank; Fairfield Shipbuilding and Engineering Limited, Glasgow; Vickers-Armstrong (Shipbuilders), Tyne; Swan, Hunter and Wigham Richardson Limited, Wallsend – also on the Tyne; Harland and Wolff Limited, Belfast, and Cammell Laird and Company (Shipbuilders and Engineers) Limited, Merseyside.

In January 1961, it was announced by the northeastern yards that for this venture, Vickers and Swan Hunter proposed to join forces in order to win. The plan was to construct the hull at the Wallsend yard, birthplace of the *Mauretania*, and to fit it out a couple of miles upstream at Vickers' Walker Naval Yard. It was a powerful combination. Both firms were at the forefront of ship construction and were arguably the most technically advanced shipbuilders in Britain. Additionally, Vickers' Barrow-in-Furness yard had

*The Vickers/Swan Hunter consortium was too far-sighted for its own good. In 1961 it submitted a tender for an all-steel quadruple-screw vessel, but also for a smaller alloy and steel vessel with two propellers instead of four. This much smaller, lighter, more modern concept suddenly made Cunard think twice.*

produced the 45,000-ton *Oriana* for Orient Lines in 1960, a revolutionary ship embodying many new design concepts valuable to the builders of *Q3* and to the eventual owners.

## Worsening Trading Results

Tenders were to be received by the end of July 1961, but the process was not to be a smooth one. At the Cunard AGM in May 1961 desperate shareholders urged the immediate cancellation of the *Q3* project because of worsening trading results. Even the supposedly forward-looking airline acquisition, Cunard Eagle Airways, was losing money, unable to compete with the non-stop direct services of PanAm and BOAC.

The *Queen Mary* and *Queen Elizabeth* were doing badly too – sometimes sailing with as few as

200 passengers – and losing the company in the region of £2 million a year each. Yet despite the indication that times were not good for an inflexible transatlantic passenger ship, the *Q3* project sailed serenely on – receiving a major boost when the North Atlantic Shipping Bill became an Act of Parliament in June 1961, thus allowing Cunard to proceed as planned.

The joint bid from Vickers Armstrong and Swan Hunter Wigham Richardson became the favoured tender, with reports indicating that their bid was the lowest at £28 million and that they offered an earlier completion date that would allow Cunard to take advantage of the 1965 summer season.

So Cunard decided to award the contract to the Vickers/Swan Hunter consortium, but the consortium's own competence and far-sightedness was its undoing. For not only did it submit a tender for the all-steel quadruple-screw vessel Cunard had in mind, but also for a smaller alloy and steel vessel with two propellers instead of four. It was this much smaller, lighter, more modern concept that made Cunard pause.

## Second Thoughts

Even Sir John Brocklebank himself belatedly began to wonder if the all-steel four-screw *Q3* was actually the answer to Cunard's problems, and whether the more revolutionary twin-screw option wasn't preferable. On 19 October 1961, Sir John reluctantly announced that Cunard had shelved plans for *Q3*, citing rising labour and material costs that had increased the price of the ship. The government loan was not sufficient to cover the escalator clauses in the shipbuilding tenders.

In his Annual Report for that year, Sir John commented: 'You will expect me to say something about the postponement of the placing of an order for a new Express ship. In this connection I am glad to say that the two *"Queens"* have a number of working years ahead of them and an immediate decision is not, therefore, necessary.'

---

'I am glad to say that the two *"Queens"* have a number of working years ahead of them and an immediate decision is not, therefore, necessary.' *Sir John Brocklebank, chairman of Cunard*

---

Even though the cancellation of *Q3* posed Cunard a number of operational problems – not least of which was the possibility that *Queen Mary* and *Queen Elizabeth* would be retired before any replacement could now be built, it was nonetheless widely accepted in retrospect that the decision was the right one.

But not until *QE2* actually came into service eight years later would it be seen what a narrow escape the company had had, and what a triumph its last-minute conversion proved to be.

*The Bridge of* Queen Mary

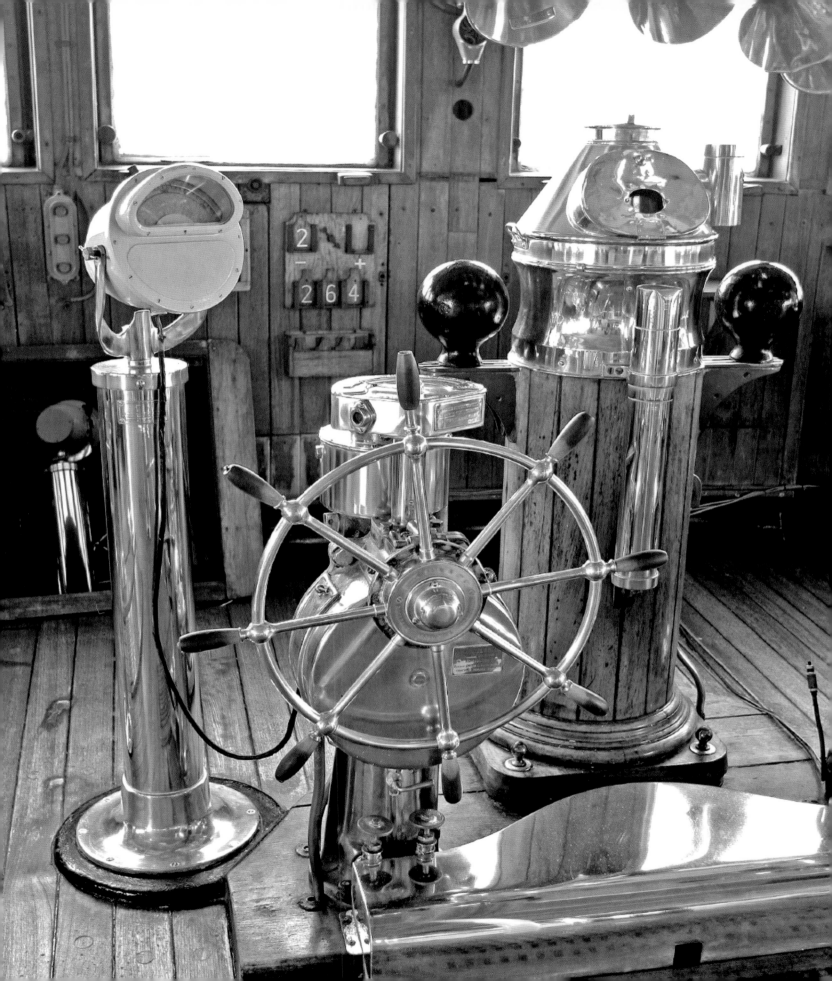

# Chapter 3
# *Drama by Design*

Cunard was saved not once, but twice, from commercially dubious projects to replace *Queen Mary* and *Queen Elizabeth*. First, by a government committee set up primarily to protect the taxpayers' investment, which overruled Cunard's insistence that only two similar large and inflexible ships would do. Second, by Vickers Armstrong and Swan Hunter Wigham Richardson, which, as an adjunct to its successful tender to build the Chandos-inspired all-steel quadruple-screw *Q3*, put forward proposals for an even smaller, more flexible aluminium-alloy and steel vessel which, largely by virtue of its reduced weight, could manage the speeds required on the Atlantic with twin screws.

Cunard suddenly underwent a conversion that would not have been out of place on the Damascus Road, abandoning even the scaled-down *Q3* for which Vickers Armstrong and Swan Hunter Wigham Richardson had successfully tendered. Instead, Cunard embarked enthusiastically on designing a smaller but fast ocean liner with the flexibility of a cruise ship.

They had little time to do it: *Queen Mary* and *Queen Elizabeth* could not go on forever – or, more to the point, Cunard could not afford for them to.

## Small Is Beautiful

In December 1962 it was announced that Cunard was planning a smaller and

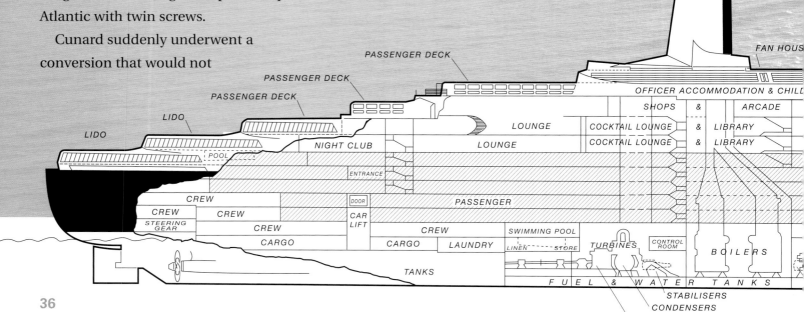

more versatile liner. Although *Q3* had been rejected on the whole for being the wrong ship for the jet age, her design embodied a number of progressive elements that would eventually be incorporated into the new *Q4* design. The most progressive ideas in *Q3's* layout and planning were brought forward and rescaled to the reduced overall dimensions of what was to be *Q4*.

Cunard planned the project to take four years to complete; delivery for the new ship would be by the end of 1966. In February 1963 Cunard announced that a decision on a replacement for *Queen Mary* would be made by the end of April that year and it was widely assumed, not least on the Tyne, that Vickers Armstrong and Swan Hunter Wigham Richardson would build a ship so clearly based not just on the groundwork done for *Q3* but more particularly on their alternative option.

Sir John Brocklebank, while refusing to be drawn, confirmed

that she would be in service by 1966 and that she would be 'quite a bombshell', saying:

> We are firmly convinced that there is a great future for a new express ship of a very different type from the present *Queens*. She must be a top flight cruise ship and a revolutionary North Atlantic unit. We are not yet ready to announce our plans for this ship but design work is well advanced.

Cunard first approached the government in July 1963 for a loan of £18 million over 25 years and while this was initially rejected by the government the Ministry of Transport wrote to Cunard on 17 October 1963 advising them that the minister, Ernest Marples, had agreed that a loan should be offered. The government decided to grant Cunard's application for a loan after considering advice from the Shipbuilding Credit Advisory Board under the chairmanship of Lord Piercy and the money was to be advanced through the government's shipbuilding credit scheme.

A loan of £17.6 million was offered for the vessel, or alternatively 80 per cent of the final building cost

*Early blueprint for Q4, later to be named QE2*

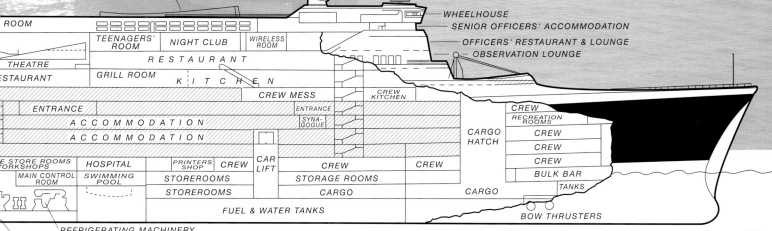

PASSENGER DECK

WHEELHOUSE
SENIOR OFFICERS' ACCOMMODATION
OFFICERS' RESTAURANT & LOUNGE
OBSERVATION LOUNGE

ROOM
THEATRE
RESTAURANT
TEENAGERS' ROOM
NIGHT CLUB
WIRELESS ROOM
RESTAURANT
GRILL ROOM
KITCHEN
CREW MESS
CREW KITCHEN
ENTRANCE
ACCOMMODATION
ENTRANCE
SYNA-GOGUE
CREW RECREATION ROOMS
ACCOMMODATION
CARGO HATCH
CREW
STORE ROOMS
ORKSHOPS
HOSPITAL
PRINTERS SHOP
CREW
CAR LIFT
CREW
CREW
CREW
MAIN CONTROL ROOM
SWIMMING POOL
STOREROOMS
STORAGE ROOMS
BULK BAR
STOREROOMS
CARGO
CARGO
TANKS
FUEL & WATER TANKS
BOW THRUSTERS
REFRIGERATING MACHINERY
TURBO-ALTERNATORS
STABILISERS

of the new liner, whichever should be the less. The terms included 4.5 per cent interest – the government lending rate of the time – over 10 years.

## Built in Britain

It was stipulated that the building contract for the construction of the new liner was to be made with a shipbuilder in the UK who had submitted the best tender. The minister would also have to give prior approval to the choice of shipbuilders invited to tender; the terms of the invitations to tender and associated documents; the final choice of the shipbuilder and the final specification of the new liner as agreed by Cunard and the shipbuilder.

Cunard also had to ensure that the new liner would be registered in the UK and that it would be classed +100 A1 by Lloyds. The offer was made public on 21 October when Cunard confirmed it was to go ahead with the building of the new ship.

The new Cunarder would be 293m (960ft) in length with a draught of 9.45m (31ft) and a gross tonnage of about 58,000. Her twin-screw turbine machinery would be capable of developing a maximum of 110,000 horsepower. Service speed would be 28.5 knots on less than half the fuel consumption of a *'Queen'*. Again, the machinery weight would only be one-third that of a *Queen* liner and the engine room complement considerably less than half. The ship would carry as many passengers as a *Queen*.

Uncluttered upper decks with two large swimming pools, lido areas that were to be the largest afloat, the use of large glass windows in promenade decks, side screens, passenger cabins and in the restaurants (themselves located above the main deck) would contribute to the ship's modern appearance and let in the maximum amount of natural daylight. A total of 1,400 passengers would be accommodated in cabins with portholes. Again, recognising that passengers expected continuing improvement in the standards of cabin comfort, Cunard gave a lot of thought to fitting the greatest possible number of actual beds rather than upper berths. Of a total passenger capacity of 2,050, all accommodated in rooms matching the highest standards of

*Q4 was designed to be narrow enough and with shallow enough draught to pass through the Panama Canal*

competitive ships, only 10 per cent would occupy upper berths.

## Cruise and Canal-friendly

These features were essential to North Atlantic service as well as cruising. *Q4* would be able to pass through the Panama Canal if required and so would be able to cruise widely.

At the end of August 1964 Cunard was in a position to invite tenders for *Q4*. The firms likely to be invited to tender were John Brown and Co., Clydebank; Cammell Laird and Co., Birkenhead; the Fairfield Shipbuilding and Engineering Company, Glasgow; Harland and Wolf, Belfast; Swan, Hunter Wigham Richardson, Wallsend-on-Tyne would combine with Vickers Armstrong, Wallsend.

Most still considered the Tyne shipyards to be the favourites for *Q4* given their likely success in attracting *Q3*. But John Brown's orderbook was the least full of all the shipyards expected to tender.

The tender document Cunard issued to the yards on 9 September 1964 consisted of 550 closely typed foolscap pages of plans and specifications. Price was to be Cunard's main consideration and the deadline for the shipyards was late November.

In mid-October Cammell Laird advised Cunard that 'regretfully' they would not be tendering for the new Cunarder. The yard's orderbook was such that it could not start work on the new ship until nearly a year after the date necessary to meet Cunard's delivery requirement.

A month later the Fairfield yard announced it was also dropping out of the competition. Again the yard cited its orderbook as the reason for not pursuing *Q4*. The tender from Harland and Wolf arrived at Cunard's Liverpool Head Office on 28 November some 48 hours before the deadline. The next tender to arrive was from John Brown and the final one (delivered by hand by the two chairmen) came from the Tyne consortium on 1 December.

The Vickers and Swan Hunter tender was for £22,547,428 and an October 1968 delivery date – provided the contract was awarded by the end of January 1965. The John Brown tender was £870,000 less than Vickers at £21,677,000 and with a significantly earlier delivery date of May 1968. Harland and Wolff, quoting £23,825,000, were easily beaten on price by both the other yards. But, fatally for them, they also would not commit to delivery before the end of 1968.

## Over-the-top Tenders

The shipyards had been asked to quote a fixed price but all three stated that they were unable to do so. At the time it was difficult to obtain fixed prices from shipbuilders for any type of ship. Likewise there was no penalty clause for late delivery of the ship – this had been discussed during the preparation of the tender for *Q3* when all the available builders indicated that they would not accept any penalty clause.

Even the lowest price, that submitted by John Brown, was £2 million more than Cunard had estimated the cost would be. Some Cunard management was adamant that *Q4* was still too expensive and may have to be cancelled, but the problem was that the ageing *Queens* would soon need to be taken out of commission.

## Frantic Cost-cutting

Dan Wallace, Cunard's naval architect, Tom Kameen, Cunard's director of engineering, and John Starks, assistant managing director of John Brown, were given the task of reducing the price of the ship and during an 'extremely hectic seven or eight days' according to Wallace, went through the specifications and managed to reduce the machinery costs by £500,000 and the hull price by £1.5 million. A plan to incorporate a sliding glass roof on the top deck was scrapped; one boiler was eliminated thus saving weight and space, and an aft cargo hatch was abandoned.

The men were also able to re-arrange the ship by pointing out anomalies in the passenger department's requirements and managed to secure berths for an additional 200 passengers within the same space.

Cunard then faced the problem that in order to obtain the benefits of the government loan it

would be necessary for the ship to be paid for before 31 December 1964. That meant that within a period of two weeks the building agreement had to be prepared, agreed and signed.

On 30 December 1964 Lord Aberconway, chairman of John Brown, and Sir John Brocklebank signed the contract for *Q4* at the Bank of England – the biggest ever British passenger ship contract in terms of value.

> 'Clydeside will have its happiest Hogmanay for years. There will be no need to lay on a special celebration.'
> *Lord Aberconway*

When the news was flashed to the Clyde, church bells rang out, and Lord Aberconway commented: 'Clydeside will have its happiest Hogmanay for years. There will be no need to lay on a special celebration.'

Sir John Brocklebank was less jubilant but no less positive when he said: 'This confirms our intention to stay in the forefront of the North

*Tom Kameen*

*Dan Wallace*

Atlantic trade. This ship will be the match of any foreseeable competitor and of any cruising liner.' In less than an hour Cunard were already receiving bookings for the new liner; 100 people, mainly Americans, registered on 30 December.

> 'This confirms our intention to stay in the forefront of the North Atlantic trade. This ship will be the match of any foreseeable competitor and of any cruising liner.'
> *Sir John Brocklebank*

Before building work could begin, of course, designs had to be prepared – first the external design and that of the internal space arrangement, followed by interior design. Neither element went smoothly.

To begin with Cunard could not make up its mind whether it wanted an old-style three-class ship, or a more modern two-class one. Being Cunard, it leant towards the conservative option, but the sheer force of evidence finally – and very belatedly – pulled it the right way, with the result that a huge redesign of the internal spaces was needed well after construction had begun.

## Designer Duo

Even the benign field of interior design was riven by dispute; not surprising, really, since the enthusiastic but non-designer wife of Cunard's chairman was given a pivotal role in the whole process. *Q4* would owe much of her design to the work of two Cunard employees – Dan Wallace and Tom Kameen. John Whitworth, later managing director of Cunard, called these two men the 'real heroes' of the *QE2* story.

Dan Wallace headed a team of six naval architects who would carry out the whole of the design and layout of the ship except for the machinery spaces and decorative effects. A Clydebank man, he had worked on the two *Queens*: he had been in *Queen Mary's* boiler room taking measurements as she was launched, and was later on the promenade deck of *Queen Elizabeth* when she too first hit the Clyde. He left the yard in 1951 when he was ship manager and joined Cunard as assistant naval architect before being

*Dan Wallace, Cunard's naval architect on Q4, was formerly employed by John Brown shipyard, and had been on board both the* Queen Mary *and* Queen Elizabeth *when they were launched.*

*The fitting of the bulbous bow, February 1967*

appointed naval architect in 1964. Dan Wallace's former bosses at the yard would now find themselves reporting to him.

Tom Kameen led a team of seven engineers who would be responsible for coordinating the design of the main turbines and auxiliary power plant and for all other main and minor machinery including generators, evaporators and the computer.

## Many Hands

John Starks headed the yard design team. The shipyard would obtain technical advice from all over Britain: Lloyd's Register of Shipping would be consulted on detailed structural designs; the Board of Trade and the British Ship Research Association would be consulted from a very early stage, while on the problem of vibration the yard would work with the National Physical Laboratory. In all, the yard would spend up to 40,000 person-weeks on design, drawing and calculation work.

Much of the work done by Cunard's design department in reducing structural complexity and weight in *Q3* would ultimately prove vital in *Q4*. The final funnel shape of *Q4* was based on initial work undertaken on that for *Q3*, which it somewhat resembled. *Q3* propulsion machinery designs were resurrected and modified for *Q4*.

Cunard had issued an interim report on the general plans in May 1964 disclosing two important decisions: the ship would carry three classes of passenger in accordance with Cunard tradition and at variance with developments among other shipping companies, and have three restaurants located above the main passenger deck

– a total break with tradition and an idea that had been developed for *Q3*. All cabins would be fitted with baths or showers and toilets. The general plans were scheduled for completion in August 1964.

## A Bulbous Bow

At the same time secret tests were being carried out at the Ship Research Laboratory on a 7m (22ft) long wax model of the hull of the proposed new ship. The most significant development from the tests was the provision of a slightly bulbous bow to reduce pitching in rough seas as well as to save considerable power compared with the traditional form. The bulbous bow concentrates high pressure in the forward part of the ship, creating suction that tends to pull the ship forwards. The model had already been tried in the 400m (1,300ft) long tank at Feltham, the longest of its kind in the world.

An exhaustive series of resistance and propulsion tests, involving four- and six-bladed propellers (the ship would eventually become the first to be specifically designed for six-bladed propellers), had been carried out at the Clydebank Experimental Tank and at the Ship Division of the National Physical Laboratory (NPL). The latter had also been involved in extensive manoeuvrability trials in proving the aft underwater hull form. Cavitation tests on models of the propellers were to be carried out shortly at Newcastle University. Vibration studies had been carried out in conjunction with the British Ship Research Association (BSRA), NPL and Pametrada, who were to construct the turbines.

## Wind-tunnel Tests

A model of the liner, complete with superstructure, had been built for testing in the NPL wind tunnel. These tests would assist in determining the optimum shape and height of the funnel to ensure that exhaust gases would be carried well clear of the decks.

The use of aluminium in *Q4* was vital to the eventual success of the ship. Using the alloy enabled the design team to reduce the liner's draught by 2.13m (7ft) when compared to the *Queens*.

'Each of us had a little magnet like children play with and we were to be seen walking round the decks of the superstructure of the *United States* leaning up against the bulkhead…if it stuck it was steel, if not it was aluminium alloy.'
**John Brown, deputy chairman of John Brown**

*One of the models used in the extensive testing of the* Q4 *design*

John Brown, deputy chairman of John Brown (though the name was coincidental), would later recall that not only did the yard have little experience of aluminium but that Cunard was very conservative when it came to aluminium usage. They were eventually won over by the benefits: a lighter, smaller ship with less power requirement, which resulted in a reduction of costs. He also recalled what some of the research into the use of aluminium on *Q4* would involve:

> We decided that it would be a good thing to find out the extent of the aluminium alloy on the *United States* liner. We were going to do it as a secret trip but Cunard decided that it must be made official so we were duly booked in and we did the trip from Southampton to Bremerhaven and back. Each of us had a little magnet like children play with and we were to be seen walking round the decks of the superstructure of the *United States* leaning up against the bulkhead with our arms behind our backs and if it stuck it was steel, if not it was aluminium alloy. So we had a very good survey of the extent of aluminium alloy on the *United States*.

The aluminium superstructure would be of all-welded aluminium – a decision that was taken after many strength calculations and discussions with Lloyds. Probably for the first time on a large ship the aluminium superstructure would be incorporated as a main longitudinal strength member with no expansion joints fitted.

## Fitted for the Panama

One of the fundamental requirements of *Q4's* design was the necessity for her to go through the Panama Canal, thus enabling the ship to undertake world cruises during the winter months. The Panama Canal Authorities indicated that they would now accept vessels up to 32.3m (106ft) beam and because the builder's estimate for the centre of gravity for *Q4's* was slightly high it was decided to increase the beam at the waterline by 30cm (1ft) to 32m (105ft). She was therefore designed to get through the Canal with only 30cm (1ft) to spare.

*Over 20 different funnel designs were tested before fixing on the characteristic shape for which* QE2 *became famous*

During January 1965 a new general arrangement plan, embodying the various economies and changes in passenger accommodation, was developed. This work would continue for the first six months of 1965 but progress in the drawing office was rather slow.

To assist in assessing passenger requirements on the selling side, the Economist Intelligence Unit was commissioned to conduct market analyses of the probable development of sea travel, particularly in relation to leisure and resort hotels. In effect it was clearly revealed that demand for scheduled services, in terms of pure transportation, would diminish, and the role of the passenger ship change in favour of resort living. Marketing considerations therefore became a crucial factor in the shaping of the design for the ship.

## Haute Cuisine

One of the most innovative features of the public room layout was the placement of the restaurants high in the ship's superstructure and not, as was usual, buried well down in the hull. On *Queen Mary* and *Queen Elizabeth* only passengers in the famed Verandah Grills had enjoyed the windows and the views they offered while dining. In the past there had been two objections to siting restaurants high up in the superstructure – one was that weight so high was undesirable and the other was

that rolling in heavy weather was felt most on the upper decks. However, using aluminium for the superstructure minimised the problem of weight high up, and the stabilisers would virtually eliminate rolling. The removal of the restaurants from within the hull of the ship would also enable more cabins with portholes to be incorporated.

The external appearance of *Q4* was the result of close cooperation between Dan Wallace and James Gardner. Gardner joined the design team shortly after construction of the ship had started. By that time the basic layout and profile of the ship had been determined by the naval architects who had to meet technical requirements for the location of such major features as the wheelhouse, funnel, swimming pools, mast etc.

During this preliminary design period, Wallace and his team paid considerable attention to the exterior appearance of the ship – indeed the early model of the ship built by the naval architects would very strongly resemble the finished product.

Gardner had the difficult task of having to work to the largely unalterable terms of reference set by the naval architects. When he was made responsible for the exterior of the ship he regarded his primary task as a visual designer as bringing order and unity to the results of functional engineering, and he had to reshape the details of the structure without upsetting any basic features of the design.

For *Q4* he started off producing a wooden sandwich model of the ship, from sheets covered with code numbers and data, first marking the vital point where the flues and ducts surfaced on top. From this, deck plans began to shape up, and it was possible to build a 1.5m (5ft) model. Towards the end it was a race to keep the model ahead of construction.

## Focal Point

In order to reduce the complexity and irregularity to a formal simplicity, a focal point was necessary. Gardner selected the wheelhouse for this, and both raised it and edged it forward so that it would dominate and appear to take the mass of the ship along with it. Gardner also made sure all the main vents came up at one point – amidships, making clear decks and an unbroken line from the Bridge to way aft.

A neat line of identical lifeboats, echoed by an orderly line of promenade windows below, gave poise and neatness to most passenger liners. However, *Q4's* boats would be irregular and assorted as some were passenger launches and some just lifeboats. This would result in the davits failing to line up with each other so Gardner specified khaki paint to lose them.

*Q4* was given an elegant prow and a series of terraces at the stern that would yield more shelter than could be obtained by a screened upper deck. Particular care was taken in the bird's-eye view of the ship, the view so often seen by the public in model exhibitions. This was achieved by ensuring that vent trunks and other similar obstructions did not pierce the lido decks and also by special care in the positioning and design of the ladder ways, pools, guard rails and windscreens. Mooring equipment was placed undercover, which would enhance the appearance as well as giving weather protection to the crew.

## Designing the Funnel

The funnel itself was developed by Cunard's technical department after months of testing in the wind tunnel at the National Physical Laboratory at Teddington in Middlesex. The final design was probably the most technically advanced funnel ever fitted to a passenger ship and perhaps the most controversial. The design and position of the single funnel added to the graceful appearance of the ship but it was not merely a design feature. The funnel was as functional and efficient in disposing of smoke and

*James Gardner*

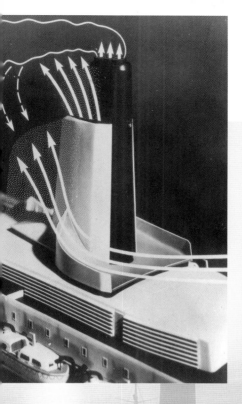

boiler gases as science and a long and exhaustive series of tests could make it.

The situation of the funnel amidships was conventional Cunard practice and the position was dictated by the disposition of the boilers, which for convenience were located next to the main machinery. This was sited amidships in order to achieve maximum strength and stability.

> 'A traditional smokestack proved out of the question after the first wind tunnel test.'
> *James Gardner*

Another advantage in positioning the funnel amidships was that it achieved the maximum shelter for deck accommodation. As the ship goes faster, smoke and exhaust gases tend to swirl downward. The factors governing this are the velocity of the smoke and exhaust gases, and the

height of the funnel. The best combination of these factors to ensure smoke-free decks required a tall funnel with a shovel-shaped scoop at the base to direct the airstream up and behind the vent. Having produced the shape to give the best overall efficiency for differing ship speeds and wind directions, the design shape was then slightly adapted for aesthetic appeal. Altogether 20 different funnel designs were produced and tested before the final design was approved.

James Gardner commented:

A traditional smokestack proved out of the question after the first wind tunnel test. In a functional stack, performance had to take complete priority, and the final structure comprises a relatively small diameter smokestack, a large air outlet vent and a wind scoop mounted on the fan house which covers the air intake.

Months were spent refining the lines of the structure to achieve the perfect relationship of the various parts. The result was the black and white funnel with a touch of Cunard red in the wind scoop. The two white masses – the funnel and the mast – were the key elements that gave the ship

her scale and dignity. The unusual mast was not needed as such but had a functional purpose as it served as an exhaust for the kitchens.

For the first time in Cunard history – although it was then current airline practice – the side of the ship would carry the name of the company below and aft of the bridge. The word Cunard was in red on the white superstructure in the distinctive letterform recently adopted by the company for its name. The wording was aluminium plate almost 1cm (⅛in) thick, manufactured and fitted at a cost of £924.

## Rooms With a View

Passenger accommodation was to be ahead of anything else then afloat. Five decks of cabins would offer three-quarters of her 2,025 passengers outside cabins, a higher proportion than any other transatlantic liner. Every cabin would have a private toilet and bath or shower – *Q4* being the first big liner to offer this. Cunard research indicated an overwhelming preference for rooms with daylight and beds as opposed to bunks, so only 15 cabins featured four berths while 145

featured three – designed for family or party use. Even when the ship was full only 178 passengers would sleep in upper berths.

The widths of the cabins were reduced, with the area saved being used to provide longer rooms. Experience from other ships showed that 2.7m (9ft) was ample for most rooms and this was adopted as standard for *Q4*. A total of 46 suites would be provided and most of the passengers would be in double or single rooms – all the 106 single rooms and 592 of the 666 double rooms would have divan beds. A greater amount of wardrobe space than had been fitted into a liner ever before was incorporated.

Two sets of sample cabins were built at the yard. The first set was constructed in the early stages and at that time the bulkheads and furniture were mainly constructed of hardboard so that they could be easily altered. The second set of sample cabins was completed in every detail, including furniture, furnishings, lighting and even the ventilation system, which was operational in order to assess the freedom from draughts.

*Gaby Schreiber, who designed the conference rooms, theatre and some suite rooms*

## Unveiling the *Queen*

On Tuesday, 4 April 1967, Cunard unveiled *Q4* for
the first time simultaneously on both sides of the
Atlantic. Chairman Sir Basil Smallpeice unveiled
a model with the emphasis on technical
achievements. He was supported by managing
director Philip Bates, naval architect Dan Wallace,
technical director Tom Kameen, and James
Gardner, responsible for the exterior lines. At
exactly the same time in the lounge on *Queen
Mary* in New York, deputy chairman Lord
Mancroft, supported by Captain Warwick, unveiled
an identical model of *Q4*. Emphasis there was on
the commercial attraction. A special stage was
created for the 1.5m (5ft) model, which was
covered by a mechanical arrangement like a closed
flower; the leaves unfolding to reveal the model on
a spotlit rotating plinth.

The first external artist's impressions were
unveiled with the caption:

The world's fastest and most powerful twin
screw liner, Cunard's *Q4*, will have more open
deck space than any other passenger ship. Two
thirds the tonnage of the *Queens*, she will carry
the same number of passengers in greater
comfort and at the same cruising speed – but
will do it on half the fuel consumption. The new
Cunarder will be the largest ship capable of
passing through the Panama and Suez canals for
worldwide cruising. Restaurants high in the ship
with sea views for all the 2,000 passengers is one
of the liner's unique features.

On 21 February 1968 the first glimpses of the
interior of *QE2* were given at a special exhibition
opened by Princess Margaret at the Design Centre
in Haymarket, London. It included full-size mock-
ups of two cabins and illustrated with diagrams
and models and photographs of how the
restaurants, bars, lounges and other sections of the
ship would look. Examples of the tableware,
furniture, carpets, furnishing fabrics, wall
coverings and other products to be used on the
liner, as well as a specially developed sign-posting
and graphics system, were also displayed. The
exhibition ran until 23 March and was arranged
jointly by Cunard and the Council of Industrial
Design. It was a calm and positive affair; which
is more than can be said for the situation in
the shipyard.

# The Class Issue

Despite significant design advances in other fields, Cunard remained firmly committed to *Q3's* three-class Atlantic service. In February 1962 it issued a statement: 'Cunard are aware there have been moves towards two class ships, but are convinced that in a ship of *Q4's* size, three classes are justified.'

Cunard was undoubtedly influenced by tradition and the fact that the new Italian liners were three-class. However, these liners were operating on a very different route, with their lower class being virtually emigrant traffic.

## Cabin Class in the Balance

The debate was between those (notably the New York office) in favour of three classes: First, Cabin and Tourist, and those who felt that because the future of the ship lay in cruising as well as the North Atlantic, she should be a two-class ship, with no Cabin Class. It continued well into the construction period. It caused delays that the yard was later able to blame on Cunard when the shipping company complained about slippage.

In March 1963 Cunard's naval architect's department produced an anti-three-class document analysing passenger capacity: in a three-class vessel it was possible to have 1,990 passengers; in a two-class vessel 2,030. The report explained that the future cruising role of the vessel would be hard to satisfy in a three-class design as there would be some public rooms that would not be used for cruising whereas the fewer rooms required by a two-class vessel would aid the conversion to one-class during cruises.

Cunard management remained undeterred, claiming that design and economic studies 'demonstrated conclusively that a ship of three-class arrangement was not only more profitable but of greater passenger appeal, in that it resulted in a more evenly scaled grading of accommodation from Tourist through Cabin to First Class.'

## Swayed by the USA

Cunard's American side for now at least had won the argument. They insisted that the American market demanded three classes and as Americans provided 75 per cent of Cunard business, it was not surprising that the Cunard board was swayed by their point of view.

The *Evening Press* reported:

> Cunard's final decision to build three passenger classes – first, cabin and tourist – into its new £22 million transatlantic express liner, has roused more controversy in the passenger liner trade than any other development in liner design in the last decade.

> The notable point about the decision is that it sails boldly against the post-war tide flowing towards the smallest possible number of segregated classes aboard a ship.

In January 1964, the shipbuilding committee of Cunard decided that a three-class ship would cost £500,000 more than a two-class ship and require 50 more people to man it. Despite this, in February 1964, the naval architect was instructed to design a three-class ship.

Captain William Law of *Carmania*, who later became captain of *QE2*, wrote in February 1964:

> Cabin Class has no place in the future. The argument is often put forward that the Cabin Class in the *Queens* (*Queen Mary* and *Queen Elizabeth*) is well booked; this is merely due to the fact that the Tourist Class is well below standard …. In a new ship with a well-designed, attractive Tourist Class there will be no need for the 'middle of the road' passenger to look for anything beyond Tourist Class.

Law pointed out that America had changed since the Second World War into a virtually classless society wherein almost anyone in the vast middle segment could afford a substantial level of comfort.

Captain Law's views were echoed in the August 1964 edition of *Modern Transport*:

> The information recently released that *Q4* will be a three-class ship is almost unbelievable. This takes us back 53 years to the *Olympic*, first of the so-called monster ships. Since then the railways, air transport and practically all shipping companies have discarded three-class carriage as seeming entirely out of date to the travelling public and proving uneconomic to the transport operator.

## Time to Decide

In May 1966 the yard advised Cunard that delivery of the vessel would be delayed to November 1968 instead of May 1968. While this meant that Cunard would lose the lucrative 1968 summer Atlantic season it allowed enough extra time for the class argument to be resolved.

Cunard finally reversed its original view on three classes. In a statement on 27 May announcing the delay in completion the company said '… a firm decision has been taken to make the new Cunarder a two class ship.'

Sir Basil Smallpeice, who by then had taken over as chairman, reported:

> In travel, separate class accommodation as a reflection of a hierarchical social stature is clearly out-of-date. …the new ship is entirely open. All passengers can walk from end to end without let or hindrance.

## A Class Apart

Dan Wallace, who led the *Q4* design team, received the orders to change the ship from three to two classes when the hull was almost completed. He made the philosophical statement that at least it was easier to re-design the ship with one fewer class than an additional one.

The design and layout of *Q4's* cabins did not undergo extensive rationalisation, except that they were no longer divided among three classes. The most expensive accommodation was arranged amidships, along the greater part of the Main, Foyer and A Decks, comprising the First Class bloc on Atlantic service.

The areas affected were primarily the public spaces on the uppermost decks. The layout of the Verandah Deck (now the Upper Deck) was completely revised; two lounges, one on the Upper Deck and one on the Boat Deck, became a single double-height area (now the Grand Lounge); and the Boat Deck was extensively revised. While all this simplified things, it was a very late decision for a ship already six months behind schedule.

# Deciding on Design

Back in October 1965 Cunard announced the team that had been appointed to create the internal designs for the new ship. Eight designers had been selected: Evelyn Pinching, Jon Bannenberg, Jean Monro, Michael Inchbald, James Gardner, David Hicks, Dennis Lennon and Gaby Schreiber. All eight had visited the *Queen Mary* and *Franconia* in Southampton and had agreed on the basic design principles for the new ship.

Lady Brocklebank was also heavily involved seemingly for no other reason than that she was the chairman's wife and was a member of the Cunard committee established to ensure that technical and operational requirements were integrated in the design schemes.

John Brocklebank commented: '...this brilliant team of designers, with several of whom we began consultations as long ago as October 1964, will join forces with Cunard and the builders to bring into being the finest ship that British brains and industry can achieve.'

### Midships Lobby
*The Midships Lobby benefited from a startlingly futuristic design.*

Not everyone agreed: the Council of Industrial Design tersely replied when asked for a view on the selection: 'Sorry, we cannot comment.' Writing in *The Times*, John Gloag, from the Royal Institute of British Architects and the Architectural Association, said: '... [we] criticise the Cunard company for entrusting the interior design of the Q4 to eight designers who do not appear to speak the same design language and...will not be directed by any coordinating mind.'

Lady Brocklebank herself was accused of endangering the design of the liner with 'British amateurishness and bungling' to which she replied: 'I know what people like and dislike.' Cunard was accused of 'acting as a brake on progress in design'.

### All Change

A month later, on 8 November 1965, Sir John resigned for health reasons as chairman of Cunard, taking his wife with him, and his successor was Sir Basil Smallpeice. One of Sir Basil's first moves, after consultation with the Council of Industrial Design, was to revise totally the design team.

Sir Basil appointed well-known designer Dennis Lennon, who would, as well as designing the

### The Lookout
*The Lookout shows signs of its 1960s heritage.*

interiors of the restaurants, be concerned with the introduction of a design signature that was immediately apparent throughout the ship. Lennon would be joint coordinator with James Gardner, who had responsibility for the exterior of the vessel.

So it was Dan Wallace and Tom Kameen's job to present the yard with a hull and engine specification as well as the detailed layout of all cabins and public rooms, and the job of the decorative design team to transform this layout into a floating hotel resort.

Gardner and Lennon's new design team consisted of Jon Bannenberg (Premium Class cabins, a swimming pool, card room and the main Tourist Class lounge); Misha Black (synagogue); Stefan Buzas and Alan Irvine (Boat Deck bar, shops, gallery and selection of the suite rooms); Crosby / Fletcher / Forbes (observation lounge and all the graphics on the ship); David Hicks (nightclub / Tourist lounge); Michael Inchbald (First Class lounge and First Class library); Jo Pattrick (officers' and crew accommodation); Gaby Schreiber (selection of suite rooms, conference room and the theatre); Elizabeth Beloe and Tony Heaton (children's room and teenage room) with Messrs Tabb, Haslehurst as technical coordinators. Lord Queensberry was

### Beloe/Heaton

*Elizabeth Beloe and Tony Heaton, in charge of the children's rooms.*

appointed consultant on tableware and Geoffrey Dunn on loose furniture.

The designers and their staffs – plus other consultants – totalled about 80 people in all and they would use over 300 suppliers of furnishings and fabrics.

### Stefan Buzas

*Stefan Buzas, who helped design the Boat Deck bar, shops and gallery.*

### David Hicks

*David Hicks, who designed the nightclub.*

# Technical Innovations

In order to reduce the height of the centre of gravity of *Q4*, about 760 tonnes of steel were added to the double-bottom structure and shell, mainly by increased thickness of plating and by closer-spaced floors and longitudinals. These increases were a substitute for permanent ballast and allowed the structure to be strengthened where corrosion or heavy-weather damage might be expected.

## New Girders

In 1955, in conjunction with the British Ship Research Association, a new type of girder had been developed and tested. This girder had large holes for the various services cut in during fabrication, the depth of the girder being increased slightly to compensate. The girder was much lighter than the standard girder and all the various ducts and pipes were designed to suit the openings. The girder was successfully used experimentally in *Sylvania* and would be used throughout *Q4*.

Positions of girders and pillars were decided at an extremely early stage in the design and were never altered. All the routes for the electrical cables, ventilation and piping were also developed early. This ensured that they were routed in the fore and aft passages or over bathrooms where lower headrooms were acceptable. A saving of 15–23cm (6–9in) per deck was obtained and resulted in a total saving of about 1.83m (6ft) from conventional construction. The Cunard engineering staff assisted by similar careful planning and were able to reduce the height to the top of the machinery spaces by about 1m (3ft). This total saving of 2.74m (9ft) provided an additional deck and was one of the major contributions to raising the standard of

## Twin Screws

*View of QE2's port propeller and rudder before the launch.*

accommodation. *Q4* would have 13 decks as opposed to 12 on the earlier *Queens* and this more than compensated for the restrictions placed on *Q4's* length and beam in order to pass through the Panama Canal, as well as restrictions on her mast and funnel heights to allow her to pass under bridges in world harbours.

## Modern Engines

*Q4's* modern turbine engines were lighter, taking up less room and needing less fuel than her predecessors. The final position of the main machinery space was fixed after many investigations into subdivision and strength. To keep the bending moment to a minimum, it had to be sited aft of amidships.

*Q4* was to be the most powerful twin-screw merchant ship afloat. The main propelling machinery, manufactured by John Brown Engineering (Clydebank)

Limited, comprised a twin-screw set of Brown/Pametrada turbines. Each set consisted of a high-pressure and low-pressure turbine driving the propeller shafting through double reduction, double helical, dual tandem gearing. The maximum combined output of the machinery was 110,000 shp at 174 rpm. The steam conditions at the turbine inlet were 800 psig and 504°C (940°F). The normal service rating would be 94,000 shp and the machinery had been designed for maximum efficiency at this power.

The main condensers were of the flow regenerative type and were built to maintain 29" Hg vacuum at normal service power and 28.86" Hg at maximum continuous shp, in each case when supplied with sea water at 15.5°C (60°F).

The steam for main propelling and all other purposes was supplied from three Foster Wheeler E.S.D II boilers which were also built under licence by John Brown Engineering (Clydebank) Limited. These boilers were the largest ever installed in a merchant vessel, each unit having a normal evaporation of 104,780 kg/hr and a maximum evaporation of 140,614 kg/hr at 850 psig and 510°C (950°F). The design of the turbines and the boilers was such that if required the machinery could operate at a temperature of 538°C (1000°F).

The generating plant comprised three turbo-alternators and was supplied by Associated Electrical Industries, each alternator having an output of 5,500 kw at 3,300 volts. These turbo-alternators were

also the largest units ever to be installed in a merchant vessel.

Compared to the earlier *Queens*, *Q4* would have one engine room instead of two, two propellers instead of four, a quarter of the engineering staff, and half the fuel consumption – 530 tonnes instead of 1,120 daily.

## Bulbous Bow

*The revolutionary bulbous bow was fitted in February 1967.*

# Construction 2

# Chapter 4
## Conflict and Construction

By the end of June 1965 the yard had developed a monthly steel-erection programme, including a construction schedule for the various trades involved in the building of units for the double bottom, oil tanks, decks and side shell. Over 1,000 tonnes of steel had been delivered to the shipyard.

Such planning was crucial to ensure on-time delivery. Three thousand men would work on the construction of *Q4* – a figure that would increase by another 500 at the peak fitting-out period. Each stage of the building was phased, with cardinal dates from the laying of the keel to the final handing over. A skeleton programme with a few fundamental details was initially established. Time, labour, materials, equipment, delivery dates and costs were then integrated into a grand plan from which the ship would take shape. Monthly targets were fixed, items such as 460,000m (1,500,000ft) of Formica and units ordered from suppliers, long delivery dates fixed for major items such as main engines and turbo-alternators. Labour resources and materials had to be related to avoid snags and delays. A computer analysed the number of men required at any given time for a particular job while forecasting progress.

The use of computers was a completely new technique to keep check on the cost and progress of the new Cunarder at any stage of its construction. The system would provide information to enable spot checks to be made at any stage of the contract and an accurate cost assessment – all at a glance in the records from the computer. All the key departments where calculations had to be progressively applied – estimating, planning, buying, production, assessment, costing and budget control – were coordinated in the vast network.

### Coordinated by Computer

To operate the system the liner was broken down into 64 blocks, each of which was handled as if it were a small ship on its own. There would be 150,000 pipes in the new Cunarder, each one of which would go through five stages – drawing, manufacture, fitting on board, attachment of valves and testing – and the computer would keep track of each pipe.

The whole operation was under the personal direction of the formidable John Rannie, managing director of John Brown. Of him Dan Wallace was later to write: 'Mr Rannie was being allowed to manage *QE2* entirely by himself, and this was the main cause of failure.'

The keel for Cunard's 172nd ship was to be laid on Friday, 2 July 1965, just two days before the 125th anniversary of the maiden voyage of *Britannia,* Cunard's first ship.

The keel for No. 736, the shipyard's orderbook number for *Q4,* was to be laid at No. 4 slipway in the East Yard of John Brown and Co., the same slipway on which *Queen Mary* and *Queen Elizabeth* and other famous Cunarders had been built. The prefabricated section of the new ship's keel consisted of three 60-tonne sections 35.7m (117ft) long, 7m (23ft) wide and 1.9m (6ft 3in) high.

Unfortunately it not had been stipulated that the prefabricated section being built in the

workshops should weigh just 40 tonnes, to be within the combined lifting capabilities of two tower cranes adjoining the slip, which with the aid of a powerful winch would lift and pull the keel section into place. A rehearsal of the ceremony on the Wednesday evening before had gone very well but this good omen turned out to be misleading.

Lady Aberconway, the wife of John Brown's chairman, was to perform the ceremony at 1000 hours, and more than a score of press and television cameramen and about 30 journalists

*Stern of the new ship overhanging the Clyde*

from London and Glasgow were there to witness the occasion. Also present were Lord Aberconway and Sir John and Lady Brocklebank.

As the process began it rapidly became clear that something was wrong. Although the keel section initially moved a few inches it then stuck and refused to move further. Seemingly the weight of the keel was greater than the two cranes could manage, and the strain on the winch threatened to tear its concrete base out of the ground.

This was not what Prime Minister Harold Wilson had in mind when he said the ship should be 'a showcase for modern Britain'. The embarrassing ceremony ended abruptly and the guests were quickly taken away to be entertained; fortunately press coverage was sympathetic.

After such a high-profile disaster, the keel section was moved without fanfare into position onto the building blocks on Monday 5 July.

## Slow Progress

For Dan Wallace, Cunard's chief naval architect, the keel-laying problems were down to 'builders' inefficiency' – a comment on the yard that gave a foretaste of the lacerating but reasoned criticism to which he was to subject them as work progressed. And work did progress – but agonisingly slowly,

After Sir John Brocklebank resigned as chairman of Cunard in November, his successor – Sir Basil Smallpeice, a veteran of the airline industry – took it upon himself to attend the December monthly progress meeting. Cunard was concerned with the slow advance. But the builders still maintained that their estimated launch date would be April 1967.

*'…it is well-known that…I had difficulty with Mr Rannie in trying to obtain from him an accurate assessment of the situation, together with adequate forward planning.' Dan Wallace, chief naval architect*

Dan Wallace later commented:

These meetings were always dominated by Mr Rannie and were most difficult as far as I was concerned. Indeed it is well-known that throughout these meetings I had difficulty with Mr Rannie in trying to obtain from him an accurate assessment of the situation, together with adequate forward planning. In the end – in my opinion – it is what caused the disastrous finish.

Throughout the first months of 1966 Cunard continually raised concerns that while good progress was being made in the drawing office, the steelwork progress was disappointing. Finally in March the yard conceded that the new liner was already six months behind schedule – the shortage of steel workers in the Clyde area allegedly being responsible for the delay. The launch was now

*Cunard decided not to call their new ship Ian S…*

rescheduled from April 1967 to September 1967, with delivery in November 1968.

By May the delay had worsened even further, and gradually a battle of blame between Cunard and John Brown escalated into total war. At a series of acrimonious meetings and exchanges of correspondence, the shipyard made it clear that in its view the main cause of the delay was Cunard's failure to confirm the final design and arrangements of the ship when the contract was signed. The yard drew particular attention to Cunard's failure to agree the design of passenger accommodation, the repositioning of the main and auxiliary machinery and the indecision on the number of classes. Cunard, while accepting that some delay could be blamed on indecision on its part, robustly took the view that the degree of change was not as big as John Brown maintained and that many of the pending changes had been apparent at the time the contract was signed back in 1964.

## Labour Shortage

The principal reason for the delay was actually a shortage of skilled labour, which the yard was reluctant to admit. Consequently, in order to keep the peace and attempt to move things along, Cunard agreed that a greater degree of blame than was the case could be placed on design alterations.

> 'Shortage of labour has had and is having a delaying effect on the ship's progress.'
> *Joint statement from Cunard and John Brown*

A joint statement issued on 27 May 1966 reflected this agreement with the words:

Since the contract was signed in December 1964, the employment situation in the shipbuilding industry has changed materially. Shortage of labour has had and is having a delaying effect on the ship's progress. It has also been decided to revise the layout of certain passenger accommodation in the ship as well as to modify the arrangements for interior design.

About two-thirds of the hull of *Q4* was completed at this time, with some items of machinery already in place and work on the lower strata of cabins begun. The loss of the lucrative summer 1968 season was a great blow to Cunard – transatlantic revenue would have been in the region of £200,000 per week.

Dan Wallace was still unconvinced of the proposed delivery date and he suggested privately it may be March 1969 before the ship would be delivered. In a memorandum to Sir Basil he stated: '…it may be realistic to aim for a November 1968 completion but the actual date is more likely to be about March 1969.'

## Of Captains and Queens

At the end of 1966, Cunard had two pieces of positive news relating to *Q4* to announce within the space of a month.

On 8 December 1966, at Cunard's first-ever Masters' Conference held in Winchester, at which 17 out of the 27 Cunard captains were present, it was announced that 54-year-old Birkenhead-born Captain William 'Bil' Warwick would be master of the new ship. Bil Warwick had joined Cunard in 1937 as third officer on *Lancastria*. His first command had been the cargo ship *Alsatia* in 1954 before he took over his first passenger ship, *Carinthia*, in 1958, and he had since commanded almost all of the ships in the Cunard fleet.

Captain Warwick was naturally extremely pleased, saying: 'It is a great honour, I had no idea I had been selected. I regard this as the chance of a lifetime – I've no doubt she will be the finest ship in the world.'

Captain Warwick was the youngest captain ever to be appointed as master of a *Queen* liner and was posted ashore immediately to keep a watching brief on the progress of the new ship and to act as liaison chief for all the departments concerned with its construction. He was given an office in London and told to visit the shipyard whenever he wanted to keep an eye on progress.

Interestingly, his son Ronald Warwick went on to become captain of *QE2* in 1990, and later became fleet commodore just as his father had. Moreover, just as Captain Bil Warwick became master of Cunard's first transatlantic liner for over 30 years, so did Commodore Ron Warwick when he was appointed master of *Queen Mary 2* in 2003.

On 12 January 1967 Buckingham Palace announced that 'The Queen, accompanied by The Duke of Edinburgh, will launch the Cunard Steamship Company's new ship at John Brown's yard, Clydebank, on Wednesday 20 September 1967.'

*Captain William Warwick on the starboard Bridge wing of his new ship*

He also complained bitterly that yard-produced minutes of joint meetings regularly contained errors and misrecordings, usually to the yard's advantage, and that getting straight answers to straight questions proved virtually impossible.

While it might have been the case that there was shortage of skilled workers, the yard was experiencing significant problems with the 3,000 it already had. The main difficulties originated in the fact that the workforce was split between 18 unions, each of which had to be considered separately in negotiations, and each of which vigilantly protected archaic demarcation rules that inevitably led to constant walkouts and downing of tools.

For example, water supplies on ships had traditionally been delivered by zinc pipes, which, being water pipes, were fitted by plumbers. But on *Q4* there was a move to copper pipes which, because they were copper, had to be fitted by coppersmiths, thus denying work to plumbers. The compromise reached was that coppersmiths would do the work, and each would be accompanied by a plumber – who would be paid to do nothing.

The first major strike came in March 1967 when the Draughtsmans' and Allied Technicians' Association began a dispute that was to last over ten weeks, and which – the yard reported to Cunard in May – meant 'that many plans will not be prepared by the previously programmed dates.'

In June, the plumbers walked out, rapidly followed by 286 electricians. Many other trades went on strike in July and August. Such stoppages continued throughout the entire time the ship was on the Clyde, each union apparently calling a strike of its members without any regard for the overall effect on the progress of the ship or on its brother unions.

Peace reigned until October 1967 when the ventilation sub-contractors went on strike, and the

*The worst period for strikes was probably from June to August 1967, when the following trades all went on strike: plumbers, electricians, welders, painters, deck and machinery engineers, apprentices, brass-finishers, stagers, red-leaders, drivers, general labourers, joiners, engineers, boilermakers and platers.*

following week all the plumbers did the same. So strike and dispute piled one on top of the other, compounding the already serious delays. But it was – and is – difficult to determine to what degree the strikes resulted from genuine grievance, from archaic demarcation, from the political motivation of a few – or whether they were just a means of causing delay, to keep the job, and hence paid employment, going longer.

## Computer Technology

On 21 July 1967 the prime minister, Harold Wilson, visited the yard to inspect progress on the new ship before having lunch with the directors of Cunard and the yard. The man who coined the phrase 'the white heat of the technological revolution' could not fail to be impressed with the fact that *Q4* was to feature the most sophisticated computer system ever to be installed in a merchant ship; it was the first to combine technical, operational and commercial functions at sea. Based on the Ferranti Argus 400 computer, the installation cost just over £100,000. The micro-miniature Argus 400 was one of the smallest and most advanced computers in the world and was the result of two years' investigation and research in which Cunard cooperated with the British Ship Research Association, the National Research Development Corporation, Ferranti and the shipbuilders. The computer system would have six

*The bow seen through the scaffolding being erected for the launch platform*

## New Materials: Steel and Aluminium

During the early build period an average of over 300 tonnes of steel a day was put into the ship – this was believed to be a record tonnage for a passenger ship. An average of 30 tonnes of aluminium was erected weekly from the time the raw material was delivered to the yard. The aluminium superstructure was the first all-welded unit in a passenger ship and 760 tonnes would be erected by the time the ship was launched.

In total 1,120 tonnes of aluminium alloy would be used – the largest amount (including some of the biggest plates) ever in the construction of a British liner. In total 30 separate multi-tonne pieces were welded together to create the superstructure for the new liner. To prevent any corrosive electrolytic interaction between the steel of the hull and the aluminium a special epoxy compound was spread along the joints between the two metals and steel rivets were used for the final connection.

Pre-fabricated sections were widely used. The heaviest, such as the double-bottom, bow and stern units weighed

QE2's *Bridge being lowered into position, April 1968*

40 tonnes. The biggest of the pre-fabricated aluminium sections was 15 tonnes. The massive stern frame was a solid cast steel unit of 66 tonnes. Each propeller bracket weighed 66 tonnes and the rudder weighed 80 tonnes.

When *Q4* was finally ready for launch, some 17,800 tonnes of steel from Colvilles of Glasgow, worth more than £1 million, had been used.

main functions: data logging, alarm scanning, machinery control, weather routing, prediction of fresh water requirements and stock control.

Nor would he have missed the significance of the ship's dual metal structure – a steel hull topped by an aluminium superstructure, one of the main differences between *Q4* and the abandoned *Q3*, a difference that so reduced the ship's weight that she could achieve 30 knots with just two screws and half the fuel consumption of the *Queens*. It was this combination that had allowed the *United States* to seize the Blue Riband as long ago as 1952.

Cunard's financial situation had worsened during 1967 and the company forecast a further £3.5 million loss on the passenger ships for that year. This was compounded by the news from John Brown in July that the contract price for *Q4* of £25.5 million would probably be increased by a further £3 million. Even if *Q4's* cost had not risen, the additional losses on the passenger ships would mean that the government's financial aid would not be adequate. Cunard warned the Board of Trade that the project was in danger of being abandoned, with major political repercussions, unless the government agreed to increase the loan.

'Even now it is impossible to tell what the final price of the *Q4* will be when she comes into service early in 1969.'
*Sir Basil Smallpeice, chairman of Cunard*

Sir Basil said:

I have seen the Board of Trade about the new loan and they are considering our request. It is to cover the increases in shipyard wages and materials since the £25,500,000 contract for the *Q4* was signed in 1964.

When the Government loan was arranged it was to cover 80 per cent of the estimated cost of the hull and machinery, but it did not take into account a substantial escalation in cost levels. Even now it is impossible to tell what the final price of the *Q4* will be when she comes into service early in 1969.

There then followed a period of intensive negotiations between Cunard and the government throughout August and September. Cunard stressed that a final decision had to be made by the time of their next board meeting on 14 September – if the news was bad the company felt it would have to give the Queen at least five days notice of the cancellation of the launch on 20 September!

In his autobiography *Of Comets and Queens* Sir Basil would later write:

We had no indication of what the Government were prepared to do by the afternoon of the 13th. Geoffrey Seligman (of S G Warburg, our merchant bankers) and I asked to see Harold Lever, the Financial Secretary to the Treasury, that evening. We met him in his flat in Eaton Square. This gave us the opportunity to present our case to him in a simple and straightforward manner, not through officials. Without a larger loan from Government, we should almost certainly have to stop building the ship; her new cost was much higher than quoted in 1964 and we could not meet it in full. He listened with evident sympathy and asked questions to fill gaps in his knowledge. He promised to let me have a written answer before or during our board meeting next morning. And with that, which was all we could have expected, Geoffrey and I retired to our respective homes and Harold Lever left – late – for a dinner engagement.

While waiting for the Financial Secretary's letter, we had time at our board meeting to consider what we would do if the Government's response proved negative. Geoffrey Seligman was with us, and so were Sir Henry Benson and Anthony Pinkney, our auditors. It was a grim prospect. We might even have to put Cunard into liquidation. At last the long-awaited letter arrived. To our great and undisguised relief, we found that our basic requirements had been substantially met.

*The 80-tonne rudder being installed*

On 19 September, on the eve of the launch, Cunard announced that agreements had been reached in the discussions with the Board of Trade. The existing loan agreement under which the government would make available a loan of £17.6 million on delivery of the ship by the shipyard to Cunard was to be replaced with a new arrangement. Under it the government was now prepared to lend in the neighbourhood of £24 million. At a time of continuing trading difficulties this new loan arrangement relieved Cunard of the strain in its cash resources involved in putting *Q4* into service.

If Cunard was worried about its financial situation it could not have been as worried as John Brown was about its own – a dire position not helped by the fact that its *Q4* tender had not allowed for any profit margin, so desperate was the yard to secure the contract. In the financial years 1962–65 the shipyard had made a loss of £4 million, and had to be subsidised by other more profitable parts of the John Brown conglomerate. Lord Aberconway was to note later that: 'there was little regret within the John Brown Group when we stopped building ships because the other parts of the group did not like their profits being whittled away to subsidise the losses of Clydebank.' Further losses were projected for the years up to 1969.

'At last the long-awaited letter arrived. To our great and undisguised relief, we found that our basic requirements had been substantially met.'
*Sir Basil Smallpeice*

But John Brown was not alone; many yards on the Clyde were struggling, as exemplified by the sudden and unexpected collapse of Fairfields in October 1965. So precarious was the situation that in February 1965 Douglas Jay, president of the Board of Trade, set up the Shipbuilding Inquiry Committee under the chairmanship of Reay Geddes to report on the best course of action for the Clyde shipyards. The Geddes Report, published in March 1966, recommended the amalgamation

*The port side propeller being attached; note the complete lack of safety equipment*

of smaller yards on the Clyde into two larger groups. Thus in January 1968 the name John Brown disappeared from shipbuilding, and the yard became part of Upper Clyde Shipbuilders. The engine works, meanwhile, was separated and became John Brown Engineering.

A secret Cunard internal memo dated 28 July 1967 discussed those who should attend the launch on 20 September. For financial reasons, invitations to company staff to attend the launch were severely restricted and were issued only to Cunard Line directors and their wives, plus a few senior members of the shore and sea staff from the

three main regional offices: Southampton (12 invitees), London (two invitees) and Liverpool (two invitees). The senior managers were balloted, but also had to meet the criteria of being in receipt of a salary of £2,250 or more and have at least 15 years' service with the company.

Even John Bannenberg and his design team, insultingly in their view, were not invited to the launch. But they went anyway, viewing proceedings with a picnic in a cornfield on the opposite side of the Clyde.

On the eve of the launch thousands turned out to take one last look at the liner on the slipway. The

*The Queen chats to shipyard director George Parker before the launch*

Queen had her first view of the liner as she flew overhead prior to landing at Abbotsinch Airport, Glasgow, at 1140 hours on 20 September. She was then driven to the shipbuilder's offices. There she was met by Admiral Sir Angus Cunninghame Graham, Lord Lieutenant of Dunbartonshire, who presented Sir Basil Smallpeice and Lord Aberconway. After a private lunch in the boardroom the Queen then made the two-minute car journey to the launching berth where she and the Duke spent 20 minutes inspecting the launching arrangements. Lord Aberconway's eight-year-old son, Michael McLaren, presented the Queen with a bouquet.

## Queen Elizabeth Launches *QE2*

At precisely 1428 hours on a sunny afternoon, in front of 30,000 Clydesiders, Her Majesty stepped forward on the launching platform and said: 'I name this ship *Queen Elizabeth the Second*. May God bless her and all who sail in her.'

There was a thin cheer in the yard as the Queen announced the name. She cut the ribbon using the same gold scissors that her mother had used to launch *Queen Elizabeth* in 1938 and her grandmother to launch *Queen Mary* in 1934. This released the bottle of wine that smashed onto the side of the newly named liner. She pressed the button that electrically released the launching trigger.

> 'I name this ship *Queen Elizabeth the Second*. May God bless her and all who sail in her.' **HM The Queen**

Then nothing happened. For 70 seconds it seemed as if the ship did not move. The Queen looked amazed; the smile slowly faded from Prince Philip's face. Workmen high up on her deck leaned over and shouted 'Give us a shove!' Shipyard director George Parker joined in the spirit of the request and bowler-hatted, he sprang to the bows and pushed. He jubilantly waved his bowler when, by a coincidence, she began to move. A little over two minutes after the Queen had named her, the new *Elizabeth* had slid smoothly into the Clyde. Newspapers the next day claimed the Queen had wept as the new ship entered the Clyde, and that Prince Philip took a white handkerchief from his pocket and handed it to her. The Queen exclaimed 'Oh, look at her, she's beautiful.'

Afterwards Cunard claimed there was nothing unusual in the delay and the ship had begun to move as soon as the Queen had pressed the button – but she had moved only a fraction of an inch at a time.

Aircraft from the No. 736 Squadron of the Fleet Air Arm flew over the ship in an anchor formation as six tugs manoeuvred her inch by inch into the fitting-out basin. The Queen and the royal party and guests then went to tea in the works canteen.

*Continued on page 78*

# Launching Q4

It was planned that the liner would glide towards the river at 35km/h (22mph) with the last shore fetters, the massive drag links, running out in a thunderous roar. There were ten bundles of them on each side of the ship. Each weighed 71 tonnes – 1,420 tonnes in all to steady the liner's journey to the river and so to the sea. The ship was expected to be travelling at 30km/h (19mph) as she hit the water, pushing away 20,320 tonnes of water – her own launching weight. A total of 150 men would be aboard the empty shell that was Q4 ready for any emergency. A further 161 men would work ashore to ensure a smooth launch.

The intricate launching calculations had been worked out by a computer – a week's work (with the normal methods) reduced to 30 minutes. Many factors had to be considered, for the river was narrow and the ship was long.

Very early on in the proceedings, John Brown had to decide the width and slope of the slipway on which the liner would slide down to the water. The effects of temperature on the launch lubricant grease mixture had to be considered and a host of other factors had all to be checked, evaluated and re-checked.

John Starks surprised local press by telling them that Q4 would suffer more stress during the launch than at any other time in her working life. He said of the launch process:

> The first step is, obviously, to make sure that it will move. When it starts to move the first thing that starts to happen is that the stern begins to lift. As it does so pressure on the forward end of the slipway is increased very considerably as it is taking the whole weight of the ship, apart from

any buoyancy that the water is taking. One must, therefore, make sure that the ship is then strong enough to take the stress at the forward end.

You also have to ensure by calculation that the ship will float off the slipway as opposed to dropping off and you also have to make sure that it is waterborne while it is reasonably clear of the slipway. The next thing that you have to decide is how far the ship can be expected to travel and you have to decide what drag chains you are going to attach at what points to prevent the ship from going too far.

What most people do not appreciate is that the ship takes a very rough ride during its launch. She bends during the course of the launch and we have to make sure that all her structure is absolutely sound. We, therefore, inspect the ship very carefully.

The most critical factor by far in the launch is the depth of water available at the aft end of the slipways. The River Clyde is extremely temperamental; sometimes the water is deficient and sometimes it is excessive. If we have too much water, the danger is that the ship will really be afloat before she is clear at the end of the slipway and the danger is that, since high water is usually associated with high wind, if she is not clear at the end of the ways she could damage herself on one of the cranes.

### Three Cheers...
QE2 *enters the Clyde for the first time.*

## A Perilous Job

The cameraman was told to film the drag chains as the ship went down the slipway; that's all he saw.

The man responsible for the slipway was Robert Craig, head foreman shipwright. He had worked at John Brown's since leaving school in 1918 and Q4 would be his 47th launch as head foreman. He built the slipway from the information given to him. Its declivity (downward inclination towards the river) was 1.27cm for every 30cm (½in to 1ft). Every square metre of the sliding and standing (fixed) ways had to bear a weight of more than 20 tonnes.

He used 5,000m (16,300ft) of 30cm (12in) square timber to build the supporting poppets (cradles) at each end of the ship. Once the ship had rested on 300 keel blocks but these had now been knocked away; the berth had been stripped of the huge bilge blocks and wedges.

Q4 rested on two sliding ways, each formed of 25 timbers 9.1m long, 1.83m wide and 30cm thick (30ft by 6ft by 1ft). The sliding and standing ways had been greased with a concoction of 9 tonnes of tallow compound, 320 litres (70 gallons) of sperm oil, 0.71

tonnes of soft black soap and 32 litres (7 gallons) of fine spindle oil.

Q4 was held by six mighty triggers, each with its 20cm (8in) wooden tongue set into the sliding ways. Wires trailed from a tiny electrical device to the button on the high platform where the Queen would perform the launching ceremony. As the Queen pressed the button the powerful trigger arms would snap back in their pits with a report like an artillery salute. Then Q4 would glide towards the river; and just in case the liner was reluctant to leave the berth, two hydraulic rams would give her a nudge – a push with the power of 84kg/cm² (1,200lb per sq in) behind it.

In the river six tugs would be waiting to handle the ship – three at the fore and three at the aft. Another would be standing by for any emergency. Lines would be rocketed from the tugs to the new Cunarder, towing lines would be secured and the new ship would move towards her fitting-out berth.

# What's in a Name?

There was considerable public and press interest in the likely name of *Q4* from the moment the contract was signed. There was pressure from Cunard's American offices for a '*Queen*' name, while the favourite in the UK – at least in the early days – was *Princess Anne*.

In January 1966 the *Daily Mirror* columnist, Cassandra, wrote:

> The next question for romanticists such as myself is to speculate on what they are going to call the new maritime giant, which is known simply as No. 736. I predict that there will be enormous pressure to christen the new Cunarder a *Queen*. But which queen?
>
> We are short of reigning queens in English history. The Normans, the Plantagenets, the Tudors, the Stuarts, the Hanoverians, the Saxe-Coburgs and the Windsors have only produced half-a-dozen in the past thousand years.
>
> Two Marys, two Elizabeths, one Anne and one Victoria. Queen Anne was a colourless nobody and Queen Victoria was a colourful somebody....

The Americans who will be the main clients for the ship would, I am sure, settle for *RMS Winston Churchill*. They are very fond of that old Anglo-American party.

Immediately before the launch more than 15,000 bets had been placed, and a Glasgow bookmaker was offering the following odds:

| | |
|---|---|
| 3 – 1 | *Sir Winston Churchill* |
| 4 – 1 | *Prince of Wales* |
| | *Prince Charles* |
| | *Princess Margaret* |
| 5 – 1 | *Britannia* |
| 6 – 1 | *Princess Anne* |
| | *John F Kennedy* |
| 8 – 1 | *Queen Victoria* |
| 10 – 1 | *Aquitania* |
| 12 – 1 | *Mauretania* |
| 14 – 1 | *Queen Elizabeth II* |
| | *Prince Philip* |
| | *Atlantic Princess* |
| 25 – 1 | *Clyde Princess* |
| | *British Princess* |

Other suggestions included *Queen of the United States, Great Britain, Ocean Queen, The Crown and Anchor, Rose of England, Twiggy, The New Elizabethan, Gloriana, Windsor Wave* and *Donald Campbell* (he had been killed a few weeks earlier).

Sir Basil Smallpeice said in July 1966, in apparent rejection of a '*Queen*' name: 'We shall have to find a name which will reflect this modern age and not recall the days of Henry Hall's band.'

*Even the styling of the name on the stern was different from earlier Cunarders*

In the event the final shortlist of three names was decided in May 1967 by Sir Basil and his deputy, Ronald Senior. Sir Basil later confirmed that the three names were *Queen Elizabeth, Princess Margaret* and *Princess Anne*. The final name was chosen by the same two men on Monday 18 September 1967. Once this was done, a message was sent to the Queen's private secretary, Sir Michael Adeane, at Balmoral – so at that stage only four people knew. The secret was kept to the very end.

Public speculation continued, and the odds on *Princess Margaret* shortened to 4 – 1 on the eve of the launch when it was announced at the last minute that she would attend the ceremony. The yard workers had a different view and chalked *Princess Anne* on the hull – allegedly Captain Warwick's preferred name.

But Cunard's chosen name was not *Princess Margaret* or *Princess Anne*, it was not *Queen Elizabeth II*, let alone *Queen Elizabeth 2*. It was simply *Queen Elizabeth*. One reason – advanced by Sir Basil Smallpeice – may have been that no British merchant ship had ever been named after a reigning monarch and the company did not wish to presume an exception being made.

But another reason concerned the sensibility of the Scots, to which Cunard, who had built over 100 ships on the Clyde in the preceding century, was well attuned. The company knew full well that in Scotland the present Queen is not Queen Elizabeth II – she is simply Queen Elizabeth. To ignore such a historical fact would reek of English arrogance and would be resented.

When the Queen proceeded at the launch ceremony to name the ship '*Queen Elizabeth the Second*' – not just '*Elizabeth*', nor even '*Elizabeth Two*' – the fleeting look of consternation on Sir Basil's face was obvious to the millions of television viewers tuned in to the historic event.

## Breaking With Tradition

But it is difficult to know if it was a look of surprised delight that the Queen had, of her own choosing, decided to ignore tradition and to confer her name on a merchant ship. That would have been a singular honour from the monarch. Or, conversely, if it was a look of concern deriving from a knowledge of what complications would ensue. Probably a bit of both.

As soon as the Queen had surprised everyone, including Sir Basil, controversy began. In England the name was criticised as being unimaginative, but in Scotland it was damned as 'insulting', 'provocative' and 'disgraceful'. Arthur Donaldson, chairman of the Scottish Nationalist Party, said: 'It could not be a bigger insult to the people of Scotland.' More than 500 calls were made to the various offices of Cunard in the UK, most of which, however, congratulated the company on the choice.

In his autobiography Sir Basil maintained that he 'could hardly contain' his delight when the Queen conferred her name in full on the ship. But he proposed the use of the Arabic '2' as it would not have been appropriate to use the 'official designation of the Queen as sovereign' – that is, Roman Numerals – in advertising.

Cunard issued a release in February 1968 saying that the Arabic 2 rather than the Roman II was chosen 'for clarity at a distance' on the stern of the ship.

For the public, confusion rather than clarity was the result: *QE2* is still regularly referred to in print as *QEII*.

*The fly-past by No.736 squadron of the Fleet Air Arm*

There the Queen was presented with a small speedboat for the Royal Yacht *Britannia* – built on the same berth as *QE2*. A delighted Queen thanked Lord Aberconway and suggested it may be appropriate to call it John Brown and paint it in Cunard colours, to which Prince Philip retorted: 'Why not call it Cunard and paint it brown?'

Earlier that year plans had been put in place by Cunard to ensure the offices in Montreal and New York were advised of the name just as soon as it was known. Each office would have a model of *Q4* and the company proposed to keep a hotline from Glasgow to Montreal and New York. The moment the name was announced by the Queen both offices would be informed of the name and perform a little ceremony round their own respective models. Staff in the offices would immediately place the name of the ship on her stern, and crack a suitably miniature bottle of champagne on her bows with, the company hoped, the guests cheering!

Over a thousand firms and 500 subcontractors were involved in supplying fitments for the new ship, and lorry-loads of items from all over the country were arriving at the yard – ranging from fibre-glass lifeboats from Surrey, to the rudder from Sweden. But all the efforts to deliver what the great ship needed continued to be undermined by labour problems. On 11 October 1967 all joiners in the shipyard withdrew their labour to enforce a claim for increased payments. They came back on 15 October, but nine days later on 20 October the coppersmiths and plumbers went on strike following a lengthy dispute regarding demands for increased wages. The men returned to work on 29 November.

## Unofficial Strike Action

Then 41 cranemen, in violation of a union agreement that had recently been concluded and ratified by the Ministry of Labour, went on unofficial strike on 20 November. This resulted in the yard having to suspend a further 153 men from various trades with a threat that further men would have to be suspended if the stoppage was not ended quickly. The cranemen returned to work on 24 November and those suspended returned three days later.

In December 1967 Dan Wallace wrote:

I have advised the builders that in my opinion there must be a considerable improvement in the general rate of progress if the vessel is to be completed by the end of November 1968. The builders, while not sharing this view, agree the whole matter of progress must be fully reviewed at the next meeting on 21 February.

> 'I have advised the builders that in my opinion there must be a considerable improvement in the general rate of progress if the vessel is to be completed by the end of November 1968.'
>
> *Dan Wallace*

On 18 January 1968 *QE2* received minor damage during a gale. An aluminium unit, consisting of deck plating and bulkheads, was badly damaged and required renewal. Two public-room windows were smashed and damage was also done to an aluminium bulkhead, five gangways, 30 wooden blocks, a gangway platform and welder's platform. Aluminium superstructure on the starboard side of the upper deck aft was buckled and several pieces of liner furniture were damaged when bricks from another building fell through the roof of a joiners' shop.

But strikes and acts of God were only part of the toxic mix conspiring to compound the delays. Another was a Clydebank hobby known euphemistically as 'squirrelling' but which most people would recognise as theft.

In August 1967 Bob Arnott, later to become *QE2's* longest-serving captain, was appointed chief officer, and his initial duties before the ship came into service were to oversee aspects of construction on Cunard's behalf. He soon became aware of the practice of 'squirrelling', which was explained to him as not just being a lucrative perk but, rather like some of the

QE2 *and shipyard worker in the fitting-out berth*

strikes, a means of keeping a good job going longer. That was not how he saw it, though, preferring as he did the epithet 'larceny on a grand scale'.

No doubt *QE2* was not the first ship to suffer from the practice, but it was so prevalent that Arnott later recalled that: 'Some of the yard workers were stealing the ship faster than the others could build it.'

## Fixed Prices

There was a thriving trade around Glasgow of materials removed from the ship, a trade that was so organised that items even had a fixed retail price including delivery. Paint was £1 a gallon, light fittings (including shades) from the cabins just 5 shillings (25 pence) and Formica sold at 10 shillings (50 pence) for 2.4m by 1.2m (8ft by 4ft) sections.

When rolls of carpet for the public rooms were laid out, they were found to have front room-shaped sections, complete with window bay, cut out of them as if by a giant pastry-cutter. There were certainly some cosy and expensively carpeted living rooms in Clydebank that winter.

By way of example, Arnott cites one electrician whose home was raided by the police, who was found to have removed from the ship 27m (30yd) of carpet, two chests-of-drawers, a wall cabinet, three bookcases, three lounge stools, 55m (180ft) of fibreglass, five lamps, 36 litres (8 gallons) of paint, plus crockery and soft furnishings. In mitigation

the man's solicitor implied such activity was the norm. 'My client just walked off the ship with the stuff,' he said.

It was regular practice for workers to walk out of the yard concealing items beneath their clothes – items ranging from copper piping to towels. Ironically, Bob Arnott noted, most of the stolen material had to be carried past the police station adjacent to the dock gates, but the prevailing attitude of the police was that although an ocean liner was being stolen piece by piece in front of them, there was little they could do about it.

> 'They consistently underestimate the complicated nature of the ship and all their programmes tend to leave too much to be completed at the end of the vessel.'
> *Dan Wallace on the builders*

*QE2* made her first 'trip' since launching when she was winched just 15m (50ft) further into her fitting-out basin to bring her stern in from the Clyde. Until this time the stern had been sticking out into the river to enable a heavy crane to lower machinery into the engine room. Engines, condensers and boilers were now in place and about 2,300 men were employed.

Dan Wallace was still very frustrated at the lack of information from the builders and their reluctance to plan realistically:

They consistently underestimate the complicated nature of the ship and all their programmes tend to leave too much to be completed at the end of the vessel. The fact that crew accommodation and Tourist accommodation is now almost ready for final inspection misleads them into a false sense of progress. The vessel still lacks supervisory staff.

By March 1968 progress was improving and preliminary final inspections of some Tourist and crew accommodation on Four, Five and Six Decks were taking place. Cunard was keen to have the ship handed over by the end of November 1968, while the yard saw this as the time for the ship to leave the yard for trials.

By April 1968 the Signal, Sports and Boat Decks were well underway, and by late spring the Bridge was in place, still minus its wings, and the funnel had been seated but there was still no mast. The name *Queen Elizabeth 2* was emblazoned on the

*The start of another day for the shipyard workers at Clydebank*

81

*The funnel was hoisted on board in two sections. Here the lower section is being fitted on 18 April 1968.*

hull – formal approval having recently been received from the registrar general of the Board of Trade in Cardiff to use *Queen Elizabeth 2*. The registrar general also confirmed the allocation of the signal letters GBTT (originally used by the *Queen Mary*) at the same time. Dan Wallace felt at this time that the ship was '2/3 months behind schedule'.

## Serious Disagreement

There was serious disagreement between Cunard and the builders about where the problems lay. The yard felt that the public rooms were more problematic and attention should be focused on them, while Cunard felt the accommodation was

furthest behind and that is where the focus should be. But such disputes to Dan Wallace were symptomatic, and he felt the real problem lay with yard management, and particularly John Rannie, managing director of the yard. 'I was becoming increasingly concerned at this time about Mr Rannie's general handling of the situation but found it difficult to know what to do, remembering at this time that he was still regarded as "the king of shipbuilders".'

April 1968 also saw yet more problems with labour when the Otis Elevator Company reported that its workforce had gone on strike. Then the sheet iron workers went on strike for over two months. These troubles were followed in May by all the insulators and pipe-coverers going on strike.

On 7 May 1968 Sir Basil wrote to Anthony Hepper, chairman of the newly formed Upper Clyde Shipbuilders:

I know full well that you are anxious that the ship should be delivered in time because of the publicity attached to the ship worldwide.

…even four weeks delay would therefore be a very serious matter from our point of view, to say nothing of your own.

…The main thing is to get the ship to sea on time. It is always possible to have certain work done while the ship is at sea so long as it is out of sight and hidden from the view of passengers.

But, as if in answer to Sir Basil's call to 'get a move on', on 4 June 1968 30 plumbers and engineers employed by one of the subcontractors went on strike and did not return until 11 June.

In July 1968, as the first wisps of smoke were to be seen emanating from the funnel, Cunard announced that the gross tonnage of *QE2* had increased by 7,000 tons to 65,000 tons. The main reason for the increase was the difficulties of the direct calculations on which the original estimates were made. As *QE2's* design developed it was possible to increase the volume of the superstructure as a result of the rigid weight-saving policy that was adopted. Because of Cunard's design approach, each passenger on *QE2* would have, on average, 60 per cent more space than travellers on the bigger *Queen Elizabeth.*

## More Strikes

Cunard by now was resigned to even more delay, and to the fact that the earliest possible date on which *QE2* could satisfactorily be completed would be 19 December. On 16 July 1968 welders in the yard withdrew their labour following a demand for increased wages (they returned on 22 July) and the next day saw the painters going on strike (returning a week later). On 31 July the deck and machinery engineers, apprentices and brass-finishers withdrew their labour and returned the following day.

Ever hopeful, Cunard announced on 24 July that *QE2* would sail a special four-day inaugural shakedown cruise in conjunction with a selected charity, the National Society for Cancer Relief, followed by a four-day mini maiden cruise departing 10 January 1969 with fares from £98. She would formally enter service on 17 January 1969 with a 13-day 1,500 nautical mile Southampton to New York sailing, calling at Le Havre, Las Palmas, Barbados and Kingston. First Class fares would be £366 and Tourist Class £190. The ship would then make Caribbean cruises from New York before returning to Southampton on 26 March after a 15-day voyage from New York calling at Barbados, Las Palmas, Madeira, Lisbon and Le Havre. Her 1969 season would also include 27 Atlantic crossings – 13 eastbound and 14 westbound – with First Class fares from £185 and Tourist Class from £102 depending on the season.

The company reported that over 8,000 names of people who wished to be on the maiden voyage had been registered over the previous ten years on both sides of the Atlantic.

'The only thing *QE2* has in common with other ships is that she floats. The only thing she has in common with other great Cunarders is a legend called service.'
*Advertisement for* QE2

*E Stairway takes shape*

The campaign to promote the ship was unlike any other. The slogan was 'Ships have been boring long enough' and typical advertisements would read:

> For years, ships have been boring their way across the seas. Now, Cunard has launched the ultimate weapon against boredom at sea. The *QE2*. The new *Queen Elizabeth 2*. The only thing *QE2* has in common with other ships is that she floats. The only thing she has in common with other great Cunarders is a legend called service. Stepping aboard *QE2* is like stepping 20 years into the future. Whatever your preconceptions about her, she's bound to take you by surprise.

Cunard's managing director Philip Bates left the passenger division of Cunard for the cargo division in summer 1968. Dan Wallace in his usual perceptive and forthright way would update the new managing director, former company secretary John Whitworth:

> …unless there is a serious dispute we should still meet our completion date of 19 December. The degree to which the ship will be complete then depends on how successful we are in avoiding further labour problems. … Mr Rannie and Mr Parker have been extremely successful in resolving minor recent disputes. I am now satisfied that although far from perfect, the general organisation and planning in the shipyard is reasonably efficient and the building is under complete control…. From the foregoing you will gather that unless there is a sudden change in the next ten days, you will be able to proceed with details of the Charity Christmas Cruise.

But right on cue, on 5 August, 29 stagers withdrew their labour. That same day 477 general labourers, helpers, red-leaders and drivers also went on strike. Both groups returned two days later, but were immediately followed by the joiners employed by the decorative contractors striking for six days on 15 August, then five days later by 432 shipyard engineers striking for 12 days. Before the month of August 1968 had finished 1,100 boilermakers and 233 platers were also on strike.

## Promises, Promises

On 4 September 1968 Anthony Hepper wrote to Sir Basil: 'I fully understand your concern with regard to *QE2*. On Monday I spent a couple of hours with John Rannie and at the time of writing we are confident we shall keep our delivery promised.' This promise was for delivery on 19 December 1968.

---

'…unless there is a serious dispute we should still meet our completion date of 19 December. … the standard and finish in the accommodation will vary, dependent upon the manpower available….' *Dan Wallace*

---

Just a week later basin trials were delayed by an hour when 464 dock and shipyard engineers and apprentices went on strike. On 1 October 1968 the employees of the ventilation subcontractors went on strike. A week later a subcontractor's plumbers also withdrew their labour.

The level of work deteriorated during October as the labour problems were increasing. Dan Wallace

would later comment: 'I found it almost impossible to make them [the builders] realise the seriousness of this problem…. I fear that in some areas the vessel will not be complete by 19 December, in

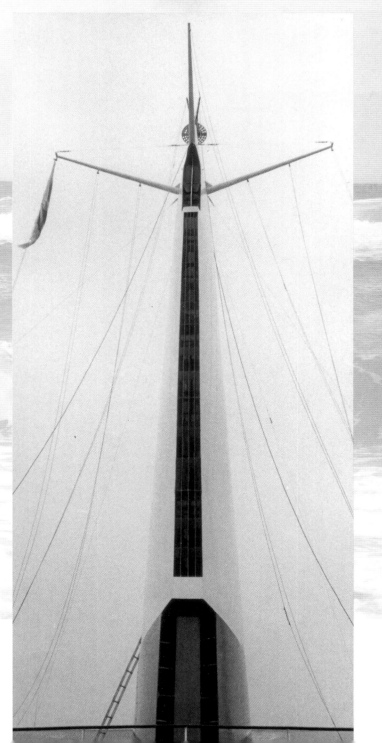

QE2's *masthead stands over 61m (200ft) above her keel*

which case the builders will require working on the vessel until 10 January.'

Dan Wallace still felt at this time that the ship would be reasonably complete for her maiden Atlantic voyage on 19 January, except for three blocks of accommodation. It was also recognised at this time by Cunard that the remaining accommodation would not be complete in detail but would be of an acceptable standard to embark passengers, and that there would be some commissioning faults in the ship during the early voyages.

The ship had the first of many royal visits under her new name of *QE2* on 19 November 1968 when Prince Charles was on board as the ship left her birthplace for the first time – Cunard was shrewd enough to realise that a forthcoming royal visit would ensure the yard remained focused. A special holiday had been declared for the locals and thousands assembled on the fields and shores along the Clyde. Six tugs eased her from the fitting-out berth, where she had been since 20 September 1967, and she used her own engines for the first time. She made 6 knots for the 10-mile journey.

John Rannie and Sir Basil escorted Prince Charles who spoke with some of the shipyard workers. John Whitworth would later recall how the prince ran up the 'down' escalator in the main galley, and how he was on the Bridge as the new liner gave three blasts of her whistle. Captain Warwick recalled how the prince's eyes lit up when he was asked if he would like to press the button to sound the whistle, which he did.

> It was her first time on her engine, and she went like a daisy. I was most agreeably surprised. There were no flaps, and everything went very well.'
> ### *Captain Warwick*

Internally, the ship looked unfinished but Cunard hoped that by 19 December she would be reasonably complete, and by 17 January she would be in a reasonable condition. John Rannie claimed to the press and on TV that QE2 was ahead of schedule by about ten days. The Prince was steered away from most of the incomplete work.

## Scrapes and Scratches

As the liner left the fitting-out basin she nudged the wooden wharf-side and scraped about 6 metres off her paint causing a plume of smoke because of the friction of the liner's hull against the wharf. The ship itself was undamaged. And upon arrival in Greenock she lost some more paint as she gave a slight lurch to starboard and a metre of orange paint was scraped away when her starboard side came into contact with the dock entrance.

QE2 entered the Inchgreen Dry-dock that evening. Cunard called the departure from the yard and the dry-docking 'a significant achievement' for the yard and Captain Warwick commented: 'It was her first time on her engine, and she went like a daisy. I was most agreeably surprised. There were no flaps, and everything went very well.'

Cunard continued to express its concern at the volume of outstanding work and pressed for improved organisation and supervision on the part of the builders but the situation deteriorated rapidly after the arrival in the dry-dock. Delays caused by strike action were further compounded by wholesale vandalism, which served no purpose other than to delay completion and so preserve jobs in Clydebank a little longer. On one occasion the Queen's Room was deliberately flooded with oil, and on another, leather walls covering 'D' Stairway were slashed.

Dan Wallace later wrote:

Unfortunately, Mr Rannie continued to carry out the duties of a Personnel Director and had no assistance with the labour problems, with the result that his assistant managers were often left without a leader. His deputy – Mr McLaughlin – tried to organise the ship from a cabin but never

*Captain Warwick, HRH Prince Charles and Sir Basil Smallpeice on* QE2's *port Bridge wing as she sails down the Clyde*

attempted to inspect the ship and we all have very vivid memories of his constant assurances that all was well.

All the managers on the ship were dominated by Mr Rannie and were either unable or unwilling to take action themselves. Only a few of them were efficient and very quickly the yard's programme of inspections became meaningless.

---

'…Mr Rannie was at Clydebank arranging for the sacking of some 500 joiners and 200 electricians. He appears to have done this without consulting any of his colleagues and this was a most crucial action which caused very considerable labour unrest…' *Dan Wallace*

---

*QE2's* preliminary sea trials commenced two days later than planned due to severe gales. Such was the organisational confusion on board, however, little realistic attempt was made to benefit from the extra time gained. Wallace noted:

> …prior to the ship leaving the dry-dock…Mr Rannie was at Clydebank arranging for the sacking of some 500 joiners and 200 electricians. He appears to have done this without consulting any of his colleagues and this was a most crucial action which caused very considerable labour unrest and horrified Mr Rannie's colleagues who

were well aware of the fact that there was still much work to be done.

At 1700 hours on Tuesday, 26 November 1968, *QE2* left the dry-dock in Greenock for preliminary sea trials. On the Wednesday she was off the Isle of Arran for the measured mile where she achieved 164 revolutions per minute with speeds in excess of 29 knots. But the trial finished on the morning of 30 November having been abandoned because of contamination of the steam and feed system by oil fuel. She was again dry-docked on 30 November for cleaning and decontamination.

A meeting between senior Cunard and yard management took place on board on 1 December to discuss the mechanical problems as well as the unfinished state of the ship. Dan Wallace reported to John Whitworth that in his view 'Mr Rannie had lost control of the situation.'

When John Whitworth raised this concern with Anthony Hepper, the latter responded that it would not be politic to change John Rannie's leadership at that time but did agree for John Starks, the technical director, to take on greater responsibility.

## Charity Cruise Cancelled

Her main trials to the Canaries, due to start on 4 December, were postponed. The first of the 'mini-maiden voyages' that had been scheduled for the new ship, the Christmas charity cruise, was now also cancelled due to the delay. Cunard made an

undisclosed payment to the charity to compensate for their loss.

At this stage 1,600 workmen and crew were aboard. The cleaning operation as a result of the contamination added considerably to the difficulties of finishing the accommodation. Lighting supply was very limited with some black-outs, and heating was also extremely limited.

> '…we expressed grave concern about the prospects of completing the ship by 23 December and pressed again for better organisation and more manpower.'
> *John Whitworth, managing director of Cunard*

On 1 December an onboard meeting between Cunard and the builders decided that technical trials would be resumed between 16 and 18 December and that acceptance trials would begin on 23 December. This meant the postponement of the ship's arrival at Southampton and delivery until 1 January. The builders were still confident about completion on schedule but John Whitworth would later recall: '…we expressed grave concern about the prospects of completing the ship by 23 December and pressed again for better organisation and more manpower.'

On 9 December John Whitworth, Dan Wallace and Tom Kameen undertook a detailed inspection of the accommodation as a result of which all three became fearful that, in the absence of a marked acceleration of progress, the ship would be in no fit state to undertake her first commercial voyage on 10 January with passenger service and amenities operating to the required standards. The overtime ban imposed by joiners and electricians was still in place and there was only a small night shift working.

The incomplete areas were mainly blocks of passenger accommodation on Two and Three Decks and the ancillary public-room areas on Boat Deck. Although the female ratings' accommodation had been ready to receive them, it had suffered some damage due to pilferage of electrical fittings. Most of the male ratings' accommodation was inhabitable but had become dirty through use by workmen and had also suffered from pilferage. Cunard accepted that these blocks would probably still not be complete when the ship entered service but that the ship was in a condition to provide an acceptable standard of passenger service and amenities.

## Completion Date?

The builders relented and agreed to transfer substantial and specific numbers of joiners and electricians from other divisions. They maintained that the ship would be substantially complete by 23 December and wholly complete by 1 January. The builders estimated that there was a shortage of 100 man/weeks of joiners and 50 man/weeks of electricians (on the return of the ship from acceptance trials on 2 January revised figures of 1,500 men for at least three weeks were issued). It was agreed 250 workmen could sail on the acceptance trials. Plans were in hand to clear passengers from unfinished areas if they were still incomplete by 10 January.

Cunard was now in a desperate situation and concluded that it was essential to get the ship away from the Clyde on 23 December in almost any condition provided she had obtained her passenger certificate. The company had realised that if it failed to achieve this it faced the prospect of endless delays and deliberate attempts by the labour force to prolong the work.

## Passenger Certificate

A passenger certificate was required for the December acceptance trials and to achieve that the ship needed to be registered. It was decided that the ship should be registered in Cunard Line's name in order to avoid the necessity of re-registering the ship on 19 December.

Cleaning completed, she left for a second trial in the Irish Sea on 17 December for three days of trials. John Whitworth would later recall:

On 17 December the ship left dry-dock for an anchorage and it was then discovered by Cunard that although a large number of men had been sent ashore some 1,200 still remained in the ship. The engine rooms were also found to be under only-manual control and the Builders proposed to start the technical trials in these conditions. Cunard's Technical Director refused to permit this and the trials finally started on the morning of 18 December.

This trial consisted of stopping, starting, going astern and manoeuvring at full speed and a full technical trial, during which the speed was gradually increased to 177 rpm, at which the full power of 110,000 shp was developed. No vibration or imperfect running was detected. A full visual inspection of the main gearing was made and everything was found to be in perfect condition.

Believing that a satisfactory conclusion was in view the chairmen of the respective companies agreed that they would join the ship by helicopter while she was coming up the English Channel so that at a meeting on 31 December (instead of 1 January for the builders' tax purposes), Sir Basil would hand over a cheque for the final amount due and take delivery of the ship.

## Acceptance Trials

The next stage of the process was the acceptance trials, necessary before the final amount was paid. These trials were a voyage to tropical waters, during which the air conditioning was to be given a thorough try-out. It was agreed that it would be necessary to carry 450 workmen on the acceptance trials to continue the work of finishing the ship. Cunard had to quickly arrange for over 500 of its employees and their families to act as guinea pigs.

Sir Basil was due to join them but his wife had been taken into hospital so he left his deputy Lord Mancroft in charge and flew back to London from Glasgow. The ship embarked passengers for these trials on the evening of 22 December. John Whitworth would describe how he was 'disturbed' at the condition of the accommodation. The whole of Five Deck was allocated to yard workmen and of the 698 cabins on One, Two, Three and Four Decks, 234 were uninhabitable and all the remainder had substantial defects. Considerable re-berthing of the guinea pig 'passengers' had to be undertaken.

The Board of Trade surveyor in charge of the ship advised Cunard that he was unable to issue a passenger certificate which was essential if the ship were to proceed to sea with passengers unless considerable work had been done to make the ship safe for them. The yard arranged for a substantial number of electricians and joiners to work overnight primarily to block off the uncompleted areas and make them safe electrically by isolating electrical circuits and taping up bare wires.

At 0830 hours on 23 December a passenger certificate was finally issued and QE2 quietly left the Clyde – not to return for 22 years – and was worked up to 150 rpm in the normal way.

The trials were to be comprehensive sea trials. On the technical side the main and auxiliary machinery would be tested including simulated breakdowns and damage conditions. The equipment would be overloaded intentionally. On the hotel side the 570 'passengers' would have to simulate a full ship so they were put into groups

QE2 *on acceptance trials*

and asked to turn up at specific times for particular functions. They had been instructed to order anything from the menus in order to test the kitchens. Each would fill out a form once they had completed a task.

## Strictest Secrecy

So sensitive was Cunard about the unfinished state of the ship that the 'strictest secrecy' was to be enforced and all communications between the ship and the UK were to be sent in code for the chairman's attention. The use of the radio telephone was to be avoided as far as possible.

It was now apparent to the company that it would be unrealistic to maintain the 10 and 17 January voyages. This was not only due to the extent of the uncompleted work but also the fact that many items of the ship's equipment had not been properly commissioned by the builders and when put into operation were found to be defective. A press party of 71 was due to join the ship in Las Palmas on 28 December and it was difficult to find enough cabins for them, even in an unfinished state.

Trouble with the engines during the acceptance trials soon overshadowed all such considerations. First the starboard and then the port engine malfunctioned. After four days of problems, on 28 December *QE2* limped into the port of Las Palmas.

Sir Basil and Anthony Hepper joined the ship there at around 2000 hours and went straight into a meeting in the Card Room that lasted until 0400 hours the next morning. It was agreed that delivery would not take place upon arrival in Southampton. The Board of Trade surveyor would withdraw the passenger certificate as soon as the ship had berthed in Southampton – the certificate would not be reissued until 17 April 1969.

'I would like to pay a very well deserved tribute to the efforts of all Cunard officers and crew. They are demonstrating their ability – under most difficult circumstances as a result of the volume of this uncompleted work – daily to improve and bring the ship up to the standard of passenger requirements for the new markets that we are seeking.'
*Sir Basil Smallpeice*

They are demonstrating their ability – under most difficult circumstances as a result of the volume of this uncompleted work – daily to improve and bring the ship up to the standard of passenger requirements for the new markets that we are seeking. I cannot speak too highly of what our Cunard men and women on board have accomplished.

Commenting on Sir Basil's statement, Anthony Hepper said he was quite certain that *QE2* was going to be a very fine ship, a ship of which Cunard was going to be very proud, and of which they as shipbuilders would be very proud for many years to come. The yard was committed to handing over *QE2* in an absolutely first-class state. He confirmed that it would not be less than three weeks from 1 January but an exact date for handing over could not be given until after arrival in Southampton.

Anthony Hepper also explained that the delay led to another problem, that of their own management. John Rannie, the special director in charge of the ship, was retiring on 31 December. This would mean Upper Clyde Shipbuilders would have to make other managerial arrangements for

At 0930 hours on 29 December a joint press conference (also broadcast throughout *QE2's* public address system to keep the ship's company informed) was held and Sir Basil confirmed that Cunard would not be taking delivery of *QE2* on her return to Southampton citing two main reasons. The major reason was the degree of uncompleted builders' work in the passenger spaces of the ship including the areas that serviced them. The second, but subsidiary, reason was the technical problems that had arisen with both sets of main machinery during the trials. Sir Basil commented:

I would like to pay a very well deserved tribute to the efforts of all Cunard officers and crew.

the remainder of the period to see the ship handed over to Cunard. Hepper personally assumed control of the operation assisted by John Starks (technical director) who would now become project manager for the operation.

## Costs Written Off

The 10 and 17 January cruises were cancelled (at an estimated loss to Cunard of £500,000) and the visit for more than 2,000 travel agents on 2 January was also cancelled. The expensive advertising and marketing programme was wasted. In addition, the crew – trained and in readiness – had now to be retained on standby with full pay. That high cost would also have to be written off.

QE2 had broken down and neither Cunard nor the yard knew what had caused the damage let alone how to cure it. The Pametrada turbines that had been approved by Cunard for QE2 were a tried and tested design. QE2's previous speed trials demonstrated that these turbines were fully capable of achieving their required performance. The fault was major, could not be rectified at sea and would take some time to repair. To take the ship back to the Clyde was just not practical – Southampton was the nearest port so QE2 headed 'home'. It was decided to proceed at half speed (14 knots), which gave an acceptable vibration level; any increase in vibration could be immediately countered by a reduction in revolutions.

During most of Monday, Tuesday and Wednesday the ship proceeded homeward without further incident. Her arrival in Southampton was one day later than originally planned and the 'splendid arrival' that had been organised (which was to feature the Hampshire Police Band, balloons and the mayor and other VIPs meeting the ship by launch) was cancelled.

The engineering difficulties did prove to be a blessing in disguise for the yard as it now gave them extra time to complete the unfinished passenger accommodation. Some 400 men were brought to Southampton from Clydebank to join those already on board, and Vosper-Thorneycroft was engaged by Upper Clyde Shipbuilders to act as contractors in Southampton.

## Broken Turbine Blades

On QE2's arrival in Southampton the turbines were opened, and it was revealed that blades in both rotors had sustained damage – hundreds of blades had been stripped from the main body of the rotor hub. Many of the broken blades were piled up against each other near the horizontal joints while some were wedged in the nozzle passages. The neighbouring nozzles were extensively distorted, and cracking could be seen at the bases, or roots, of other blades. It was immediately clear that a major repair, requiring entirely new blades, would be needed.

*This detail shows clearly the damage to the 9th and 10th stages of the blades in the starboard high-pressure turbine rotor*

## Engine Trouble

The acceptance trials seemed to be going well until the morning of Christmas Eve when vibration began to be noticed in the starboard engine. Since no vibration had been detected during the voyage up to that point, the cause was deemed to be the result of an oil leak from a small bore pipe, and the effect of cold oil on a hot part of the turbines. When no change was detected after a short while, speed was reduced to allow the turbines to be investigated – but by late afternoon the situation was much worse and the engine had to be stopped altogether.

The investigation that ensued was finally completed at dawn on Christmas Day, and the turbines restarted – slowly at first, and then at an increasing speed. All seemed to be going well until the following day when the starboard turbine again began to vibrate. Despite continuing investigations and the exploration of a number of theories as to the cause, the vibration persisted.

A bad situation got worse later on Boxing Day when vibration began on the port engine – vibration that gradually increased until the speed was reduced. On 28 December the ship was at Las Palmas, where she was at anchor all day.

An investigating team, under the leadership of Sir Arnold Lindley, President of the Institute of Mechanical Engineers, was established to assess the cause of the damage and to find a solution to the problem.

Upper Clyde Shipbuilders remained responsible for the ship during this completion period. Cunard Line Limited, acting as agents for and on behalf of the builders, undertook the care, maintenance and security of the ship including the operation of the ship's machinery in accordance with the builder's requirements, using the ship's crew and shore personnel for these purposes with all costs and liabilities attributable to the builders.

'Cunard will not accept delivery until after the ship's turbines have been thoroughly re-tested and proved in further basin trials, speed trials and a prolonged acceptance trial under maintained pressure, followed by further inspection.'

*Sir Basil Smallpeice*

The examination showed, in simple terms, there were design faults in the blades, and that steam supply nozzles that directed steam to the blades were both too numerous and of inadequate quality. The resulting vibration caused blades to crack or shear, and each one so affected damaged

*Previous page: Crowds greet QE2 on her maiden arrival in Southampton, January 1969*

its immediate neighbours. Once identified, the problem was rapidly remedied.

The port turbine rotor arrived back in Southampton by road and was inspected at Vospers on the evening of Saturday, 1 March, with the arrival and inspection of the starboard rotor following shortly afterwards. The port rotor was re-installed on 5 March. On 7 January the yard indicated to Cunard that the major work would be completed by 31 January but also provided a secondary date of 14 February to allow for cleaning and commissioning. There were around 1,500 men working on board at this time.

## No Further Payments

On 9 January Sir Basil took the monumental step of instructing Cunard's chief accountant that no further payments should be made to the yard, and a week later Cunard issued this statement:

> Cunard will not accept delivery until after the ship's turbines have been thoroughly re-tested and proved in further basin trials, speed trials and a prolonged acceptance trial under maintained pressure, followed by further inspection. It is impossible to say when this programme of correction, testing and proving of the ship's power plant can be completed.

The shipyard refused Cunard's request in mid-January for one of its own independent

consultants to visit the yard and inspect the rotors. The yard stated that it had been agreed at an earlier meeting that it would be their responsibility to report back and make available reports on tests etc. when these became available and that as well as appointing their own consultant they had also consulted a well-known American turbine builder as well as placing evidence and conclusions before a panel of experts for their consideration. This panel would include experts from Rolls Royce, the National Gas Turbines Establishment, the Central Electricity Generating Board and the Department of Engineering at the University of Cambridge.

---

*'Despite the optimism of the Builders, Mr Wallace reported to me on 15 January his concern at the general lack of progress.... He regarded their estimated completion dates of 31 January/14 February as totally unrealistic.' John Whitworth*

---

Questions about *QE2* were raised in the House of Commons with MPs asking for an enquiry into all the troubles and delays. The Minister of Technology, Anthony Wedgwood Benn, responded that he did not believe a formal enquiry would serve any purpose at all. Reports of widespread pilfering during the building of the liner were raised in the House of Lords and the government spokesman, Lord Beswick, responded that that was a matter for the management.

John Whitworth would later write:

Despite the optimism of the Builders, Mr Wallace reported to me on 15 January his concern at the general lack of progress. He had sent the Builders formal letters regarding a number of aspects…. He reported further on 28 January to the effect that the Builders were becoming increasingly behind schedule; he regarded their estimated completion dates of 31 January/14 February as totally unrealistic.

Despite this, Upper Clyde Shipbuilders were still reducing the numbers of men working on board. On 28 January there were 1,300 UCS men on board; the number on 27 March was 340.

## Independent Assessment

On 10 February 1969 Anthony Wedgwood Benn met Sir Basil, Sir George Gardner (Chairman of John Brown Engineering) and Anthony Hepper to ask Sir Arnold Lindley to make an independent technical assessment and to report back to the Ministry of Technology.

Two days later Cunard announced:

You will have learnt, from the various news sources, that the Minister of Technology has called for an independent assessment of the troubles besetting the *QE2's* power plant.

It now becomes apparent that the ship cannot be delivered to us by the builders before mid-April and therefore the Easter Cruise due to depart on 3 April cannot take place.

---

'You should be aware that we consider that we have a claim against your Company in respect of the losses suffered by us as a consequence of delay in delivery of the vessel….'
*Frank Leach, Cunard's company secretary, to UCS*

---

On 12 February Cunard's company secretary Frank Leach wrote to his counterpart at the yard, P Russell:

We accept that your expenditure certificates should be met, on our part, by the appropriate payment but only in so far as the expenditure has been well spent and has produced an acceptable product. The expenditure so far incurred and paid by us on the turbines and associated machinery has been rendered valueless because of the inability of the turbines to operate, and we are doing no more than withholding amounts against the payments already made to you in respect of work now found to be quite unacceptable.

You should be aware that we consider that we have a claim against your Company in respect of the losses suffered by us as a consequence of delay in delivery of the vessel….

On 19 February 1968 Lord Aberconway wrote to Sir Basil to complain about some of things Sir Basil had supposedly been saying to the press about the problems. Sir Basil was accused of claiming that John Brown Engineering's attitude 'made one wonder what reliance could be placed on statements made at their press conference' held in Glasgow on 5 February; also that the turbines might need to be replaced with a new set designed and manufactured to Cunard's satisfaction and that Cunard would require a guarantee of the turbines for the life of the ship.

Lord Aberconway retorted that for Cunard to talk of replacing the turbines after one failure, was quite premature. Also that a guarantee for the lifetime of the ship would go far beyond the terms of the contract. It was also suggested that Cunard had specified turbines of Pametrada design and approved them.

> 'Cunard did not specify the turbines of Pametrada design exclusively, nor did we approve the actual designs. The choice and approval of designs lay with the builders.' *Sir Basil Smallpeice*

## Tony Benn remembers his part in the building of *QE2*

*QE2* was a very important ship, not just in terms of jobs on Clydeside but also in terms of what she would mean for Britain. It was obvious even then.

I was very, very keen to get this ship built, but it was a difficult and stressful time. Shipbuilding was a funny industry, run by gentry who had inherited a yard or two from their grandfathers but who had very little knowledge of engineering. They would go to their clubs in Glasgow in the afternoons in the hope of picking up an order or two from a friend. It's no wonder the industry was in trouble.

I have no doubt at all that John Brown's would not have survived to complete *QE2* had Upper Clyde Shipbuilders not been created to prevent the de-industrialisation of the Clyde and to direct investment into the yards.

I recall trying to bring peace in some of the disputes, but it was hard not to take the workers' side. They were treated in a bloody awful way – almost as serfs. They were highly skilled craftsmen, and though they might have lacked a university education they knew the ship and what needed to be done intimately. Far more so, in my view, than many of those running the yard who couldn't mend a puncture in a bicycle, and who didn't have to be at work, outside, at 5 on a cold Glasgow morning.

# Fixing the Faults

Cunard appointed Booz Allen & Hamilton to initiate a system of recording individual defects on punched cards which would then be run through Cunard's computer to produce a printout listing each defect individually. This work would continue from mid-January until mid-March and the final printout based on information up to 12 March gave the following figures:

| | |
|---|---|
| Total recorded defects | 19,500 |
| Defects rectified by Builders | 11,000 |
| Defects passed by Cunard | 5,500 |

Machinery spaces and a number of general items on the hull side were excluded in the above figures.

John Whitworth commented:

> Progress meetings were held regularly at weekly intervals during February and March. They followed a consistent pattern. The Builders continued to under-estimate the volume of outstanding work and were continually over-optimistic about completion; their assurances in this respect were constantly proved to be false by Mr Wallace's inspections and Booz-Allen's printouts.

Sir Basil responded: '…I am satisfied that my comments following the press conference on 5 February were, at the time and in the circumstances, justified,' and that 'Cunard did not specify the turbines of Pametrada design exclusively, nor did we approve the actual designs. The choice and approval of designs lay with the builders.' Lord Aberconway finalised his next letter thanking Sir Basil for his response with, as Sir Basil said: 'Altogether not the sort of acknowledgement I should have expected to a "slap-down" letter!'

## A Substantial Claim

Cunard had been advised by their legal counsel that a substantial claim could be made against UCS but the company would have to pay the balance of the contract price prior to pursuing the claim. Cunard had no legal right to hold back an amount in respect of claims the company thought it may have had for loss on profits due to the late delivery. Such a claim would have been a 'disagreement' between the parties which had to be referred to arbitration.

Sir Basil wrote to Lord Aberconway after the publication of Sir Arnold's report:

> We have all had an opportunity of considering the report of Sir Arnold Lindley to the Minister of Technology dated 28 February 1969 on his independent assessment of the *Queen Elizabeth 2* turbines, the contents of which, I understand, have been accepted by John Brown

*Tugs bring* QE2 *into Southampton, January 1969*

Engineering (Clydebank) Limited, Upper Clyde Shipbuilders and ourselves.

---

'When *QE2* sails from Southampton on 2 May she will be as perfect as a ship can be. Her accommodation and public rooms will be 100% complete and there will be no doubt about the reliability of her engines.' *Sir Basil Smallpeice*

---

The Directors of Cunard Line Limited must now consider the steps to be taken to formulate the Company's claim against Upper Clyde Shipbuilders Limited for the delay in delivery of the ship.

Finally on 3 March 1969 Cunard announced that *QE2* would make her maiden voyage from Southampton to New York on 2 May. In making the announcement Sir Basil said:

When *QE2* sails from Southampton on 2 May she will be as perfect as a ship can be. Her accommodation and public rooms will be 100% complete and there will be no doubt about the reliability of her engines. Sir Arnold Lindley's assessment of her turbine troubles sponsored by the British Government and published last Friday means that her technical problems have been positively identified and resolved. There is no foreseeable reason why we should not get delivery of the ship in the last half of April.

*Queen Elizabeth 2* will more than fulfil the promises made to her prospective passengers as to her performance. She will be the most superb example of the shipbuilder's craft the world has yet seen. *QE2* is certainly a new place to visit between New York and London or Paris.

Basin trials were undertaken on 23 March and *QE2* finally left Southampton on Tuesday 25 March for three days of builders' technical trials. Sir Arnold Lindley was on board. Sir Arnold proclaimed the three days of testing as 'extremely satisfactory' and he was able to give the liner a 'maker's guarantee'.

Captain Warwick commented:

We put the engines to full astern and the ship pulled up in a mile-and-a-half in seven minutes. This was something completely new to me in efficiency. We kept the engines going and went backwards at 14 knots for 30 minutes passing ships we had previously overtaken.

Upon return to Southampton *QE2* was dry-docked again before proceeding on an eight-day acceptance trial from 30 March to 7 April, which took her to tropical waters and back to Southampton.

The trials proved most successful with excellent turbine performance. The turbines were opened again and examined after *QE2's*

Passengers enjoying QE2's *lido decks on the Preview Cruise*

return to Southampton and the stages that had previously given trouble were found to be satisfactory.

## No Guarantees

Sir Basil was most keen to obtain a 2–3 year guarantee from the builders but UCS would not budge on this point, claiming that the turbines had been the subject of an independent technical assessment by Sir Arnold. On 14 April over 300 VIPs were entertained on board at a private function hosted by Sir Basil and Captain Warwick.

> 'We put the engines to full astern and the ship pulled up in a mile-and-a-half in seven minutes. This was something completely new to me in efficiency.'
> *Captain Warwick*

On Friday, 18 April, *QE2* officially became a Cunard ship when she was finally handed over to her owners by a simple exchange of letters reserving all rights or claims on both sides. Unusually the handing-over took place in London at a private ceremony because Sir Basil would be 'flying out of the country immediately afterwards'. With three triumphant blasts on her whistle the Cunard flag was hauled up by coxswain Andrew McGregor at 1315 hours as the Upper Clyde Shipbuilders' flag – which had been flown over the liner since her arrival in Southampton on 2 January

– was lowered. The flag raising was at first scheduled for 12 noon, but because of a delay in the London ceremony the UCS flag remained in place on *QE2* for another hour.

On 18 April 1969 Cunard made a payment of £2,072,000 and the yard paid Cunard £792,000. At the same time Cunard borrowed from the Board of Trade the remainder of the government loan (£1.9 million) under the loan agreement made in September 1967. This would result in a net inflow of cash to the company of £620,000.

On the same day a list of outstanding items and tests in all areas of the ship were agreed by both Cunard and UCS – it came to 216 pages. These items were progressively rectified throughout 1969.

*QE2* had cost £28,825,185 – and in terms of stress, worry, anxiety, frustration and anger of all those concerned, probably a great deal more. But was she worth it?

*A memo circulated within Cunard in December 1971 revealed that the final cost of QE2 had been £28,825,185 and that the gross book value of the ship was £20 million. Other costs revealed were £54,980 agreed with John Brown Engineering for the repairs to the turbines and £21,317 for items stolen or damaged at the shipyard.*

# QE2 in Service 3

# Chapter 5
# Making an Impression

To the weary relief of Cunard, *QE2* finally entered service on 22 April 1969 with an eight-day Preview Cruise to Las Palmas, Tenerife and Lisbon. Only 1,350 passengers boarded, well below the ship's capacity, but they were given a rousing send-off by hundreds of onlookers, balloons and a band; all was going well until two stowaways were discovered on board – and the ship had to turn back to rendezvous with a pilot cutter south of Nab Tower, But, fortunately, that was not a foretaste of what was to come – and the ship's first cruise passed without incident.

*QE2* returned to Southampton on 30 April, and immediately preparations began for a visit by the Queen and the Duke of Edinburgh the following day – just before *QE2* was to set off on her maiden transatlantic voyage. The royal party spent several hours on board, taking both lunch and a tour.

In his autobiography *Of Comets and Queens* Sir Basil noted:

> …we were passing through the Queen's Room…Lord Mancroft pointed out to the Queen the Oscar Nemon bust of herself. The Queen commented: 'He is a great perfectionist, isn't he? I have now sat seven times for this bust, and each time he finds something wrong with it. "That's no good," he says and wrenches my head off' – using her hands as she spoke to demonstrate his wringing her neck.

The Queen also asked the chief engineer to explain in non-technical language what was wrong with the ship's engines. He answered in the plainest layman's terms possible: 'Well ma'am, instead of going chug, chug, they went clang, clang….'

> 'Well ma'am, instead of going chug, chug, they went clang, clang….'
> *Chief engineer explaining the engine problems to the Queen*

Two days earlier, a special five-pence stamp three times the normal size was issued by the Post Office showing the liner on a background of

turquoise blue. But turquoise was the one colour not in evidence as she prepared for her maiden voyage; driving rain persisted for the whole day, and lifted only as the ship was pulling away. The departure was delayed slightly by baggage loading problems, as well as a police search necessitated by a hoax bomb scare.

But nothing detracted from the warmth of the ship's send-off, aided by music from the Royal Corps of Transport and a fly-past by Buccaneer jets of 736 Squadron of the Fleet Air Arm – the same squadron that had saluted the ship's launch.

The Ocean Terminal was packed with over 3,000 well-wishers who had turned out to cheer her on her way. Bright streamers criss-crossed from ship to shore and a thousand balloons were released from the dockside. A flotilla of small boats escorted the ship to the open sea. Among them were fire tugs that saluted QE2 in their own fashion, sending jets of water arching high into the sky. Schoolchildren from Fawley and surrounding areas lined the shores at Calshot.

*The Queen, with Captain (later Commodore) WE Warwick, admires a figurehead of Britannia carved by Charles Moore and presented to Cunard by Lloyds of London*

Some people had waited a long time for this moment: a Mr Taylor had booked his passage ten years earlier, and he brought with him the newspaper cutting from April 1959 announcing Cunard's intention to build two new superliners that had prompted him to make a reservation the same day. With plenty of time to get ready, Mr Taylor made the sailing without difficulty – but two passengers from London missed the ship. They were finally able to board by taking a boat out to *QE2* from the dockhead.

At the ship's first port-of-call in Le Havre, *QE2* was given the biggest welcome the port had laid on since the liner *France* had paid her first visit. *QE2* graced the port for just two hours before she was finally on her way on the true maiden voyage – non-stop to New York – at 2130 hours.

The steaming time from Le Havre to Ambrose Light was four days, 16 hours and 35 minutes, which gave an average speed of 28.02 knots. Thousands turned out to welcome the new *Queen* in New York on 7 May. Hundreds of small craft escorted her to Pier 92 and helicopters carrying dozens of press photographers buzzed around her.

Mayor John Lindsay boarded the ship on the seaward side of the Verrazano Bridge, along with other civic dignitaries and press for the last leg of her journey. He honoured Cunard by officially proclaiming it '*QE2* Day' in New York.

During a short ceremony in the Queen's Room Sir Basil presented to Mayor Lindsay a gold medallion to commemorate the ship's first arrival in the city. The gold medal, inscribed on one side with an outline of *QE2*, had caused a little bother both with the Bank of England and the United States Treasury Department. The first had not wanted the gold to leave the country, and the latter didn't want it to come in unless it went directly to Fort Knox. The letter authorising the importation was not issued until Mayor Lindsay gave an assurance that he would not melt the medal down for its gold content. Mayor Lindsay in turn presented Sir Basil with a glass seahorse; the little seahorse, thankfully, raised no bureaucratic obstacles whatsoever.

*QE2* remained in New York for two days and various receptions took place. Many guests were astonished by the modern leather and chrome vibrancy of the new Cunarder and how different she was from the muted art deco of the earlier *Queens*.

Most passengers boarded *QE2* on Two Deck and immediately met the full impact of the designers' ingenuity in the dazzlingly modern Midships Lobby. The lobby was circular with a sunken seating area, navy carpets, walls lined with navy hide and sofas covered in green leather. The ceiling was silvered fibreglass which flowed to the outer walls in concentric circles like the pattern made by a stone dropped in a pool. A central column was covered in white fibreglass and white painted ribs that emanated from the mirror finish of the ceiling.

## Views in All Directions

Ascending to the highest deck, Signal, passengers found an observation platform giving spectacular views in all directions. On Sports Deck below, apart from the usual shipboard games, could be found the Children's Room including a crèche and a cinema.

One deck down on the Boat Deck and decorated in Indian laurel veneer was the 736 Club, named after the shipyard number by which *QE2* was known, and the venue for the evening discotheque. Next was the 24-hour Coffee Shop and the Juke Box which was orientated towards the young and had

an area set aside for pin tables and a juke box. To the port side could be found the London Gallery, featuring showcases for the display of small objects as well as pictures. Midships on Boat Deck was the balcony of the Theatre and the shops with several showcase windows.

Beyond the shopping arcade doors was the top level of the Double Room, the main tourist-class lounge and the largest and most dramatic room on the ship. With an area of 1,850m$^2$ (20,000 sq ft) and seating for about 800, the room glowed in shades of red from scarlet through to plum. From the upper gallery a great stainless steel, curved staircase, with treads 1.5m (5ft) wide, swept down into the lower room.

Upper Deck below was the home for the principal tourist-class public rooms. Forward was the Lookout, a two-level room where passengers could enjoy views overlooking the bow of the ship. Aft was the red, white and blue *Britannia* Restaurant with seating for 815 passengers. The 500-seat Theatre was a room with four principal functions: a theatre, a cinema, a conference room and, on Sundays, a church. The Theatre Bar adjacent featured a wall of bright red fibreglass moulded in an egg-box pattern and a red piano. A more restrained atmosphere was to be found in the Upper Deck Library opposite – a cool, quiet room with a thick beige carpet, blue leather-lined cases for the books, big leather sofas and a great circular

*The original aft decks with swimming pools are shown here*

rosewood table with a top partly lined in leather. Aft of the Double Room was Double Down Bar.

The principal first-class public rooms were to be found on the Quarter Deck. Forward, and discreetly accessible by a circular staircase up from its own private bar on One Deck was the Grill Room. This exclusive and exquisitely decorated extra-tariff room had a capacity of 100 and was decorated in Bordeaux red leather and velvet with shiny metal trim. The *Columbia* Restaurant, decorated in ochre leather, extended the full width of the ship and was divided into smaller areas with the use of bronze-tinted glass screens. The ceiling was in gold aluminium and the chairs, as in the *Britannia* Restaurant, were specially designed by Robert Heritage.

Aft of the *Columbia* Restaurant, on the starboard side, was the Midships Bar with sumptuous curved sofas in rich green leather and mohair velvet, and walls lined with the same material. On the port side was the Quarter Deck Library, where Michael

Inchbald used traditional ship finishes of wood and brass to achieve a peaceful effect.

The white and silver Queen's Room was a brilliantly successful space-age yet elegant main lounge with a sunny garden room atmosphere by day. A slotted white ceiling gave an airy trellised effect and the structural columns were encased in great trumpets of white fibreglass complemented by the white fibreglass space-age chairs which had bases of this trumpet shape in reverse and were upholstered in natural hide. Rounding off the main public areas was the *Q4* Room aft, a nightclub that had the added appeal of opening up to the swimming pool.

## Four Swimming Pools

There were, in fact, four swimming pools on *QE2* – on the Quarter Deck, One Deck, Six Deck and on Seven Deck. Elsewhere could be found passengers' launderettes, the Beauty Shop, a Synagogue, Purser's Office, a hospital and Turkish Baths.

Passenger cabins could be found on One to Five Decks. There was immense variety, from suites that consisted of one, two or three main rooms as required, through to family cabins where two rooms were adjoining and sharing a bathroom, to smaller single-berth rooms. There were many permutations of colour and room arrangements.

Crew accommodation and facilities on *QE2* were among the finest afloat and colours were chosen to make the rooms cheerful and attractive. There were four messes and five recreation rooms for the various ranks.

The whole ship was as strikingly redolent of the sixties as her predecessors had been of the thirties; obviously so, maybe – but almost everyone was surprised.

---

'One cruise, and I've done over 40 on *QE2*, there was lobster on the menu. As a joke I said to the restaurant manager "Is this from Maine?" "No sir," says he, "but your next one will be." Lo and behold, docked in Naples, he announced "Your lobster, Sir Jimmy, just flown in from Maine" – and it had. That's *QE2* style.' ***Sir Jimmy Savile***

---

*QE2* began her return journey, her first eastbound crossing, on 9 May, with Lord Mountbatten on board. He was the first of many celebrities to travel on *QE2* and in the initial voyages she carried Lynn Redgrave, Peter Sellers, Ringo Starr, Count Basie and Gracie Fields. Attracting celebrities has remained a *QE2* forte, and she has been host to more than any other ship. Regulars include David Bowie, Rod Stewart and Sir Jimmy Savile.

On 16 May, while outward bound through Spithead on her second westbound voyage, *QE2* passed through

the multi-national fleet of NATO that HM The Queen was reviewing from the Royal Yacht *Britannia*. *QE2*'s whistle sounded a greeting as she drew abreast of the Royal Yacht.

Captain Warwick signalled: 'Captain Warwick and the ship's company of *Queen Elizabeth 2* … send their best wishes and hope Her Majesty will have an enjoyable day reviewing the NATO fleet.' Her Majesty replied: 'I am grateful for your signal. I send you and all on board my best wishes. Bon Voyage. Elizabeth R.'

On 29 May 1969 HRH The Duke of Edinburgh paid a visit to *QE2* to present awards on behalf of the Council of Industrial Design in a ceremony that took place in the Theatre. The Duke was given a behind-the-scenes tour of the ship by Sir Basil Smallpeice and Captain Warwick, which included crew spaces, the Boiler Room and the Engine Room, prior to lunch in the *Columbia* Restaurant. The design of the chairs in the *Columbia* and *Britannia* Restaurants received an award.

Lord Snowdon, along with other members of the royal family, had seen designs in various stages of preparation. He telegrammed Dennis Lennon on

*The original Queen's Room with sixties-style furniture*

30 May 1969, after he had seen the finished ship, saying: 'What you have personally achieved with *QE2* makes one proud to be British…the mood is breathtaking. Many congratulations.'

---

'What you have personally achieved with *QE2* makes one proud to be British…'
*Lord Snowdon to designer Dennis Lennon*

---

At the annual shareholders' meeting in London in June of that year Sir Basil reported that *QE2* was right on target in making the profits Cunard expected from her. Sir Basil had confirmed the day before the meeting that passenger numbers were increasing and that *QE2* had just brought 1,868 passengers from America to France and the UK, earning a total gross revenue on this single one-way voyage of over $700,000.

But there were still doubts about Cunard's future. On 7 August Lord Mancroft, Cunard's chairman, while speaking on board at a ceremony attended by the officers and chief petty officers of the 736 Squadron of the Fleet Air Arm, tried to allay those fears. He gave an assurance that *QE2* would stay under the Cunard flag for the duration of her anticipated 30-year career: 'People who say she will be transferred to P&O or go to the Americans will have to think again.'

*QE2*'s 25,000th passenger, 24-year-old Nancy Moorehead from Ohio, was welcomed aboard on 14 August by Captain Warwick and honoured in a brief ceremony before the ship sailed on her eighth eastbound transatlantic voyage.

## Weathering the Storms

It's inevitable that a ship like *QE2*, travelling tens of thousands of nautical miles a year across all oceans of the world, will from time to time be challenged by storms of a kind not encountered by cruise ships hugging the coasts in warm and shallow seas. But *QE2* is built to withstand the most ferocious weather, as she has from time to time been able to prove.

The first such occasion was in October of that year, when the ship ran into three severe storms in succession on an eastbound crossing. Force 11 winds and 15m (50ft) waves were the norm for several days and Captain Storey was forced to reduce speed significantly in order to minimise passenger discomfort. The ship eventually arrived

*Captain (later Commodore) WE Warwick*

in New York ten hours late – dishevelled but undamaged. Both the captain and Cunard felt that *QE2* had proved her seaworthiness in conditions that would have defeated other ships. They noted that she rode the storms far better than either *Queen Mary* or *Queen Elizabeth*.

## First Overhaul

*QE2* was due to enter the King George V dry-dock in Southampton for her first scheduled overhaul on 29 October. The turbines, which had had to be repaired before the ship was handed over to Cunard, were examined by experts who wanted to see the condition of the blading after six months in service. The examination of the turbines was made in accordance with an agreement between Cunard and the Board of Trade when *QE2* was handed over after her second set of trials. *QE2* had operated without main machinery trouble, reaching speeds of over 30 knots, since those trials. The Board of Trade expert who inspected the starboard high-pressure turbine was so pleased with its condition that he did not even bother to look at the twin port-side turbine, which was also damaged after the original proving trials.

Sir Basil Smallpeice was able to announce that month that Cunard had repaid £2.5 million – one-eighth – of the government loans provided for the 'world's most sophisticated ship', and in so doing he commented:

Some people often speak as though Cunard has been accorded by the Government some specially privileged financial position in respect of the *QE2*. If another shipowner were to order (say) five container ships costing £6 million each, he would be able to borrow, on normal terms, the regular 80 per cent (£24 million) and would have only to repay some £2 million by the end of this year, leaving £22 million outstanding.

Compared with this, Cunard will have reduced the amount outstanding on the *QE2* loans to only £17 million, the difference of £5 million having been provided entirely out of our own funds.

At the same time Cunard announced that during *QE2*'s six-month transatlantic season of 12 round-trip voyages she had carried 40,752 passengers – which meant she had been 84 per cent full.

In early January 1970 Captain Warwick was obliged to turn *QE2* into a battering ram as he forced his way into New York's icebound harbour. Then, having beaten the freeze-up, he had to dock the liner without the aid of tugs, which were not icebound but strike-bound. Gently, without any fuss, Captain Warwick manoeuvred her into the berth – and came across ice 15cm (6in) thick off Pier 92. The captain put *QE2* astern four times before charging at the ice, and finally broke through. He said later: 'I never thought I would have to use a £30 million ship as an ice-breaker.'

In March 1970 HRH Princess Margaret paid an informal visit to *QE2* while the liner was berthed in Barbados. Accompanied by Lord Snowdon, who had already expressed admiration for the design of *QE2*, and a party of 13, Princess Margaret toured all the public rooms of the ship before she and her party were entertained to cocktails by Captain Warwick in his room prior to dining in the Grill Room. After their dinner of smoked salmon, caviar, chicken kiev and champagne sorbet, the royal party visited the kitchens, engine room, control rooms, shaft tunnel and finally the Bridge.

## Man Overboard

Although 'Man Overboard' is a well-known phrase, people rarely go overboard accidentally these days. This was far more common in the days of sailing ships when sailors went aloft to tend to the sails, often in the most atrocious conditions, and lost their grip on icy rigging. But even now such things do occasionally occur – and *QE2*'s first experience of it was between Barbados and Madeira in March 1970. As soon as the alert was given to the Bridge, the ship slowed from 28 knots and within 15 minutes had completed a 'Williamson Turn' to put her on a reciprocal course. Lookouts scanned the waves and finally the body of a crew member was spotted, and recovered from the sea. Unfortunately he could not be saved – and nor was it ever discovered what caused the fall.

*QE2*'s most popular cruises over the years have been those to the Mediterranean, and the first began on 22 April when the ship left Southampton for a 15-day sailing to Gibraltar, Athens, Istanbul, Naples and Lisbon.

In June 1970 *QE2* crossed the Atlantic westbound in a record time of 3 days, 20 hours and 42 minutes, an average speed of 30.36 knots – a speed that she has never exceeded since on a westbound run.

In a year of firsts, *QE2* achieved her first medical rescue from another ship during an eastbound transatlantic crossing in June 1970. A distress call was received from a small German ship, *Zosmarr*, en route to Boston, seeking assistance for a sick seaman. As soon as *QE2*'s principal medical officer had determined from the radioed descriptions of the patient's symptoms that the seaman's life could be at risk without proper attention, *QE2* altered course and sailed at full speed towards *Zosmarr*. On the way, she ran into dense fog and the two ships were only able to rendezvous through radio contact. When they were close to each other, just after midnight, *QE2*'s doctor was taken by one of the ship's launches to find *Zosmarr* , which was not easy in fog and darkness. It was achieved by means of an officer on the Bridge tracking the launch and the *Zosmarr* on the radar, and issuing instructions to the launch, travelling blind, by walkie-talkie. Despite the drama of the night, the sick seaman

*QE2 in the Caribbean in the early 1970s*

was safely transferred to *QE2*. He made a full recovery.

*QE2*'s first long cruise was a 37-day 'Three Continents' voyage from New York that Cunard dramatically called 'the cruise of the 1970s'. The voyage would include stops at Las Palmas, Dakar, Luanda, Durban, Cape Town, Rio de Janeiro, Bahia, Curacao and St Thomas before *QE2* returned to New York.

On 8 January 1971, while cruising off the Leeward Islands in the Caribbean, the French Line's *Antilles* was in the vicinity of Mustique when she struck an uncharted reef. Oil in the engine room caught fire, and, as the blaze spread, the 635 people on board were forced to abandon ship. Again, thanks to her speed, *QE2* – anchored off St Lucia – was able to reach the scene in just over

three hours. It was dark when *QE2* arrived at 2230 hours, but the scene was lit by fire and explosions from the sinking *Antilles*.

---

'You could almost feel the heat. We were terrified that there were still people on the ship.' **QE2** *passenger on the sinking of the* **Antilles**

---

One *QE2* passenger said: 'You could almost feel the heat. We were terrified that there were still people on the ship.' By then the passengers from the *Antilles* had been transferred in the ship's lifeboats principally to Mustique. During the dash

to the scene comprehensive preparations had been made as there was little certainty of what would be found: the hospital was on full alert, the kitchens on standby, and the housekeeping department assembled stacks of blankets. Although *QE2* had a number of empty cabins available on that sailing since she was carrying only 1,000 passengers, lists were prepared of those willing to give up their cabins for survivors.

In the end *QE2* picked up 300 stranded passengers from Mustique – a transfer made difficult by heavy swells as the ship was too big to dock. By early the following morning all the *Antilles*' passengers had been accounted for – all uninjured – and *QE2* sailed for Barbados where the rescued were set ashore. Apart, that is, from 85 *Antilles*' passengers who decided to continue their Caribbean cruise on the Cunard ship.

Much less exciting was the appointment, by Cunard, of consultants McKinsey & Co to undertake a review of the company. The subsequent report was very critical of the prospects for *QE2*. McKinsey recommended that serious consideration should be given to laying up *QE2* as the vessel was forecast to lose £1.7 million in 1972 and approximately £4.4 million by 1975. Fortunately, Cunard paid not the slightest attention and continued to make profits from *QE2*.

But, sophisticated though the ship may have been – technically the most sophisticated afloat at the time – she was abruptly reminded on 5 March 1971 how something as humble as jellyfish could bring her to an embarrassing halt.

While in Trinidad, on a 14-day cruise from New York, *QE2* was anchored about 2km (1 mile) from shore and the sea around the ship was white – the effect of thousands of jellyfish. They were so numerous that they had been affecting the operation of the ship's launches and slowing down the ship-to-shore service.

## Jellyfish Alert

Shortly after sailing at 1800 hours *QE2* experienced a shut-down of all machinery and a complete loss of power. The engineers, having initially kept one of the main water inlet valves closed throughout the ship's stay at the anchorage, had opened it on leaving. As *QE2* increased speed the water had ceased to circulate properly and the shut-down had occurred.

The ship's officers were initially without radar but, after managing to get the radar going, they discovered that the ship was 8km (5 miles) from the nearest land; a satisfactory distance except that the wind was blowing onshore. The problem was further compounded by the discovery that there was deep water right up to the land so that anchoring was not an option and *QE2*'s drift towards the rocky coastline could not be prevented.

The chief engineer requested that ratings be despatched to the engine room to help with the 'turning gear'. Turbines run at such high temperatures that the blades must be kept turning to prevent damage. Normally the 'turning gear' was operated electrically but on this occasion the electric motor was not operable and the gear had to be worked by hand. The ratings had to endure extremely high temperatures in the engine room so could only tolerate a minute or so before becoming exhausted.

*QE2* continued to drift towards the coast and it was estimated that she would be in danger within three or four hours but it was not known how long it would take a rescue tug to arrive from Port of Spain. Fortunately the wind changed, preventing the ship getting closer to land. *QE2* was stopped for four hours, but finally the engineers de-jellied the intakes and she continued on her way.

A poignant meeting took place in Aruba in mid March 1971 when *QE2* met, for the first and only time, her namesake *Queen Elizabeth*, by now renamed *Seawise University* and about

QE2 *cruising in the Caribbean*

to undertake her voyage to the Far East and eventual destruction in Hong Kong. Both vessels exchanged farewells as *QE2* sailed away, an act the then managing director Lord Mancroft described as 'painfully moving'.

About the same time, Sir Basil Smallpeice, chairman of Cunard, received a call from Nigel Broackes, chairman of Trafalgar House Investments, an aggressive young company specialising in construction, requesting a meeting. This resulted in Trafalgar House buying Cunard, a company with an independent existence of 131 years, for just £27.3 million – less than *QE2* had cost to build. The last meeting of the board of Cunard as an independent company took place on 25 August. Sir Basil stayed on the Trafalgar House board for another five months and then '...with sadness in my heart, I let myself quietly over the side and went ashore.' Ironically, Trafalgar House went on to buy John Brown and its Clydebank shipyard company, birthplace of *QE2*.

## Drug Smuggling

In September that year *QE2* was embroiled in a £16 million heroin smuggling plot when a massive consignment of the drug was expertly hidden in a Jaguar loaded in the ship's garage in Southampton. A US Federal agent commented that the cache was so neatly stored: 'that it appeared as if they had put the heroin in and then built the car around it'.

> '...with sadness in my heart, I let myself quietly over the side and went ashore.'
> *Sir Basil Smallpeice on his retirement*

The haul was the second largest quantity ever seized in New York, and the US authorities had the perpetrators under surveillance for some time before the seizure. Police followed the case from the UK, where the new Jaguar XJ6 was bought, to France where the 90kg (200lb) shipment of heroin was thought to have originated. When the car was offloaded in New York, police spent five days following it around the city. They saw it change hands twice before they moved in to make their arrests. The car was dismantled and 180 plastic bags containing the heroin were found.

The car's floorboards had been remodelled to make a hollow area underneath where some of the drugs were hidden. Other bags were found in the transmission and in hollow compartments of the doors and door-frames. In Southampton, a local garage had steam-cleaned the car before shipment, unaware of the police and Customs surveillance. Even Captain Mortimer Hehir, Master of *QE2*, did not know of the operation until he read about it in the papers when he got back to the UK.

In April 27-year-old Jean Orsini and a 37-year-old Cuban, Luis Gomez, were jailed for 25 years and fined $35,000 each in New York for smuggling

the drugs. An accomplice, another Cuban, George Warren Perez (48) was jailed for seven years and fined $7,000. And drugs were soon followed by guns!

On 20 October 1971, when *QE2* had sailed for Southampton from Cobh in Ireland, after landing passengers from New York, six suitcases were left unclaimed on the quayside. The smart blue and green suitcases looked harmless enough until 127kg (20-stone) Irish porter Gerry Sharkey attempted to lift them. Unable to do so because of their weight, he alerted the customs authorities and subsequently a cache of arms intended for the IRA was discovered.

## Gun Running

The arms were removed to Cork police HQ while the police interviewed the passengers to see if they had seen anything unusual on the voyage. Police also visited the homes of known IRA sympathisers in County Cork. Although nobody claimed the cases when *QE2* docked, police believed someone had travelled with them. The cases were marked with a label with the name 'G Walsh' on it. The search for the mystery passenger continued.

The plot failed because the smugglers had packed their suitcases too well. The one that proved too much for the porter to lift tipped the scales at 100kg (220lb). Police confirmed that if the arms had been lighter, then no one would have noticed. Ten or a dozen suitcases instead of six would have been stored overnight and would not have attracted attention – then the building could have been raided by the IRA.

On 7 April in the following year the first telephone call from a ship at sea via earth satellite was received in Cunard's London offices from *QE2*, which was cruising in the Caribbean. Cunard chairman Victor Matthews took the call from Captain Mortimer Hehir and later reported that: 'It was an exceptionally clear call, better than a lot of local calls.'

A second 10-hour late arrival in New York as a result of serious storms occurred when, on an eastbound crossing in April 1972, *QE2* had to reduce speed to just five knots as a result of 15m (50ft) waves. To compound the delay, the ship then had to anchor off Southampton for over 21 hours waiting for the storm to abate. But again, *QE2* proved her excellent sea-keeping qualities, and while the journey may have been uncomfortable the ship rode the storm without difficulty and arrived virtually unscathed.

## Change of Plan

*QE2* had to cancel her scheduled call at Cherbourg – thus missing a civil ceremony to mark the return of Cunard to that port after an absence of several years during which Le Havre was the continental port of call. The 197 European-bound passengers were later taken by ferry or charter aircraft from Southampton.

The actors Robert Wagner and Natalie Wood were among the 1,200 passengers and described the storm as 'a great experience – it was very exciting'. Some passengers were bruised and shaken and three crewmen were hurt, one with a broken thumb, another with a broken collarbone, and the third with a wrist injury.

> '...a great experience – it was very exciting.' ***Robert Wagner and Natalie Wood on 1972 storm***

Crockery and glass worth £2,500 was broken and eight armoured glass windows on Upper Deck were smashed, though there was no flooding. Also damaged were two pianos that came loose from their moorings when the ship rolled at an angle of up to 22 degrees.

> '...she took a terrific lurch to port, and dozens of diners were hurled from chairs, and crockery and food were everywhere.' ***Staff Captain Bob Arnott***

Captain Hehir arranged for free champagne to be served to all passengers on the last night as some compensation for the rough ride. For most of the voyage the captain had been on the Bridge. He made broadcasts to keep passengers informed about what was happening and at the cabaret show on the last night of the voyage he met the passengers for the first time and received a standing ovation.

Staff Captain Bob Arnott later wrote:

As I was entering the *Columbia* Restaurant to take my place at the Captain's Table, she took a terrific lurch to port, and dozens of diners were hurled from chairs, and crockery and food were everywhere. When she settled down, I proceeded to my table (although my natural instinct was to go to the Bridge to see what was going on), picking up prone passengers as I went.

The 600 female passengers were presented with bouquets on disembarking. Oakley and Watling of Southampton received an order for between 500 and 600 boxes of flowers to be put on board *QE2*. Jack Spalding, a director of the firm, said: 'It was a rush order, and we sent a lorry for the flowers which came mostly from the Worthing area. There were carnations, tulips and iris. The lorry returned on Saturday morning and ten of the staff worked all day preparing the flowers....'

In addition, all passengers were presented with a signed 'Storm Certificate' and a map showing the area of the storm. It showed the liner's two tracks, the one intended and one taken, much farther south in an effort to avoid the worst of the weather. The certificates stated:

This is to record that on her North Atlantic voyage leaving New York on the 16 April 1972, for Southampton, England, *Queen Elizabeth 2*, of 65,863 gross tons, encountered exceptionally severe weather in position Latitude 42° 18' North, Longitude 55° 52' West.

During this storm, winds reached in excess of 100 mph. Combined with heavy swell, waves were encountered of 50 feet in height.

This weather caused even the *Queen Elizabeth 2*, with her exceptional size and sea-keeping qualities, to lie hove to for 21½ hours between 17th and 19th April 1972, until the storm abated.

I commend all passengers in sharing this unique experience with great cheerfulness and calm.

*Mortimer Hehir*
*Captain*

At a press conference given after arrival, Captain Hehir said: 'It was the worst weather I have ever experienced, not so much in its intensity as in its duration. Nobody in the ship could recall winds of that velocity lasting so long. At times there was nothing to be seen all round the liner but spume and spray. It was a fantastic sight.'

Captain Hehir recalled that two bad rolls of 40 degrees had occurred as he tried to get back on an

---

**QUEEN ELIZABETH 2**

## STORM CERTIFICATE

This is to record that on her North Atlantic voyage, leaving New York on the 16th April 1972, for Southampton, England, RMS QUEEN ELIZABETH 2, of 65,863 gross tons, encountered exceptionally severe weather in position Latitude 42°18' North, Longitude 55°52' West.

During this storm, winds reached speeds in excess of 100mph. Combined with a heavy swell, waves were encountered of 50 feet in height.

This weather caused even the QUEEN ELIZABETH 2, with her exceptional size and sea-keeping qualities, to lie hove to for 21½ hours between 17th and 19th April 1972, until the storm abated.

I commend all passengers in sharing this unique experience with great cheerfulness and calm.

Captain

easterly course to head home after having steered towards the African coast: 'It was freak weather with rogue seas. At times the swell was crashing down green on the foredeck and I was a bit worried that it might carry away the anchor cables or damage the capstan, but all seems to be well.'

He said that *QE2* had exceptional sea-keeping qualities, and that she had come through the ordeal extremely well; better, he thought, than the older *Queens* would have done. Describing the scene in the restaurant after the second of the big rolls that occurred on 18 April, Bert Weedon, the virtuoso guitarist, said: 'It was a fantastic sight. As the liner went over, everything shot off the tables – crockery, glasses, food and bowls of fruit. The floor was just one glorious mess. But the crew moved in quickly, cleared it up as best they could, and brought around more coffee.'

---

'It was a fantastic sight. As the liner went over, everything shot off the tables – crockery, glasses, food and bowls of fruit.'

*Virtuoso guitarist Bert Weedon*

---

*QE2* was already scheduled to move into Southampton's King George V dry-dock immediately after the crossing. The programme of work – cleaning, painting and other essential maintenance – turned out to be even more welcome than usual.

That year *QE2* continued to receive more than her fair share of excitement when an extortionist tried to hold the ship to ransom. On Wednesday 17 May 1972 a telephone call was received at Cunard's New York office, taken by Charles Dickson, vice-president finance and operations of the company's American organisation.

## 'Blasted Out of the Sea'

Speaking with what was described as a New York accent, the caller demanded that Cunard pay him $350,000 or *QE2* would be 'blasted out of the sea'. The caller went on to say that he had accomplices on board the ship who would detonate depth charges concealed in bulkheads if the money wasn't paid. In the days before the term 'suicide bombers' entered the language, most people would have dismissed the idea of two accomplices willingly killing themselves as absurd, and the extortionist tried to add plausibility by saying that one was a terminally ill cancer patient, and the other a former convict 'with nothing to lose'.

Although Dickson and his bosses thought from the outset that it was just an elaborate hoax, it was too big a risk to ignore the extortionist's demand, especially with more than 2,150 passengers and crew on board. They decided to call in the FBI, and also contacted Cunard's managing director, Norman Thompson in London, who in turn at once called in his chairman, Victor Matthews. The latter concurred with the view that: 'this is probably a con trick and a very clever one, but we cannot take any chances'.

Back in those days the Provisional IRA terrorist campaign, with strong support from American sympathisers, was at its peak, and there were fears that for IRA bombers the world-famous *QE2* would be a prime target.

Within minutes Scotland Yard and the British Ministry of Defence were notified, and an emergency meeting of chiefs of staff was held. The ministry decided to send out four bomb-disposal experts to drop by parachute into the Atlantic as close as possible to *QE2* – a decision taken by Admiral Sir Michael Pollock, Chief of Naval Staff and First Sea Lord, together with Air Chief Marshal Sir Denis Spotwood.

Details of the parachute drop were worked out by the joint defence planning and operational staff. The Royal Marines and the Army were asked to each provide two top bomb-disposal experts. Urgent phone calls were made to service units to get the four-man team together.

*QE2* had left New York for Southampton via Cherbourg on Monday 15 May under the command of Captain Bill Law. The 1,438 passengers included the conductor, Leopold Stokowski, and Mr George Kelly, uncle of Princess Grace of Monaco.

A coded message was sent late at night on 17 May from Cunard's Lower Regent Street office in London to Captain Law and Chief Officer Bob Arnott stating:

THREAT OF EXPLOSION
TO DESTROY SHIP
UNLESS DEMAND CASH
PAYMENT MET.
EXPLOSIVES SET ON SIX
SEPARATE DECKS.
AUTHORITIES ADVISE
TAKE ALL NECESSARY
PRECAUTIONS. TWO
ACCOMPLICES MAY BE
ON BOARD. MONITOR
ALL CABLES,
TELEPHONE MESSAGES.

*Captain William Law*

*A Nimrod aircraft of the type used for reconnaissance and communications during the bomb alert*

Every possible security arrangement was initiated and a discreet search was carried out. By chance, the ship's own security department had just undergone special training in bomb detection. Bob Arnott later recalled:

As soon as the first alert had come in, we had started standard procedures. In spite of the threat that the bombs wouldn't be found, our search routines are so thorough that it was unlikely that there were any hiding places on *QE2* we didn't know about. Intensive inspections from *QE2*'s masthead to her keel-base discovered absolutely nothing.

Money was obtained with which to pay the ransom in New York while, in Britain, the RAF readied two aircraft: a Hercules which would fly out a bomb-disposal team and an RAF Nimrod, which would be used for communications. In the interim an RAF Nimrod reconnaissance aircraft had taken off from St Magwan to advise on sea and weather conditions for the proposed air drop and to act as a communications centre between the threatened liner and the police and defence experts in Britain.

Captain Law, following the standard Cunard policy of keeping passengers fully informed in an emergency, announced in the afternoon of 18 May:

Ladies and Gentlemen, we have received information concerning a threat of a bomb explosion on board this ship some time during this voyage. We have received such threats in the past which have so far turned out to be hoaxes. However, we always take them seriously and take every possible precaution.

On this occasion we are being assisted by the British government who are sending out bomb-disposal experts who will be parachuted into the sea and picked up by boat and brought aboard.

Generally, passengers remained calm, and retired New York bank vice-president Purcell Roberston said at the time: 'Everyone stayed cool. The bridge game went on as usual. The bar had the same number of drinkers. The only big difference was that dinner was a bit late.'

Cunard advised the world that *QE2* was 'on time and flat out' on her way to Cherbourg.

'Ladies and Gentlemen, we have received information concerning a threat of a bomb explosion on board this ship some time during this voyage.'
*Announcement by Captain Law, 18 May 1972*

The military bomb-disposal team consisted of four men: Captain Robert Williams (29), Sergeant Clifford Oliver (32), Lieutenant Richard Clifford (26) and Corporal Thomas Jones (28). Together the men represented the Special Air Service (SAS) and the Special Boat Service (SBS) .

At about 1630 hours *QE2* reduced speed in order to hove-to and embark the military parachutists in a position 740 nautical miles due east of Cape Race, Newfoundland. A coded message from Cunard gave *QE2* precise and secret instructions for the ocean rendezvous.

The company also asked the officers to check if any passengers matched up to the ex-con and cancer victim descriptions. So far as the officers could tell, no matches were found. In replying to the instructions, the ship was asked in 'cloak and dagger' style to refer to the military men as 'friends', and the alleged shipboard gang of extortionists as 'special passengers'.

The Nimrod appeared just after 1700 hours, and at 1808 hours, an RAF Hercules was sighted carrying the four members of the bomb-disposal team. The craft was right on target after flying 1380 nautical miles from Lyneham in Wiltshire, and excited passengers lined the ship's rails to watch as the four parachutists appeared, dropping from beneath the low cloud base into the sea at the liner's starboard bow.

## Parachuting into the Sea

That low cloud proved to be a serious problem in dropping the parachutists into the sea near to *QE2*. The pilot made a few test runs and then, because the cloud was too low to permit a safe jump from below the cloud base, on the final run, after establishing the position of the launch which had been lowered from *QE2*, went back up to 250m (800ft). A few minutes later the first two parachutists appeared out of the cloud and landed in the sea just ahead of *QE2*. The Hercules then undertook a second run, and the last two parachutists came down with equal precision.

For the benefit of those not on deck to witness the landings, an announcement was made by Bob Arnott saying that the four parachutists had been safely picked up and were all fit and well. The bomb-disposal experts were taken to the Bridge

*An RAF Hercules of the kind used to parachute in the bomb-disposal team*

where their leader, Captain Williams, was introduced to Captain Law. The army commander reached inside his wetsuit and produced a copy of that day's newspaper, which he presented to an astonished captain.

---

'Everyone stayed cool. The bridge game went on as usual. The bar had the same number of drinkers. The only big difference was that dinner was a bit late.'

*Passenger Purcell Robertson*

---

*QE2* was under way again at just before 1930 hours, and as dinner began, the military began a search of strategic points in the passenger accommodation and baggage storage rooms. Meanwhile a board meeting in London discussed how the two accomplices on board would know when the money had been paid; it was finally reasoned that in the circumstances, it wouldn't be too difficult for them to pick up a radio signal from the American coast.

Cunard was manning phones in London and Southampton to reassure anxious relatives of passengers that no bombs had been found. In mid-afternoon on Thursday 18 May, a handwritten special-delivery letter arrived at the Cunard offices in New York – postage due 28 cents – addressed to Charles Dickson. The extortionist ordered Dickson to take the $350,000 to a designated phone booth and await a call.

## The FBI Keep Watch

Charles Dickson set off with the cash, found the booth, and the phone rang. Dickson recognised the voice, which gave him instructions to go to a washroom of a nearby café where there would be a further message taped under a washbasin. The caller warned that two guns would be trained on Mr Dickson the whole time. Dickson did as he was ordered and found the message, which told him to drive over Bear Mountain Bridge to the town of Beacon, and leave the money at a spot in an out-of-town parking lot. An attached diagram showed its location. Once again, Dickson did as he was told while the FBI kept watch at a discreet distance.

All day and night the FBI kept surveillance on the spot where the money had been left but

*The threat to bomb* QE2 *made headlines; this is from the* Daily Telegraph

no one came to pick it up and the next day it was returned to Cunard. The bomb scare proved, as was suspected, to be without foundation and nothing was found. When the pay-up-or-else deadline had passed, life on *QE2* returned to normal, the public radio communications system was re-opened and the next 24 hours was blocked with calls from the world's press, TV and radio reporters, and passengers telling anxious relatives and friends ashore that they were safe.

In the Wardroom the four bomb-disposal men were toasted by the ship's officers, and, in response, Captain Williams said: 'I've always wanted to sail on this marvellous ship, but what a hell of a way this was to get onto the passenger list.'

But as one very relieved American passenger said after the dramatic mid-Atlantic meeting between ship and security forces: 'It was very comforting to think Britain can still reach out.'

All the bomb disposal experts were awarded the Queen's Commendation for Brave Conduct. One of them was later named 'Man of the Year' by the Royal Navy.

## Mid-Atlantic threat to 2,000 lives

# ANTI-BOMB SQUAD PARACHUTE TO QE2

The QE2.

## Cunard will pay $350,000 ransom

FOUR bomb disposal experts were parachuted to the liner QE 2 in mid-Atlantic last night after Cunard was told six bombs would be exploded on board unless a ransom of $350,000 (£140,000) was paid.

Cunard ordered its New York staff to pay the ransom, which was demanded in an anonymous telephone call to the New York

For their part, Cunard invited each of the servicemen to take a free trip on *QE2*.

Richard Patton, the Cunard boss in America, said of Charles Dickson: 'He was at times in great personal danger but when I asked him how he felt at the worst moments, his only complaint was that his mouth was dry. I'm proud to have such a man working for Cunard.'

On 21 June 1972 a New York shoe salesman, Joseph Lindisi, was arrested at his shop, 'Joseph's Bootery', and charged with extortion plots against *QE2* and American Airlines. He was subsequently found guilty and sentenced to 20 years' imprisonment pending a psychiatric examination. The FBI was satisfied that there had been no bombs aboard *QE2*, no accomplices, and that it had all been the work of a lone con-man.

*Continued on page 134*

# The 1972 Refit

Trafalgar House, Cunard's new owner, was convinced that *QE2* was a potential money-maker and, given time, would prove to be a winner. It undertook a complete survey of the liner during the first six months of ownership, and began planning for *QE2*'s first major refit. In total, £1.8 million would be spent on modifications to the two-year-old ship.

*QE2* arrived at Vosper Thorneycroft in Southampton on 13 October 1972 and during the next three weeks some drastic alterations were made. The most striking addition was the block of ten penthouse suites on the Sports (lower level) and Signal (upper) decks in the existing circular open area slightly behind the mast. This resulted in the loss of the observation platform on Signal Deck and the outdoor children's area and pool on Sports Deck.

## 100 Welders on Board

The preliminary work was carried out while *QE2* was at sea shuttling across the Atlantic during the summer of 1972 with over 100 welders from the Vosper Thornycroft yard on board. The preparations on the ship and the prefabrication of the block at the shipyard had to be exact to ensure a proper fit.

Cunard and Vosper Thornycroft designed the aluminium alloy complex so that it could be fitted out and furnished in two halves, port and starboard, on the quayside, ready to be lifted by floating crane on to *QE2*. E C Payter and Co of Bilston, Staffordshire, started work on 30 June. By the end of July prefabricated sections were on the quay in Southampton and work there started with Bilston platers and welders assembling the two halves. At the beginning of September Vosper Thornycroft started work on the internal partitions.

*The new Queen's Grill*

Each block was 26m long by 8m wide (80ft by 24ft) and weighed about 50 tonnes. The aluminium alloy structure was lined with electrical and plumbing services together with the fixed joinery and glazing.

The installation started with Southampton's 150-tonne floating crane bringing the port side cabin unit from berth 40 and lowering it onto *QE2*'s top deck. The new starboard cabin unit was loaded the same way. *QE2* then left her berth for the dry-dock where the new cabins were installed.

The new block featured two 80m² (793 sq ft) luxury duplex apartments, the Queen Anne and Trafalgar Suites, each featuring two dressing rooms, a private cocktail bar with refrigerator, two bathrooms and a window facing forward, and two 5m by 6m (15ft by 18ft) teak-decked furnished balconies. The Trafalgar Suite was designed to resemble Lord Nelson's quarters on *HMS Victory* while the Queen Anne was decorated in 18th-century style.

The eight penthouses were made up of pairs of cabins, each 35m² (355 sq ft) with a communicating door, so that they could provide a separate bedroom and dayroom. The penthouses were decorated in modern or traditional décor.

Other alterations to passenger accommodation included the construction (in the existing shopping arcade) of ten additional staterooms (eight doubles and two singles) on Boat, while cabins for 300 passengers were refurbished.

## Total Luxury

These additions necessitated the creation of a new dining area, lounge and galley that had to offer an 'atmosphere of total luxury'. The Boat Deck Coffee Shop, Juke Box Room for teenagers and the 736 Casino and Nightclub were therefore converted into the Queen's Grill, Queen's Grill Lounge and dedicated galley.

The original Grill Room on Quarter Deck was closed and the space became part of the *Columbia* Restaurant, expanded to a capacity of 810. Passengers previously assigned to the Grill Room would now dine in the Queen's Grill. The *Britannia* Restaurant was also enlarged forward to a capacity of 792 using space occupied by the Lookout Bar.

To service the *Britannia* Restaurant, a new galley was constructed in the area formerly occupied by the Lookout Bar. Previously used by the original three restaurants on board, the main galley was now dedicated to the *Columbia* Restaurant. The area was reconstructed according to a sophisticated American design and incorporated a new larder, washing-up area and confectioners' shop.

Elsewhere the existing Boat Deck shopping area (midships on Boat Deck between D and E Stairways) was relocated further aft into the upper level of the Double Room, which involved the removal of the Double Up Bar; a new Casino was built in the space occupied by the Library and Port Foyer midships on Upper Deck; the One Deck Shop was moved from One Deck

to a new location on Boat Deck near the new shopping arcade; the London Gallery on the Boat Deck was removed and replaced by a Reading Room; the Double Room had its stage extended and its capacity enlarged to 500; and the loss of the 736 Club Disco meant that the new disco and entertainment location became the Theatre Bar on Upper Deck.

The refit took longer than had been anticipated; *QE2* thus left Southampton two-and-a-half days late. The delay cost Cunard £100,000 in air transport for passengers in the UK and France who could not wait for the liner, and hotel bills for other passengers.

The addition of the penthouse suites resulted in *QE2*'s gross tonnage being increased from 65,863 grt to 66,851 grt.

*The Double Room with the shops relocated to the upper level*

But how had a shoe salesman managed to come up with such a dramatic scenario? The answer is he didn't: one of his classmates at an English class at Hunter College, Manhattan, had unwittingly done it for him. A Barbara Shelvey, as part of her course work, had written a short story just a few weeks earlier, which featured an ex-convict who found no joy in life and a Mrs Garth, terminal cancer patient, who were booked on a Cunarder. They planned to hijack the liner, commit a robbery and escape in one of the ship's launches. The class teacher, Professor Philip Freund, read the story to the class – and the rest is history! When Professor Freund read of the unfolding event on *QE2* he had noted the similarity and called the FBI.

## Security Measures

The event did have a long-lasting effect in making Cunard extraordinarily security conscious, and in November 1972 Cunard banned sightseeing parties and visitors with passengers. 'These visitors are too many to allow proper security to be exercised and our time in port is too short to maintain the standards of service we require,' the company said.

In April 1973 *QE2* was chartered by Mr Oscar Rudnik of Massachusetts-based Assured Travel of Worcester. His plan was to use the ship to take passengers from Southampton to Israel for the 25th Anniversary of the state's birth. Two cruises were planned – an Easter/Passover Cruise from 14 to 28 April, and a Silver Independence Day Cruise from 28 April to 13 May.

Naturally, given the tense situation in the Middle East, it was assumed that *QE2* could be attacked by Arab activists at some point during the cruise. As a result, security was extremely tight and even involved the Ministry of Defence.

So, while the passengers due to sail on this noteworthy voyage may have felt secure as a result of the significant measures taken, there weren't actually many of them to benefit from it. Widespread publicity about the potential threat and the consequent security acted as a great deterrent to travellers, and instead of the anticipated 1,200 passengers on each cruise there were half that number. The crew complement remained virtually the same, however, so service levels were never better. An addition to the crew was a complement of 11 rabbis to ensure that the entire main kitchen and restaurant complied with the strictest kosher requirements.

When the liner put into Southampton on 12 April, the number of guards on the gangways was tripled and frogmen continuously inspected the area around the berthed ship. Lorries were searched as they delivered stores. Police vans and cars were to be seen inside and outside the docks

*QE2 in New York in the seventies*

and more than 20 police were stationed on the area leading to *QE2*'s gangways. Some police wore yellow armbands and were believed to be armed but the authorities would not confirm this.

'There was never any problem over the liner's crew. The majority of them are from the old *Queen* ships, and they look on this voyage as just another job of work.'
*National Union of Seamen on the cruise to Israel*

The National Union of Seamen, on behalf of the crew, demanded £50 danger money for the voyage plus four years' wages should they fall victim to Arab terrorists during the voyage, while at the same time claiming: 'There was never any problem

over the liner's crew. The majority of them are from the old *Queen* ships, and they look on this voyage as just another job of work.'

Still on the subject of money, MPs demanded to know who was paying for the security. Cunard was, so that particular complaint went no further.

The passengers, who were mostly American Jews, arrived at Heathrow aboard six chartered El-Al or TWA jets, and were given a huge police escort to Southampton. Fifteen coaches were used to transport them and police were on duty at vulnerable points on the route. On arrival at the docks they had to pass through eight checkpoints before they embarked. They and their luggage went through electronic doorways, and security opened and searched some of the cases. There was also a rigorous check on crew members.

SAS members were carried on board throughout the voyage to guard strategic areas – and such was the sensitivity surrounding the arrangements of the SAS, that the Irish crew members were given leave for the duration of the cruise just in case any might identify the SAS men to the IRA. In addition, the ship carried 30 Royal Marines, many armed, and sniffer dogs alert for explosives!

Dockers handling baggage for *QE2* stopped work, asking that in the event of death caused by terrorist action through baggage explosives, relatives should be granted four years' wages, similar to the liner's crew. The management agreed and work resumed after 30 minutes.

*QE2* left 40 minutes late because the last jet into Heathrow had been delayed. Helicopters – believed to form part of the security system – circled over the ship as tugs took her out into Southampton Water. Thousands of people, attracted by the publicity the liner had received, thronged the waterfront in the afternoon sunshine to see her sail away on Sunday 15 April.

Her first port-of-call was Lisbon on 17 April, where the authorities took the precaution of closing the Salazar Bridge while *QE2* passed beneath. The passenger terminal was closed to all visitors and passengers were searched before being permitted to rejoin the ship if they went ashore. Portuguese frogmen made regular searches of the ship's hull during her 12-hour call there.

## First Visit to Israel

The liner took a northern passage through the Mediterranean in order to keep distant from the North African coast, largely in order to avoid seeming unduly provocative. *QE2*'s arrival at Ashdod on 21 April marked her inaugural visit to Israel and was a unique occasion for Ashdod itself – the first-ever visit by a passenger liner. *QE2* stayed four days in Ashdod prior to proceeding to Haifa where the former prime minister of Israel, David Ben Gurion, visited the ship. After a few days she returned to Ashdod.

Anti-personnel devices were detonated in the harbour at night around the floodlit ship in order to deter unfriendly divers. On 29 April the passengers from the Easter/Passover Cruise flew home and the

*President Anwar Sadat of Egypt*

*Colonel Gadaffi, president of Libya*

passengers for the Silver Independence Day Cruise joined the ship for a reversal of the itinerary. *QE2* spent just over two weeks in Israel before leaving on 8 May under similar strict security, arriving home on Sunday 13 May.

Despite all the security arrangements, Staff Captain Doug Ridley described the cruise as 'monotonous' from his perspective: 'The only threats I know of are what we have read in the newspapers.' But, of course, the staff captain didn't know everything – and a man who did made some astounding revelations the following year.

In July 1974 President Anwar Sadat of Egypt revealed in a BBC *Panorama* interview that he personally had countermanded an order to torpedo *QE2*. President Sadat said that he was awoken early one morning and asked to confirm orders to an Egyptian submarine issued by President Gadaffi of Libya, with whom Egypt was sharing a political and military alliance at the time.

---

'The only threats I know of are what we have read in the newspapers.'
**Staff Captain Doug Ridley**

---

Sadat immediately countermanded Gadaffi's orders which had been to sink *QE2* to avenge the Libyan airliner shot down by Israel over Sinai late in 1972, killing more than 100 passengers. Sadat claimed that when he found out about the plan to sink the *QE2* he only had two hours in which to countermand the order: 'Fortunately he [Gadaffi] tried to use one of my submarines rather than his own. I was told about this at 1.30 a.m. and I stayed up until 3.30 a.m. making sure the submarine captain had returned to Alexandria.'

During a cruise to Bermuda in April 1974, memories of the ship's acceptance trials came flooding back to many senior officers. Early one morning, all power on the ship failed. There were no lights, no lifts, no refrigerators, no air conditioning, no cooking facilities and no water. Fortunately, the ship – although drifting without power – was far from land, and thus in no immediate danger. But conditions were unfavourable. Unfortunately for the chief engineer the problem did not affect just one boiler, and not even two – but all three.

Despite having very limited facilities, and minimal lighting supplied from emergency generators, the passengers remained remarkably stoical about their plight. But it could not be allowed to continue. Although steam was raised in one boiler later in the evening, and the ship moved slowly for an hour or so, the respite didn't last –

and it became clear that major time-consuming repairs needed to be carried out. After 24 hours without refrigeration, perishable food had to be fed to the fish; but more disturbingly, water – in the absence of a working desalination plant – was getting very short.

There was no choice but to offload the passengers. On the Bridge Captain Jackson set about convincing Victor Matthews, then chairman of Cunard and based in London, that a Norwegian cruise ship, *Sea Venture* – currently in Hamilton, Bermuda, for three days – should be despatched to pick up *QE2*'s passengers. There were problems with this plan as transferring over 1,000 passengers, many elderly, from one ship to another at sea would never be easy; but in addition, *Sea Venture* was much smaller than *QE2* and was licensed to carry only 600 passengers. But matters were urgent, and *Sea Venture* set off from Hamilton immediately – leaving 400 passengers behind. In the meantime, special dispensation was obtained to allow *Sea Venture* to embark significantly more people than she was licensed to carry.

*Sea Venture* reached *QE2* the following day, and began the lengthy process of transferring the passengers. The operation was hindered by the fact that *QE2*'s boats could not be lowered, so the whole job fell to *Sea Venture*'s lifeboats. The first passengers took to the lifeboats for the 300m (300yd) journey to *Sea Venture* at 0730 hours, and the long job began in earnest. It was difficult, though blessed with calm weather, and people kept cheerful – to the extent that some joked that *Sea Venture* wasn't quite up to *QE2* standards and that they would prefer to stay. What began at 0730 was finally completed at 1530 – and a much overcrowded *Sea Venture* set off for Bermuda.

The rescued *QE2* passengers were ferried to the airport in Bermuda, where two Cunard-chartered 747s were waiting to return them to New York – and relieved *Sea Venture* passengers, many of whom had thought their ship was sailing away without them, reclaimed their ship.

## Worsening Weather

*QE2*'s ordeal was nearly over when two Moran tugs started the tow. A 30-hour marathon then began which was delayed near its end when the weather, which had held so providentially throughout the rescue, deteriorated: 4m (15ft) waves prevented the tugs from reaching a safe anchorage for several hours.

Once *QE2* was safely anchored offshore – she was too large to tie up in Hamilton – work began to repair the ship. About 11 tonnes of replacement boiler tubes and 10 tonnes of special equipment and chemicals to flush out *QE2*'s boilers were ferried out to the liner. Captain Peter Jackson commented that he felt pretty helpless when deprived of the immense power from the boilers: 'I am convinced that this will never happen again. We are going to have extra safeguards to ensure it does not.'

It was estimated that the breakdown and emergency plans now had cost Cunard £700,000, which almost wiped out the profit *QE2* was expected to make in 1974. The bill included the use of *Sea Venture*, chartering the aeroplanes, hiring the tugs, and cancellation of the Easter cruise.

Cunard's technical director, R Greig, commented on the problems:

The *QE2*'s turbines were shut down when a water line running through a fuel tank ruptured and contaminated the boiler system with oil. The ship is powered by two turbines, turned by super-heated steam. The steam is generated in hundreds of feet of two-inch tubing, heated by oil-fuelled furnaces.

When oil gets into the steam lines, it adheres to the walls of the tubes and prevents the transfer of the heat. Eventually a bubble forms on the wall of the tube and it bursts.

One tube burst on the aft boiler on Monday and the ship was shut down. Because our first concern is the safety and comfort of the passengers, we tried to fire up the starboard boiler 17 hours later and about seven tubes ruptured.

By 11 April preliminary repairs were complete and the boilers had been purged so *QE2* was able to sail to New York at 16 knots using two boilers. She arrived there on 13 April. Further work at Todd's shipyard involved 30 of her 3,000 boiler tubes being replaced.

*QE2* sailed from New York for Southampton on 16 April, still on only two boilers but achieving an average of 24.5 knots. She carried 1,377 passengers and the voyage home took six days instead of the usual five. Another first took place on the crossing when a backgammon tournament for the richest purse ever offered took place on board. Sponsored by Alfred Dunhill, the tournament's $70,000 (£30,000) prize money attracted 32 of the world's top players to compete during the voyage. The tournament was won by Charles Benson, a racing correspondent for a London daily newspaper.

At a press conference held after her arrival Captain Jackson confirmed that the problem was at first 'a mechanical matter compounded by human error'.

*Captain Peter Jackson*

*QE2* was scheduled for four days of maintenance upon arrival. While in Southampton, engineers continued to work around the clock trying to get No.3 boiler repaired, cleaned and tested before the next voyage. This boiler had suffered the worst damage by oil contamination in the emergency. About 5,000 litres (1,000 gallons) of cleansing fluid was pumped round it, and to speed up the operation a hole was cut in the hull to allow a 5cm (2in) pipe to be connected from a quayside tank.

## Return to Service

On 25 April she left for her scheduled Mediterranean cruise. A helicopter team from the Army Air Corps' famous Blue Eagles flew past in salute several times and other ships in port sounded their sirens in salute at *QE2*'s return to service. During the cruise engineers managed to return the ship to full power on the passage from Southampton to Naples. *QE2* achieved 31 knots on a trial run, her fastest since she made her official trials six years earlier.

The impending withdrawal of the *France* in October 1974 prompted Cunard in August to announce:

> With the withdrawal of the *SS France* there have been press comments, particularly in America, to the effect that this is the absolute end of transatlantic traffic. This is not so, in fact in 1975 the Cunard passenger liner *Queen Elizabeth 2* will increase its crossings of the Atlantic to 31, providing 52,000 berths for travellers sailing from Southampton and New York, with calls at Cherbourg for passengers embarking and disembarking for the continent.

This is a 35 per cent increase on *Queen Elizabeth 2*'s 1974 Atlantic sailings programme.

After the withdrawal of the *France*, *QE2* became the largest liner in the world – a position she held until May 1980 when *France* returned to service as *Norway*.

---

'a mechanical matter compounded by human error' *Captain Peter Jackson on the power failure*

---

On 23 August 1974 Cunard confirmed that *QE2* would be refitted in Rotterdam during her annual overhaul in December 1974 – the first time the vessel would go to a non-UK yard for refitting – as Vosper Thornycroft Ltd were unable to take it on because of prior work.

On 25 September 1974, during a northerly gale, *QE2* was cutting her way through the heavy swell of the Mediterranean between Naples and Barcelona, when red distress rockets were seen at 0215 hours.

Captain Peter Jackson responded promptly to the call for help. In order to avoid causing further damage to the French yacht *Stephanie*, which was in immediate danger of sinking, he stopped some way off and allowed *QE2* to drift over to the

QE2 *(1972–1977)*

stricken vessel. Six male survivors were rescued from almost-certain death. The flare that the captain had seen had been their last but one.

While in Cherbourg on 28 October 1974 bad weather delayed *QE2*'s scheduled departure time of 1800 hours. At 2200 hours there was a lull in the weather and it was agreed between the French pilot and Captain Hehir to take her out. As she was leaving Cherbourg she was caught by a violent 110km/h (70mph) gust of wind. One cable snapped, injuring two dockers, and then two lines became tangled in the propellers. The ship drifted helplessly for 50m (50yd) broadside on before crashing into the Normandie Quay.

During the incident a gash was made in the ship's side, portside aft in the area of the crew cabins. The gash measured 10m long by 1cm deep (30ft by 2in) and was approximately 5m (15ft) above water level on Five Deck. One of the two French dockers had to have a leg amputated, and only a desperate struggle by *QE2*'s captain to hold the ship against the gale saved the men from being crushed to death. Twelve Tourist Class and ten crew cabins were in the affected area and were

damaged either by the indent or the cut in the fire sprinkler line that flooded them. *QE2* returned to port for an examination of the damage by marine surveyors.

---

'We used to play a sort of game where I would ask for something unusual for dinner the following night and they took pride in being able to provide it. One night I requested Spam, as we knew it during and after the war. The following evening four waiters, led by the maitre d', bore a gigantic silver tureen to the table. With great ceremony the ornate lid was removed – and there sat a tin of Spam – US Army rations.' *Leslie Thomas*

---

There were 1,630 passengers on board and a number chose to abandon their trip and fly to New York instead. *QE2*'s subsequent departure from Cherbourg to New York was delayed 48 hours and the ship sailed on 30 October.

December saw *QE2* in the news again when 200 crew members had to be flown out to join the ship in Gibraltar. They had refused to sail when she left Southampton for her Christmas cruise – a move not supported by either the crew's liaison committee or the National Union of Seamen. The crew members were unhappy with new scheduled working times designed to help reduce *QE2* overheads by £60,000. Cunard was keen to reduce

*Captain Robin Woodall*

the £50,000 daily costs of keeping *QE2* in service.

The year ended on a more positive note, however, with *QE2* achieving her revenue targets despite 'massive' fuel cost increases of 13.5 per cent on published fares; an early season depression in the UK (including a miners' strike and the introduction of the three-day working week); a 15–20 per cent decline in overall US traffic to Europe; the breakdown off Bermuda; and the nostalgia factor for the *France*. Her 21 Atlantic crossings saw her carry 27,948 passengers, which represented a load factor of 75.8 per cent.

## A Fistful of Dollars

Cunard had announced in May 1973 that *QE2* would undertake her first World Cruise in early 1975. Such a massive undertaking required a colossal amount of logistical planning, and to this end Captain Robin Woodall was despatched with 'a folder full of tickets, a fistful of dollars and a case of charts' to visit 28 proposed ports and report back on all aspects of their facilities, including their ability to handle the 1,000 tonnes of rubbish the ship would unload. All told, Captain Woodall travelled 60,000km (38,000 miles) in 52 days.

This first world cruise would depart on 10 January from New York, take an easterly direction, last 80 days and call at 24 ports in 19 countries. *QE2* had been designed to transit the Panama Canal and now she would for the first time. Fares ranged from £2,070 to £8,510.

Among the many VIP lecturers on board were the Duke and Duchess of Bedford, Lord Lichfield, Lillian Gish, Moira Shearer, Ludovic Kennedy and TV traveller Alan Whicker, who said that *QE2* was 'a space capsule drifting round the world in a delightful way'. This cast was supported by 31 musicians and 22 entertainers.

For the first World Cruise her home port of Southampton sent gifts that were presented by the captain at special receptions to maiden ports of call: Los Angeles, Acapulco, Mombasa, Mahé in the Seychelles and Bali. The gifts were gavels and striking plates made from 500-year-old New Forest oak taken from the Wool House and Tudor Merchants store in Southampton.

On 25 March *QE2* passed through the Panama Canal for the first time and thus became the largest

*At Cape Town local firms were picking up the largest orders that they had ever had. One firm was delivering 25,000 litres (5,500 gallons) of milk, 11,000 cups of yoghurt, and 6,500 litres (1,400 gallons) of cream. A ship's chandler in Cape Town received his biggest ever order too: 1,000 live crayfish, 14.5 tonnes of other fish, 12 tonnes of poultry, 40 tonnes of canned Cape fruit, 450kg (1,000lb) of kippers and 7 tonnes of frozen vegetables.*

passenger liner ever to do so, taking the record from the *Bremen*, which had gone through the canal in 1939. *QE2* paid a toll of £15,768 – the biggest fee ever – for the transit and took 11 hours to do it watched by thousands of locals. Special preparatory arrangements had to be made including folding back the hinged roofs of the control houses at the locks to allow the ship's 37m (118ft) wide Bridge to pass. It was a nerve-racking approach for the captain as in the locks the ship had less than 30cm (12in) to spare on each side, and there was much speculation about what would happen if the *QE2*'s builders had got their measurements wrong.

---

'The first time I travelled on the great *QE2* was in the company of the late, lamented Marj Proops and the ever lively Jimmy Savile. The latter ran round and round the top deck in his shorts while Marj and I propped up the bar. To sail on such a vessel is to know why Britain was once the envy of the world.'

*Dame Beryl Bainbridge*

---

On 7 July 1975 Sir Basil Smallpeice, who had by now retired as chairman of Cunard, was woken in the middle of the night by a man claiming to be an army officer. He was questioned about *QE2* and asked to attend a meeting the following day with a mysterious and unnamed colonel. Sir Basil attended the meeting, but after pointing out he no longer had any influence over *QE2*, he was abruptly dismissed. Sir Basil reported the matter to Sir Michael Cary, the permanent secretary of the Ministry of Defence. It was the last he heard of it. The odd affair of what was dubbed the '*QE2* Plot' was revealed many years later with the release of official papers. A planned coup against the British government – allegedly involving Lord Mountbatten – would have resulted in the plotters requisitioning *QE2* in order to detain members of the Cabinet on board.

In late October 1975 *QE2* arrived at the Vosper Thorneycroft repairs division in Southampton to undergo a three-week routine overhaul that turned out to be anything other than routine. While the ship was in port, on 17 November, a 180kg (400lb) cache of explosives was discovered in a block of flats close to the Eastern Docks. Believing that *QE2* might have been used to bring the explosives from America, where they would probably have been supplied by IRA sympathisers, the authorities undertook a comprehensive search of *QE2*. The bomb squad, customs officers, the police and the army joined forces to search every room and compartment, using sniffer dogs in an attempt to detect gelignite. But despite the intense efforts, nothing was found and nothing indicated a link between the cache and *QE2*. Despite the

QE2 has hosted more than its share of celebrities. Clockwise from top left: David Bowie, Rod Stewart, Ringo Starr, Peter Sellers, Sir Jimmy Savile.

interruption to the normal workflow, *QE2*'s overhaul was completed on time.

On 4 December 1975 *QE2* completed her first million nautical miles while sailing between Antigua and Boston. This seemed at the time to be a major event, not least in view of the predictions of many about *QE2*'s gloomy future: but since then she has gone on to rack up over five million nautical miles!

## Running Aground

Later that month, as the ship was leaving the port of Nassau, under the command of Mortimer Hehir, the ship's bulbous bow struck a coral reef. The resulting significant damage, including a fracture to the bow and damaged plating, was held to be the responsibility of the captain. But *QE2* officers weren't so sure – and on a subsequent visit a number of them dived in the area to establish what had actually happened. They discovered that the part of the reef that the ship had struck was not marked on charts, and in so doing exonerated Captain Hehir of blame.

A temporary repair to the damage was effected, but on the voyage to New York the temporary patch started to leak and *QE2* began to take on water again. Her speed was reduced to 15.5 knots and Cunard had her diverted to Newport News in Norfolk, Virginia, for further inspection and repairs. The 1,181 passengers were disembarked here and 500 were repatriated to New York on a specially chartered train.

*QE2* was put into dry-dock for 48 hours where a 2.5m (8ft) steel plate was welded into place. She eventually arrived in New York on 8 January and sailed that day on a revised nine-day (instead of 14-day) Caribbean cruise.

More trouble followed while *QE2* was 80 nautical miles off the Scilly Isles on 23 July 1976, when the flexible coupling drive connecting the starboard main engine high-pressure rotor and the reduction gearbox ruptured. Lubricating oil under pressure was released into the main engine room and ignited. A severe fire and explosion followed and burned for 20 minutes with flames shooting up the funnel's ventilating shaft about 30m (100ft) away, blackening and buckling the funnel casing high above the passenger decks. A 22-year-old engineer, Kenneth Lyon from Liverpool, was seriously burned while tackling the fire.

With one boiler out of action *QE2* limped back to Southampton where the affected boiler had to be replaced by dry-docking the liner and cutting an access hole in her side to remove the damaged

*Captain Mortimer Hehir*

machinery and install its replacement. Similar damage to an older ship would, perhaps, have resulted in its premature scrapping. *QE2* returned to service on 3 August and four crewmembers later received awards from the Secretary of State for Industry for putting out the fire.

Unbelievably another alleged IRA plot to blow up the ship in dry-dock in Southampton was discovered in November 1976 – and this time, unlike the previous year, it turned out to be real.

Three men had been found with 874 sticks of high explosives stored on a Southampton estate. The plot failed because when the explosives were delivered from IRA safehouses in London, the three made so much noise that neighbours called the police. Detectives kept watch on the storeroom for ten days. When they raided it, they found 160kg (350lb) of explosives – enough to make 50 bombs.

At the same time police also searched *QE2* while she was in dry-dock and found detonator devices. The bombers had planned to blow the ship up during her next voyage. Two of the men lived in Southampton and worked on board *QE2*. The two, William Baker and James Bennett, were sentenced to 20 years while a third, Bernard McCaffrey – who had allowed his premises in Southampton to be used – received 14 years.

On 2 December 1976 *QE2* ran into a really foul night of Atlantic weather. The 12.5-tonne bow anchor came adrift and ripped a hole in the bulbous bow on its way into the sea. Constant pumping evicted the unwelcome Atlantic water. *QE2* was diverted to Boston for repairs that involved fitting metal patches inside and out. The ship had to be tilted slightly by ballasting to enable workmen to repair the gash. Work was completed in time to allow *QE2* to sail on her Caribbean cruise on schedule, though the cruise passengers had to be brought to Boston from New York by plane and train.

All in all, *QE2* was more than ready for the following month's scheduled refit…

# Chapter 6

# A Decade for Decision

In the more leisurely sixties and early seventies *QE2* had her annual overhaul at Southampton, when every inch of the ship would be checked over, cleaned, renewed or replaced. However, special repairs in January 1977 required part of the annual work to be moved to Bayonne, New Jersey, where *QE2* was dry-docked for 10 days. Economically, having the repairs done in the United States also made sense for Cunard: *QE2* was able to start her winter cruise season earlier without having to make late winter crossings of the Atlantic when they were poorly subscribed.

A new turbine was built in Scotland and air-freighted to New York to replace the one damaged in an engine-room fire that had occurred the year before off the Scilly Islands. Permanent repairs were also made to the bulbous bow, which was damaged when *QE2* struck the coral reef the month before.

The wide-ranging appeal of *QE2* was demonstrated vividly by the headlines made during *QE2's* 1977 World Cruise. There was one story about a pantry maid from New Jersey who had saved for six years to go on the voyage, and another about a woman who took a suite for herself and one for her clothes as she changed three times a day and never wore the same outfit twice.

*The Sunday Times* of Ceylon in February 1977 said:

> The majestic *Queen Elizabeth 2* arrived in Sri Lanka to a rousing welcome yesterday morning. There was a stirring tattoo of drums as the massive 67,104-ton luxury liner sailed in to take its place on the quay named after Her Majesty Queen Elizabeth II…. For a moment the onlooker seemed to have been transported to a different time when air travel

*QE2 in New York after her 1977 refit with the Twin Towers of the World Trade Center in the background*

had yet to become popular and colonial ports thrived as gaily-dressed passengers disgorged by the luxury liner waited for the tourist coaches to take them to Mount Lavinia, Kandy and Pinnawela elephant park.

When the ship docked in Hong Kong in early March, 700 passengers took a tour to China – the largest single group of tourists to be admitted into mainland China for many years. For her arrival in

Bombay the Ballard Pier was dredged to take *QE2*, and the victorious England cricket team was entertained on board.

Once the French liner *France* was withdrawn from service in 1974, *QE2's* partner on the transatlantic service had gone, along with the tradition of each radio room competing to be the first to spot the other ship as they passed in mid-Atlantic and to signal the other's national anthem.

Concorde then became *QE2's* logical partner in crossing the Atlantic. Cunard linked *QE2* and Concorde in October 1977 for a series of supersonic fly cruises – First Class on the ship to New York, four nights at the St Regis, four at the Watergate Hotel in Washington and then back by Concorde to London; 40 places were offered at $2,270 each. This became one of Cunard's most popular packages, and soon the company was the biggest purchaser of Concorde seats in the world. Over the next five or six years it is likely that *QE2* saved Concorde from the scrapheap – a true irony.

## Helicopter Landing

A southwesterly gale with heavy swells of 5m (15ft) accompanied *QE2* all the way from New York at the end of September, and the weather was still so bad that on her approach to Southampton the pilot had to be landed on the liner by helicopter for the first – and, so far, only time.

In an interview about Trafalgar's purchase of Cunard, Victor Matthews made the following comments about *QE2*:

The gamble was the *QE2*. Everything we had been told led us to believe that it had no future. McKinsey had undertaken a report and recommended she would be laid up as quickly as possible. Losses, they said, would get progressively worse, and by the fourth year they could be as high as $11 million.

The cruising market had deteriorated and the number of people who crossed the Atlantic because they would not fly was diminishing.

…we steeled ourselves, despite the expert's advice, to operate *QE2* for anything from one to five years as a cost we should bear. We had no track record but we just had a feeling about it.

I went to see her in Southampton for the first time. She struck me as a 'floating hotel' – something quite strange to me as a naval man. I looked upon ships as things with ladders to climb up – not lifts. She impressed me very much so we then decided to try and win with her. We offered some cheap cruises and loss leader sales programmes.

We went into profit almost the first year with new ideas such as 'sail one way – fly the other' and world cruises. She went from success to success and last year made a profit of $9.5 million though, because of the harder pound, it will be something like $5.7 million this year.

The biggest problems facing *QE2* and affecting her overall profitability were labour costs, the frequent mechanical breakdowns of her turbines and boilers and the price increase of bunkering oil, which went up from $20 to $70 a tonne.

'The gamble was the *QE2*. Everything we had been told led us to believe that it had no future.' *Chairman Sir Victor Matthews*

# The 1977 Refit

This refit took place at the Bethlehem Steel Corporation Shipyard in Bayonne, New Jersey, between 3 and 12 December 1977.

The Tourist-Class *Britannia* Restaurant on Upper Deck was remodelled and renamed the Tables of the World. Dennis Lennon redesigned the whole area, dividing the restaurant into five sections representing regions *QE2* visited: England, France, Spain, Italy and the Far East. Each area was decorated in an appropriate national motif. Lennon described the new look as offering 'quiet elegance and great style'; his aim being to 'make it the best, with no restrictions'.

The most dramatic change was the addition of two new luxury combination suite apartments, the Queen Mary and Queen Elizabeth suites, which were added at a cost of $1 million and became America's only contribution to the superstructure of *QE2*. The two blocks were fitted on Signal Deck forward of the 1972 penthouse block, weighed 15 tonnes each and measured 15m by 9m by 5m tall (50ft by 30ft by 16ft).

## New Luxury Suites

Preparatory construction work was undertaken over a period of several months during periodic calls at Southampton, and involved the removal of decking and setting the foundations of the new units. A team from Vosper Thornycroft carried out final preparations while *QE2* was on passage from Southampton to New York. Each module was constructed ashore at the yard adjacent to the dry-dock and was hoisted aboard (fully furnished) by crane within days of *QE2*'s arrival at Bayonne.

Both suites featured two bedrooms, sitting room, two bathrooms, two patios and a walk-in closet/dressing room. The Queen Mary and Queen Elizabeth suites were more luxurious than any other accommodation available at sea. Elsewhere additional penthouses were built on

*The QE2 lit up by night*

Sports Deck and many of the existing suites and suite rooms were completely refurbished.

Technically the work included the renewal of one turbine following a DTI inspection that found the blades showing signs of weakness. Fortunately, John Brown Engineering had a replacement turbine at their yard in Scotland. The new turbine, weighing 17 tonnes and measuring 3m by 2.1m by 2m (10ft by 7ft by 6ft), was flown out in a Lockheed Hercules aircraft. About 120 men were standing by ready to fit the new turbine when it arrived.

*QE2* left dry-dock on Monday 19 December and sailed from New York on her Christmas Cruise on 20 December. The addition of the Queen Mary and Queen Elizabeth suites increased the *QE2*'s gross tonnage from 66,851 grt to 67,107 grt.

Many outstanding items remained unfinished and had to be completed once *QE2* had returned to service. While Cunard accepted that the new suites and Tables of the World were excellent, the company was disappointed with the shipyard's performance. The refit went significantly over budget, from £2.9 million to £3.9 million.

The Journal of Commerce in Liverpool described the 1978 Great Pacific Cruise as 'making history in grand style'. The voyage covered 39,022 nautical miles, visiting 30 ports with 11 maiden calls including San Francisco, New Zealand and Australia; the call at Sydney on 24 February was the first time that a Cunard *Queen* had called at the port since the early 1940s when *Queen Mary* and *Queen Elizabeth* were troopships.

A curious incident took place off Tahiti. An officer monitoring signals picked up one intended for *Queen Mary*, whose call sign *QE2* had adopted. It came from a radio station no longer in existence.

The belief is that the signal had been bouncing around in space for at least 11 years and finally, by chance, was picked up by *QE2*.

The power the small can have over the large was demonstrated in Copenhagen that May when *QE2* was blockaded by fishing vessels protesting against government fishing regulations. They later agreed to make a special dispensation for *QE2* and allowed her to continue her cruise.

On 6 August *QE2* showed off her ultra-modern communications facilities by talking to Concorde in flight. The plane's supersonic bangs had been recorded by the ship off the Grand Banks where they were powerful enough to produce a flicker in *QE2's* wake line. From 16,000m (52,000ft) below the plane, *QE2's* captain played these back and spoke to the captain of Concorde for ten minutes. *QE2* was two days out from Southampton and Concorde an hour out of Heathrow. Both were heading for New York and during the conversation, Concorde had covered 220 nautical miles while *QE2* was making 20 knots in a not-so-calm sea. Among the passengers on Concorde were 15 who had made the transatlantic crossing the other way by *QE2*. The Concorde conversation was relayed throughout *QE2* to her passengers.

The uniqueness of the infamous 1972 storm was challenged in September when

QE2 *in a lock on the Panama Canal in 1979*

*Captain (later Commodore) Doug Ridley*

Captain Doug Ridley encountered similar severe weather that damaged the liner's forepeak railings. *QE2* ran into a storm front lying across the shipping lanes, which gave little choice for manoeuvring. The ship ploughed through Force 12 winds (the maximum on the Beaufort Scale) with some gusts being recorded up to 112km/h (70mph), and 20m (60ft) waves.

## Colossal Waves

Captain Ridley slowed the ship to 9 knots, commenting that it was one of the worst storms he had experienced in 35 years at sea. At one point a wall of water hit the liner broadside on the bow and crumpled the iron railing, and the colossal waves occasionally nearly reached the Bridge. Hundreds of pieces of china were also broken and a 136kg (300lb) boom on the bow tore loose and struck the Bridge. Captain Ridley said that the boom striking the Bridge 'sounded like a bomb'.

---

'When I fell off my chair one morning in the cabin all Lady Boothby said was "It's too early to be drunk".'

*Lord Boothby on the 1978 storm*

---

The ship was carrying 1,213 passengers, who later praised Captain Ridley and the crew for their handling of the storm. Lord Boothby, one of several passengers making the return trip, said: 'When I fell off my chair one morning in the cabin all Lady Boothby said was "It's too early to be drunk".' Another passenger, Dr Malcolm Molyneux, said: 'It was rather frightening – going up and down about 100 feet – but it was very exciting.' Captain Ridley said the storm was one of 'those freaks of the sea'.

*QE2* arrived in Southampton about 24 hours late. Repairs involved welding and patching up the bow. According to a *Newsweek* article of 25 September 1978, a woman asked Captain Ridley if he had considered calling the Coast Guard for assistance during the worst of the storm. Ridley had replied: 'Madam, firstly there was no need for help. And, secondly, if there had been a Coast Guard cutter in the area, the *Queen* would have had to help the Coast Guard.'

On 3 October 1978 *QE2* entered dry-dock for her annual overhaul in Southampton. Her return to service from this £6.7 million refit was delayed when some trade unions instigated a work slowdown that resulted in the work lasting 43 days and involved the cancellation of an Atlantic crossing and a Caribbean cruise.

> '…if there had been a Coast Guard cutter in the area, the *Queen* would have had to help the Coast Guard.'
>
> **Captain Doug Ridley**

An unusual change in *QE2's* appearance took place when Cunard was asked by the British Admiralty to test a new three-layered anti-fouling paint, the top layer of which only came in blue – a shade that was not a traditional colour for a Cunard liner. This altered the external appearance of *QE2* but was only used for a short period before shades of red were available. The *QE2's* boot-topping was repainted in a light blue self-polishing paint that helped reduce fuel bills by cutting down resistance and provided further protection to the hull.

After completing the 29 April 1979 New York to Southampton crossing (officially designated as the 'Tenth Anniversary Crossing')

*QE2* set off from Southampton for Madeira on 5 May 1979 on her official 'Tenth Anniversary Cruise'. The Mayor of Southampton saw her off with full musical farewell from the band of the Royal Marines on the quayside, a jazz band in the Ocean Terminal and the Bournemouth Girls Choir singing in the Q4 Room.

*QE2's* captain sent a telegram to HM The Queen:

Greetings to Your Majesty from all on board Cunard Line's *Queen Elizabeth 2*, on her 10th Anniversary of entering service. Since Your Majesty launched *QE2* she has sailed over one million miles under the British flag and visited 63 countries with success and goodwill.

The Queen replied: 'I wish her God Speed and you and your officers and crew every success in adding to the one million miles already sailed.'

During her ten years in service *QE2* had crossed the Atlantic nearly 270 times, sailed round the world three times, visiting all the world's major ports, and clocked up 1.5 million nautical miles of travel – several times the total distance of *HMS Ark Royal* during her long career.

On 8 March 1980 *QE2* passed through the Suez Canal for the first time and became the largest ship ever to transit both the Suez and Panama Canals on the same voyage. The Suez transit took 17 hours and cost $132,000.

Excitement was high during that 1980 World Cruise as *QE2* approached Yalta in

*Captain Bob Arnott*

Crimea – then part of the communist USSR. Relations between the communist bloc and the West were not good, and visits to the Soviet Union were neither easy nor common. Passengers were looking forward not just to setting foot on what seemed at the time to be alien soil, but to recounting their adventures when they got home. However, as is frequently the way with totalitarian states, bureaucracy and bloody-mindedness confounded all plans.

---

'I wish her God Speed and you and your officers and crew every success in adding to the one million miles already sailed.'
*HM The Queen*

---

Although all the necessary documentation had been sorted out well in advance by Cunard, as soon as the ship anchored Russian officials swarmed aboard. Their first action was to demand that all passengers going ashore assemble in the Queen's Room for a full passport inspection, which would take several hours. This was swiftly followed by a demand that all those going ashore should have a full Russian visa – which would mean many passengers would not be able to disembark at all, and was not something the Russians had specified when arrangements for the visit had been made.

But Captain Arnott was having none of it. He recalled the only tender that had set off for shore, but which had not yet reached it, and at the same time ordered the Russian officials to leave. As soon as both had been achieved, the captain upped the anchor and left. That evening, as Captain Arnott and his wife entered the restaurant for dinner, the diners rose to their feet cheering and clapping.

They may have missed Yalta, but they had been part of a satisfying little rebellion, a small blow for freedom!

The benefits of applying the new self-polishing paint were evident by 1981. *QE2* remained afloat while in the King George V dry-dock during her £3.7 million 14-day overhaul in November, as no hull cleaning was needed – nor was any work required on propellers, propeller shafts and stabilisers. The new paint did away with the need for dry-docking every year. From now on *QE2* would be overhauled every two years.

## The Falklands War

On 19 March 1982 the Argentinian army invaded the British colony of the Falkland Islands in the South Atlantic. Within days a task force had been despatched and several commercial vessels, including P&O's *Canberra*, had been requisitioned and converted for war service.

Despite constant rumours that *QE2* would also be 'called up' the ship continued as scheduled with an Atlantic crossing to New York, followed by a maiden call to Philadelphia on 25 April, where she officiated at the opening of the year-long tricentennial celebrations of the founding of the city in 1682.

However, there was no doubting that *QE2's* speed, size and facilities made her ideal for trooping, and on 3 May 1982, as *QE2* was steaming along the south coast of England bound for Southampton, the long-expected news that she had been requisitioned by the British government for use in the Falklands campaign was confirmed.

> 'Your vessel *Queen Elizabeth 2* is requisitioned by the Secretary of State for Trade under the Requisitioning of Ships Order 1982 and you are accordingly required to place her at his disposal forthwith.' *Message to* QE2 *May 1982*

Cunard received the following instructions from the government:

Your vessel *Queen Elizabeth 2* is requisitioned by the Secretary of State for Trade under the Requisitioning of Ships Order 1982 and you are accordingly required to place her at his disposal forthwith. The Master should report for directions on the employment of the vessel to Mr R Brooks Department of Trade Sea Transport Officer Southampton who will act as the principal link between the Master and all other civil and naval/military authorities until sailing.

Captain Hutcheson said that after he had broadcast the news to the passengers cheers broke out all over the ship. All future sailings of *QE2* were cancelled as Cunard did not know for how long its flagship would be requisitioned.

*Continued on page 162*

QE2 *arriving alongside in Southampton in the early 1980s*

# QE2 Prepares for War

*QE2* came alongside her berth at Southampton at midnight on 4 May 1982 and was officially requisitioned as a 'STUFT' (Ship Taken Up From Trade). The conversion work to prepare the ship for her trooping assignment began the next day. Over the next eight days the most amazing transformation took place.

*QE2*'s aft decks became helicopter landing platforms after slicing away large parts of the superstructure aft. Forward, the deck was extended towards the bow right over the capstans so that a third heli-pad could be built on the foredeck. These new landing pads were capable of handling the 8.5 tonnes of a Sea King helicopter plus cargo.

The communications equipment on board was augmented with an independent radio station. This was constructed behind the Bridge while small UHF aerials were fitted on both Bridge wings, and SCOTs (Satellite Communications Onboard Tracker) domes, shaped like hot-air balloons, were installed aft of the penthouse suites on the uppermost deck.

*QE2* could not carry fuel for much more than a one-way trip so provisions had to be made for refuelling at sea. Pipes were laid from the starboard midships baggage area on Two Deck to the huge tanks below.

Most of the pictures and valuable furniture were removed from the ship and stored ashore. Six pianos (two remained on board for entertaining), casino equipment, plants and high-cost food items were removed and stored. *QE2*'s own china, glassware and silverware was collected, packed and stored.

In an effort to protect 27km (17 miles) of carpeting from military boots, hundreds of square metres of hardboard were laid over all carpets in public rooms, passageways, stairways and in some of the cabins. Thick securely fastened canvas was laid on stairways to protect carpeting.

A total of 71 tonnes of stores and military equipment were placed on board including hundreds of extra life jackets, ammunition and additional safety appliances. The military supplied 1,000 stacking chairs and 1,000 camp beds that were set up in passenger and crew accommodation areas, Double Down Bar, the Casino and the Nursery.

A NAAFI Shop was installed in the shopping arcade selling cans of beer. The Cinema was rigged up for mass briefings. The *Q4* Room became the Officers' Bar while the Theatre Bar became an NCO Bar. The One Deck shop became a library. The various offices around the ship as well as the Reading Room, Card Room and Library became official meeting rooms.

Officers would dine in the Queen's Grill with senior NCOs being allocated to the Princess Grill and the troops eating in the *Columbia* and Tables of the World Restaurants. Even the Double Room became a mess, with plain trestle tables and chairs being installed.

## Mine Protection

To reduce the natural magnetic field of the liner and help protect her from magnetic mines, a degaussing cable was fitted inside the ship. Captain Peter Jackson was advised on 6 May that he would be in command and 650 of *QE2*'s own crew volunteered to remain with the ship throughout her war service.

On 12 May, eight days after arriving in Southampton, the formal embarkation of the 3,000 troops that made up 5 Infantry Brigade began. The Brigade comprised the Scots Guards, the Welsh Guards and the Gurkha Rifles. Bands or pipers were on hand to play as each unit boarded. A large crowd and a posse of television cameras had assembled on the quayside. *QE2* was ready to go to war. But not before the Cunard chairman Lord Matthews and the defence minister John Knott had paid a visit to the ship.

While final preparations were being made a problem developed in *QE2*'s engine room. One of her boilers had been shut down for maintenance and now a second boiler had developed a massive leak in its supply of distilled water, which could not be traced.

With the world watching, it was vital that *QE2* sail on time so at 1600 hours the underpowered ship headed down-river at 7 knots to an anchor position 3 miles off the Nab where she remained overnight. Engineers worked through the night and discovered the cause of the leak. At 0935 hours *QE2* was underway.

Ralph Bahna, Cunard's president, received the following message from the commander-in-chief of the UK Land Forces:

> I wish to express our sincere appreciation for the co-operation and flexibility experienced throughout the last eight days in planning and executing the embarkation of the *Queen Elizabeth 2* in the port of Southampton.

The professional ability and dynamic approach adopted at all levels of management has resulted in an extremely efficient and successful operation.

## *QE2* in the Falklands

During the first day at sea the troops had their first lifeboat drill and preparations were made for a rendezvous with the Royal Fleet Auxiliary vessel *Grey Rover* to practise taking on fuel using the pipes that had been laid on Two Deck.

The biggest threat was from Argentine submarines and the troops practised evacuating the ship to the upper decks. To simulate the loss of power and subsequent darkness below deck the soldiers were blindfolded and had to find their way out by touch.

*QE2* first headed for Freetown and Ascension and she was soon making 24 knots on two boilers – a speed that was increased when the third boiler was brought online on 15 May.

The troops spent their days at sea undertaking various training tasks including stripping down and reassembling arms, attending lectures, practice-firing over the side and helicopter exercises. Captain Jackson also took the opportunity to fly around his ship. An onboard newspaper, *The Leek*, was produced for the troops.

QE2 arrived in Freetown on 18 May where she took on 1,896 tonnes of fuel as well as more water in an operation that was completed three hours earlier than expected. She was underway again by 2300 hours.

A 'Crossing the Line' ceremony was held as QE2 crossed the Equator and the fine weather changed to torrential rain and fierce squalls. The weather resulted in QE2 having to stay 50 nautical miles off Ascension when she arrived on 20 May while stores and personnel were ferried between QE2 and the island by helicopters. An RAF Nimrod had reported sighting the Argentinian vessel Chubut in the area, and HMS Dumbarton Castle was stationed off QE2.

After leaving Ascension strict blackout regulations were enforced on board. Black plastic sheeting was taped over the 500-plus windows and 1,350-plus portholes. A helicopter flew around QE2 to ensure the ship was indeed blacked-out. Captain Jackson noted that it was: '… a frightening sight, to see the ship belting along at 27 knots on a black night and without a light showing'.

## Through Icefields Without Radar

On 22 May QE2 sailed in company with another Cunarder, the container ship Atlantic Causeway. In addition to being blacked-out, all navigation lights and radar was switched off – QE2 became electronically silent. She sped through the dark, through an icefield, without radar; life on the Bridge went back 50 years.

During the night of 26 and 27 May the radar was switched on every 30 minutes and at one time more than 100 icebergs could be seen on the screen. Captain Jackson would later write that 'never have I known such a harrowing experience'.

Captain Jackson: 'We knew we were a prime target and I'm thankful they never found us… in the open sea we were very vulnerable.' It would later emerge that the Argentinians had used a Boeing 707 to survey the South Atlantic in search of QE2.

The next day QE2 met HMS Antrim and the transfer of Major General Moore, Brigadier Wilson and other personnel commenced. QE2 was sailing again by early afternoon and hundreds of icebergs were spotted through the patchy fog.

Just after 1700 hours South Georgia was visible on the radar and QE2 anchored in Cumberland Bay East two hours later. A rust-streaked Canberra was waiting for QE2's arrival. The immediate plan was to transfer survivors from HMS Ardent from the P&O flagship to the Cunard flagship.

The trawler Cordella came alongside QE2 at 2120 hours and the first batch of troops were on their way to Canberra a little under two hours later. Just before midnight HMS Leeds Castle, Cordella and the tug Typhoon were alongside QE2 to transfer more troops.

From 0600 hours on 28 May the transfer from QE2 started in earnest with helicopters, QE2's own lifeboats and the trawlers Cordella, Junella, Northella, Farnella and Pict carrying troops and stores to waiting Canberra and Norland, the latter bringing to QE2 survivors from HMS Antelope. Canberra sailed at

2230 hours as snow covered the assembled ships.

The next day saw another Cunard cargo ship, *Saxonia*, and the Royal Fleet auxiliary *Stromness* rendezvous with *QE2*, the auxiliary vessel bringing survivors from *HMS Coventry*.

Captain Jackson was concerned about the deteriorating weather; icebergs had drifted in and out of the entrance to Cumberland Bay during *QE2*'s stay there. *Junella* took the last group of troops from *QE2* at just after 1600 hours and *QE2* left South Georgia.

## Bringing Survivors Home

On 3 June, after *QE2* had faced another icefield and been refuelled at sea in a Force 7 gale, Captain Jackson received orders to proceed back to Southampton. *QE2*'s work in the campaign was done and it remained for her to now bring home 640 survivors.

*QE2* neared Ascension once again on 4 June in order to transfer some of the most seriously wounded to *HMS Dumbarton Castle*. On 11 June *QE2* was home. Admiral John Fieldhouse and Lord Matthews flew out to join the ship as she made her way to Southampton.

As she passed the Needles Lighthouse at 0900 hours the Royal Yacht *Britannia* came abeam with the Queen Mother standing on the aft deck. *QE2*'s crew and warship survivors gave three cheers and the liner blew her whistle in salute.

Captain Jackson received the following message:

I am pleased to welcome you back as *QE2* returns to home waters after your tour of duty in the South Atlantic. The exploits of your own ship's company and the deeds of valour of those who served in *Antelope*, *Coventry*, and *Ardent* have been acclaimed

throughout the land and I am proud to add my personal tribute.

To which Captain Jackson replied: 'Please convey to Her Majesty Queen Elizabeth, the Queen Mother, our thanks for her kind message. Cunard's *Queen Elizabeth 2* is proud to have been of service to Her Majesty's Forces.'

As *QE2* made her way to her berth she was escorted by a flotilla of small aircraft and thousands cheered and waved from the shore as she berthed. *QE2* had sailed the 6,000 nautical miles from South Georgia to Southampton in 12 days, 12 hours and 18 minutes at an average speed of 23.23 knots.

On 13 June Admiral Sir Henry Leach wrote to Captain Jackson:

…I wanted to let you know how very grateful I and the whole Navy have been for your splendid and efficient help over the recent weeks. As you will know better than most, we did not take *QE2* up from service for a gimmick; there was nothing else suitable – and indeed there was nothing else (British) at all. The whole of your passage out and back did little for my peace of mind.

…But you made it. Thank you. Well done.

*Troops board one of the trawlers during the transfer from* QE2 *to either* Canberra *or* Norland

*HM Queen Elizabeth The Queen Mother on the aft decks of the Royal Yacht* Britannia *welcomes back the warrior* Queen

On 15 August 1982 *QE2* was back in operation, military service in the Falklands completed, extensively refitted, and with a new colour scheme. Cunard was very optimistic about the ship's future and stated: 'We are thinking of the *QE2* now as having a fairly indefinite life. We have been impressed by what we can do in only two months. We realise that we have a body within which we can replace any organ we choose when we wish to.'

After leaving Southampton for New York *QE2* broke down on 6 September. There were problems with both main boiler pumps and repairs had to be carried out over a two-day period with the ship anchored off Falmouth. Five passengers decided to leave the ship and the subsequent 10–15 September US cruise was cancelled. Clearly, some parts of that body were going to have to be replaced – and fairly soon.

> 'We are thinking of the *QE2* now as having a fairly indefinite life. …We realise that we have a body within which we can replace any organ we choose when we wish to.'
>
> *Cunard statement*

# The Peacetime Refit

It took less than a week (5–12 May) to prepare QE2 for a role as troopship but it took nine weeks to put her back together for peacetime use. On 12 June, QE2 entered the King George V dry-dock for her re-conversion back to passenger liner. The work lasted until 13 August and cost £7 million. The British government contributed £2 million for repairs and conversion with Cunard taking the opportunity to make further improvements, investing a further £5 million.

Several public areas were completely redecorated. Cunard once again utilised the services of Dennis Lennon, the original co-ordinator of all QE2's striking and sophisticated interiors in the 1960s. The Queen's Grill and associated cocktail lounge were redesigned to create a 'cool, elegant and classic ambience' and the Tables of the World was refurbished.

The Q4 Room was replaced by the new versatile Club Lido. This was the first phase of Cunard's plans to revamp this entire area (phase two, involving the installation of the Magrodome, would be completed in the 1983 refit). By day, the Club Lido would be a casual gathering place with an open-air buffet. By night, the area would provide dancing and entertainment. The bar was repositioned temporarily to the portside and sliding smoked glass doors were fitted at the after end leading onto the open deck. This created a much lighter and more versatile room. The new décor consisted of orange, sleek reds, dark greens and slate greys. New recessed lighting was installed.

## First Floating Spa

The indoor swimming pool complex on Six Deck was completely revamped and transformed into the 'world's first floating spa'. Facilities included a large mirrored exercise area with ballet barres, a pool with a teak platform for hydrocalisthenics, three large jacuzzi whirlpool baths (replacing the Turkish Baths), saunas and a climate-controlled gymnasium.

In total 27km (17 miles) of carpeting were cleaned and renewed where necessary, the Burma teak decking was replaced, thousands of metres of flooring and trim were scrubbed and polished, and artwork, furniture and china was brought out of storage and replaced on board.

On return to service after the Falklands, the most noticeable change by far was the external colour scheme of QE2. On the instruction of Cunard's chairman Lord Matthews, the black hull was repainted in a light pebble grey that was almost white. The boot-topping remained red but the ship's name and homeport on the bow and stern were painted black. For the first time, the funnel was in traditional Cunard red with two black bands. Each black band was 20cm (8in) wide.

According to Cunard:

> The new colours of the ship, both inside and out, reflect the new spirit of QE2 and her crew while respecting a tradition of luxury and service…

> The painting of the funnel in traditional Cunard red and black is to emphasise Queen Elizabeth 2's continued dedication to the high standards set by her predecessors.

Most reaction to the new colour scheme, apart from the funnel, was unfavourable, and noted maritime historian John Maxtone-Graham wrote:

> I had reservations about it; although putting the company's colours up on the funnel was long overdue, the pale grey hull seemed a mistake. From a distance, it read white and was not flattering. The Sidney Greenstreet principle was at work: a fat man in a white suit looks fatter. The QE2's light-coloured hull sprawled and, worse, showed its middle age.

On 7 August 1982, QE2 put to sea for 24 hours of engine trials following the refit. On 15 August, the pride of the British merchant fleet sailed from Southampton, with a full complement of passengers, destined for New York. The Queen was back.

*QE2* completed an Atlantic crossing in November and arrived in Southampton having endured a ferocious storm that smashed fine bone china and even overturned a grand piano. Captain Peter Jackson said the hurricane-force winds were among the worst he had ever seen in his 44-year career at sea. 'The sea was a fury of whiteness, but the ship behaved extremely well and seemed to find its own way through the waves.' Remarkably, seasickness among passengers was said to have been only slightly worse than normal – many were more keen to take snaps of the waves than to take to their beds.

'The sea was a fury of whiteness, but the ship behaved extremely well and seemed to find its own way through the waves.'
*Captain Peter Jackson on the 1982 storm*

On 2 December Queen Elizabeth The Queen Mother paid her first visit to *QE2* while the ship was berthed in Southampton. She arrived in the docks by helicopter and was met by Lord Matthews, chairman of Cunard, prior to being introduced to Captain Jackson and the ship's officers. The Queen Mother unveiled the Admiralty

Falklands Plaque while in the Queen's Room before touring *QE2*.

The Queen Mother remarked during her visit:

When I launched her predecessor, that great liner the *Queen Elizabeth*, I was confident that the Cunard tradition symbolised the spirit and strength of the British merchant marine. That my belief was justified was clearly shown by the record of the *Queen Elizabeth* in World War II and by her achievements in the years which followed.

Once again, some nine months ago, in time of our country's need, the Merchant Navy was called upon to support Her Majesty's Armed Forces. The record of 5 Brigade, who travelled south in *Queen Elizabeth 2*, is now part of history, and I am delighted that it is represented here today.

When this ship, her mission completed, was nearing Southampton, I was proud to be able to welcome her and all those aboard to a homecoming so richly deserved.

It is right that splendid exploits should be recorded.

On 16 January Captain Jackson retired just before the Cunard flagship set off on her 'Circle Pacific and Orient Odyssey' cruise. The voyage also saw another first when BBC TV's *Whicker's World* was filmed on board for six weeks, as *QE2* circled the Pacific, which resulted in a four-part documentary about life 'upstairs and downstairs' on board.

---

*'The record of 5 Brigade, who travelled south in Queen Elizabeth 2, is now part of history, and I am delighted that it is represented here today.'*
**The Queen Mother**

---

On Friday 16 March at 1500 hours *QE2* completed two million nautical miles while in Chinese waters north of Hong Kong.

The new pale grey hull of *QE2* soon proved to be impractical as well as unpopular. The pebble grey was difficult to maintain in a pristine form and no matter how careful the tugs in ports were, *QE2* always lost some of her paint or obtained scuff marks from tugs nudging bows. Evidence of close contact with dockside fenders also always showed. The light colour also disclosed unsightly streaks of rust dribbling down the vessel's sides from portholes and hawser pipes.

## Whicker's World

Her external appearance as she circled the Pacific during her 1983 World Cruise drew many criticisms. The fact that this voyage was subject to the close scrutiny of the *Whicker's World* documentary emphasised, when broadcast, the poor external condition of the ship. A full

*The short-lived 'new look' QE2 arrives in New York, August 1982*

stem-to-stern clean-up was undertaken halfway through the voyage in Hong Kong, and passengers were amused to see dozens of Chinese workers dangling by ropes over the side carrying out repairs to the paintwork.

Ever since *QE2* came into service the ship had suffered from occasional but severe technical problems – notably turbine and boiler faults. After her return to service from the Falklands and throughout 1983 the number of technical difficulties increased.

A faulty engine prevented the liner calling at Naples during a Mediterranean cruise in May 1983. She had to call at Genoa instead and sail home from Lisbon at a reduced speed. The subsequent five-day crossing to New York was extended to six days.

The problems centred on the starboard low-pressure turbine. It was clear to Cunard at this stage that the turbine required replacement, but the dilemma facing the company was the out-of-service time that would be required to effect the replacement and whether the casing would also need replacing. It was decided finally to undertake work on the ship in June.

Cunard cancelled the scheduled six-day Iberian Isles Cruise (10–16 June) and the following two Atlantic crossings (16 June from Southampton and 21 June from New York) in order to obtain 17 days in which to do the necessary work while *QE2*

remained alongside her berth in Southampton. The work and cancellations cost Cunard £2.5 million, and included removing the problem turbine and sending it back to its maker, John Brown Engineering, to be repaired and refitted later in the year.

## Cunard Colours

After a reasonable trial period it was decided by Cunard to return the hull to the original colouring, and the company had planned to do this during *QE2's* scheduled dry-docking at the end of 1983. However, the repainting was done during these emergency repairs to *QE2's* turbines. The one true success of the aborted scheme, the funnel in traditional Cunard colours, remained – and is the same today. Cunard funnels have been red and black since the company began in 1840, and many – including Charles Dickens – have remarked on the welcoming and comforting sight of a red funnel towering above a foreign port. The return to tradition was long overdue.

*QE2* returned to service but it became clear that the turbine troubles had not been rectified, as overheating soon occurred in one of the two low-power turbines. It was thought that the high-speed dash to the Falklands may have caused the damage.

Cunard cancelled two further transatlantic crossings (22 July from Southampton and 27 July from New York) in order to obtain a further ten-day work period with *QE2* alongside her berth again. The work and cancellations cost Cunard a further £1 million, taking the total cost of the two unscheduled overhauls to £3.5 million, with *QE2* out of service for 27 days in a seven-week period.

On 1 August *QE2* put to sea for engine trials in the Channel and the next day she sailed for New York with 1,750 passengers; she got there without mechanical problems.

But as *QE2* entered the mid-1980s the escalating number of serious breakdowns forced Cunard to contemplate some serious options for their flagship, the most famous ship in the world. The choice was simple: build a replacement or undertake what would almost certainly be a costly re-engining. *QE2* was still ideal for the role of transatlantic liner and cruise ship, but her increasingly troublesome turbine machinery was cause for concern. The rise in fuel prices and the increasing crew costs were also compounding the problems faced by Cunard.

In the event Cunard came to the most momentous decision of *QE2's* life; she would be re-engined. It would be the biggest ship re-engining ever undertaken anywhere and was equivalent to a heart transplant for a human.

In the summer of 1983, shipyard representatives from all over the world were invited to Southampton where they were introduced to the project to convert *QE2*. It was to be the first stage in a project that would see months of exhaustive research, testings and costings being undertaken. But the re-engining lay in the future.

*Menu from the December 1982 lunch signed by HM Queen Elizabeth The Queen Mother and Lord Matthews, chairman of Cunard*

Luncheon
on the occasion of the visit of
Her Majesty Queen Elizabeth,
The Queen Mother,
on board Queen Elizabeth 2
to unveil the South Atlantic Plaque,
2nd December 1982

Host: The Lord Matthews

Luncheon

Coquille of Fresh Lobster

Roast Saddle of Southdown Lamb

Fresh Broccoli Spears,
Parisienne Potatoes

Fresh Pear, Liqueur Sauce

Petits Fours

Selection of
English Cheeses with Celery

Coffee

Wines

Batard Montrachet 1980
(Moillard)

Chateau Gruaud Larose 1966
Second Growth St Julien

As if 1983 hadn't been difficult enough, *QE2* was stranded in Cherbourg in November when a tugmen's dispute in Southampton resulted in the closure of that port. The company had to undertake the enormous logistical exercise of getting *QE2's* 1,800 passengers home from France. They were flown from Cherbourg to Bournemouth and her embarking passengers were taken to France by cross-Channel ferries.

The announcement that *QE2* would be sent to the Lloyd Werft Shipyard in Germany for her annual overhaul in November 1983 generated a lot of adverse attention in the British press. The news was even carried in many American papers, but little attention was paid to the fact that the major British shipyards had admitted that they could not carry out the work on time. Nor was much attention paid to the fact that Cunard had already spent £11 million on the ship in British yards since June 1982 refitting, refurbishing and completing new facilities. On completion of this £4.5 million refit, the total spent with British firms would rise to £13.5 million as £2.5 million of this contract was spent on British subcontractors.

The second phase of the new Club Lido area was undertaken with the installation of the

QE2 *and* Sagafjord *(top right) in Sydney,*
*St Valentine's Day 1985*

Magrodome, a retractable glazed sunroof placed over the Quarter Deck swimming pool. The Magrodome telescopic glass roof was designed by MacGregor-Navire. The Magrodome was specially designed for *QE2* so that the entire enclosure blended with the *Queen*'s existing lines; there was the maximum ratio possible of glass to metal; it was completely unobtrusive when in the stowed position and provided the largest possible daylight opening.

## The Magnificent Magrodome

The opening, which was 19.2m wide and 13.8m long (62ft by 45ft), consisted of two pairs of electronically operated panels, the inboard of each pair being the driven panel that pulled the outboard panel to the stowage at the side. Special features of the design were the panels' compact dimensions, which totalled only 1.5m (5ft) deep when stowed, and the heating coils attached beneath the metal members to prevent condensation. The open vista characteristic of the Magrodome, with its almost 90 per cent glass, allowed maximum visibility of the sky from relatively acute angles. The metal structure was reduced to a minimum with some of the smaller members only 200mm (8in) wide. The average size of the glass panels was 3.3m by 1.4m (11ft by 4ft).

The newly enclosed space would be air-conditioned when the Magrodome was shut, while an air curtain system was fitted to protect the Club Lido inner area when the dome was closed.

Extensive preparations were made prior to the installation: fabrication, assembly and testing of the entire unit was carried out ashore prior to fitting. The after end of the Club Lido was sliced away as the *QE2* crossed the Atlantic. Then, working to exacting specifications, the deck was prepared for the Magrodome, which was being finished at Bremerhaven.

---

'I made many valued friendships aboard the *QE2*, which are still maintained, and my fondest memory is being on the Bridge (with the captain's permission) and docking the ship in Gibraltar.'
*Sir Cyril Smith*

---

Two days after *QE2's* arrival at the yard (28 November), the huge Magrodome structure was slowly lifted from the yard by a powerful crane and positioned over the *QE2's* deck. Once the positioning appeared exact, the Magrodome was lowered onto the liner and welded into place.

On Monday 12 December, *QE2* left the yard and headed for Southampton. However the delays incurred at the start of the refit due to storms and now engine problems delayed *QE2's* return to service. Her first cruise left Southampton more than 24 hours late.

Cunard cemented the *QE2*/*Concorde* relationship still further in 1984 by agreeing to charter 168 Concorde flights between London and New York. It also chartered Concordes to take passengers to and from ports all over the world as part of *QE2's* World Cruise – including two to Tel Aviv, the first time that Concorde had flown to Israel. On completion of her 1984 World Cruise, *QE2* had visited 145 different ports worldwide. New York was the most visited port with 325 calls while Southampton was second with 240.

## A Floating Harrods

On 14 June the first sea-going branch of Harrods was opened, located on One Deck. Originally the actress Hermione Gingold was to open the shop but she did not turn up, so Captain Bob Arnott did the honours instead.

A special meeting took place in Southampton on 26 July when *QE2* and *Norway* (formerly *QE2's* transatlantic rival *France*) were berthed in the city simultaneously – the two largest passengers ships in the world together.

Unfortunately, unforeseen technical problems developed prior to *QE2's* departure from

Bremerhaven after her 1984 refit. In addition to general refurbishment of public rooms this had included the fitting of a new bulbous bow to replace the one that had suffered collision damage earlier in the year. The problems included the discovery of a small crack in the outer plates beneath the waterline, last-minute faults on the air-conditioning and other minor hitches. As a result, *QE2* was 24 hours late arriving in Southampton, which meant that the two-day English Channel Party Cruise, due to depart on 14 December, had to be cancelled.

As *QE2* reached New Zealand in February 1985 during her World Cruise she made further headlines when one of her passengers was discharged from the ship's hospital to the general hospital in Auckland. The Auckland hospital subsequently revealed, in a reply to a casual enquiry, that the discharged passenger was suffering from AIDS. While such a thing now would be dealt with calmly and rationally, at that time there was still much panic surrounding AIDS – not least from the UK press. This led to some hysterical reports that now sound rather old-fashioned. Even *Private Eye* magazine had a little jibe about 'cruising being dangerous'.

The 1985 World Cruise was also noted for the Concorde charters Cunard undertook that would see the maiden Concorde flight to Sydney as well as record-breaking flights to Hong Kong, Cape

*The Harrods shop aboard* QE2

Town and Rio de Janeiro. In all Cunard spent £12 million on Concorde charters in 1985 – without which the supersonic plane would have made a serious loss.

The Concorde charter to Sydney broke records – 17 hours, 3 minutes and 45 seconds. The flight arrived on 13 February in time for the special meeting the next day of *QE2* and another Cunard liner, *Sagafjord*, in Sydney.

'Whilst in mid Atlantic on an outward bound journey to New York, the captain announced that Concorde would be flying over the liner within the next 10 minutes. What seemed like the entire complement of passengers crowded the decks in anticipation. Then, there she was – Concorde, flying low over the horizon, at normal, not supersonic speed. As she passed over the funnel a huge cheer went up, and *QE2* sounded her whistle.' *Angela Rippon*

What was described by some as the 'photograph of the century' was captured on 18 May when *QE2*, the Red Arrows and Concorde were photographed at the same time in the English Channel.

During her 29 September–4 October crossing, *QE2* 'endured one of the worst gales that she has ever encountered in her sailing history', generated by Hurricane Gloria, which also caused havoc along the American Eastern Seaboard. The storm lasted for four days and ripped away the liner's foghorn, ventilation shafts, a lifeboat and part of her funnel, and pipes burst throughout the ship. The Magrodome was also damaged. *QE2's* arrival in New York was delayed by nine hours. Repairs were made during the return eastbound crossing.

In October 1985, while homeward bound from New York, an electrical fire caused a complete loss of power on board for a few hours. The damage was repaired by the ship's engineers, but *QE2* was two days late arriving in Southampton.

On 25 October it was announced that the £80 million contract to re-engine *QE2* had been awarded to the Lloyd Werft Shipyard in Bremerhaven, West Germany. *QE2* would be taken out of service from October 1986 until April 1987.

Cunard had spent over two years evaluating all the options for the project. The company had considered building a replacement but the anticipated £250 million cost was a major obstacle.

Several shipyards were invited to tender for the contract but all, including Harland and Wolff, dropped out as the process developed, leaving just two German yards: Lloyd Werft and Blohm & Voss in Hamburg. Lloyd Werft was selected as they were able to meet all of Cunard's requirements and offer a shorter conversion period. They also knew the vessel, having worked on her in 1983 and 1984.

Cunard had approached the government for aid, claiming that *QE2* was a 'magnificent ambassador' for Britain abroad that earned millions of dollars every year, employed 2,000 British workers and had proved her worth in time of the nation's need during the Falklands Campaign. The British government declined the request for a grant and loan aid.

## The Diesel Electric Option

A variety of engine proposals was considered and reduced to two – geared diesel or diesel electric. Despite no other passenger ship having a diesel-electric plant and the fact that diesel electric would mean a greater capital cost and greater operating cost, that was the option chosen as it offered greater reliability with the greatest 'redundancy factor'. *QE2* would still be able to achieve 28 knots with three out of the nine engines out of service. Diesel electric would also offer less noise and vibration (thanks to no reduction gears being needed), the greatest flexibility (the engines could be mounted in any configuration) and a simpler

conversion due to the lack of clutches and reduction gears. The company anticipated a saving of £8.5 million a year on the £17 million fuel costs alone and that the conversion would provide *QE2* with a further 20 years of useful life. This proved to be a remarkably pessimistic assessment as today, 20 years later, the diesel-electric propulsion system continues to give excellent and almost trouble-free service.

Nine diesel engines driving alternators generating electricity would provide power for two 44 megawatt electric propulsion motors and for other ship's operations. In addition 25% of the cost of the work would be spent on upgrading the passenger areas and accommodation as well as extensive work in the galleys.

A special anniversary – the 50th anniversary of *Queen Mary*'s 1936 maiden voyage – was celebrated on board in Southampton on 3 May prior to *QE2* undertaking a special crossing to New York. For that voyage Cunard launched a search for passengers who were on the 1936 voyage, and offered them passage on this special celebratory voyage at the fare they had paid 50 years earlier. Larry Adler, who had performed on the *Queen Mary*'s maiden voyage, was also on board, and vintage cars were parked at the terminal to add to the sense of occasion. The highlight of 3 May was undoubtedly the visit by HM Queen Elizabeth The Queen Mother. Her Majesty met those passengers

*QE2's new funnel being lowered into place, February 1987*

who travelled on the maiden voyage before lunching in the Princess Grill.

---

'My husband, Desmond Wilcox, ran away to sea when he was fifteen.... So when I suggested 50 years later that we two should take a cruise on the *QE2* along the Mediterranean, he was scathing. ...But he agreed to go to Southampton and take a look. He told me he had been expecting a huge, featureless sea-going block of flats. Instead he found a ship, a real wood and brass, tough but luxurious craft, burnished with love and affection by generations of sailors like him.' *Esther Rantzen*

---

Unfortunately the transatlantic crossing had to divert to Baltimore as a result of bad weather in the Atlantic. This rather upset noted film producer Desmond Wilcox who was on board making a film for his television series *The Visit*. The programme generally followed people on what were, for them, significant return visits. His plan on this occasion was to follow veterans of the *Queen Mary* maiden voyage on the return voyage to New York 50 years later. But New York was suddenly off the menu and replaced by Baltimore!

Icebergs delayed *QE2's* arrival into Southampton later that month as the liner had to alter course by several hundred nautical miles.

On 4 July 1986, *QE2* was the focal point of celebrations involving Presidents of America and France to mark the centenary of the Statue of Liberty. *QE2* held centre stage as an estimated 40,000 vessels gathered around New York for the re-dedication of the monument. In the tradition of her famous predecessors *QE2* took an emigrant family from Europe to start a new life in America. The family, from Poland, escorted the 'Freedom Torch' to the festivities – a commemorative work specially commissioned by Cunard as a gift to the American people.

In October *QE2* broke the record for turnaround in New York despite a strike by longshoremen. The 5 hour 28 minutes turnaround was 9 minutes quicker than the previous record set in November 1983 with full longshoremen facilities.

## Last Voyage as a Steamship

Maritime history was made on 20 October when she left New York for the last time as a steamship, and undertook her and Cunard's last crossing of the Atlantic under steam, ending a 146-year tradition. *QE2's* steam turbines had taken her a total of 2,622,858 nautical miles.

Five days later *QE2* arrived at Southampton for the last time as a steamship. Her arrival in Germany two days later began the race against time to complete the biggest, most complicated and most epic conversion in civil merchant

*QE2's original funnel awaiting modifications among the scrap metal just ripped out of the liner*

shipping history. The six-month out-of-service period required by the re-engining programme was also used to improve passenger areas and accommodation. In all, £25 million (25% of the overall cost) was spent on the 'hotel side' with very few parts of the ship being left untouched.

All the restaurants were refurbished with the Queen's Grill being enlarged and the Tables of the World alone undergoing a £2 million refurbishment and being renamed the *Mauretania* Restaurant. The Double Room was remodelled and renamed the Grand Lounge with the existing stainless steel stairway being removed and replaced by a new half round double-sided stairway built flanking the stage at the opposite end to the original staircase location. The original 1969 chairs and tables in the Queen's Room, likened by some to mushrooms, were replaced with new cubicle-style leather armchairs in the style of Le Corbusier.

The aft end of Upper Deck was reconfigured to feature a new Yacht Club (replacing the Double Down Bar) and a new Teen Centre and Adult Centre were built. The existing shopping arcade in the upper level of the Double Room was completely renewed and extended aft by 16m (50ft) into the open deck space which was now enclosed and incorporated into the ship's structure.

New carpets were fitted in all public rooms, alleyways, staircases and most passenger cabins. In

total, 32km (20 miles) of new carpets, all specially designed and made for the specific rooms, were woven. Altogether, 24,500m² (270,000 sq ft) of old carpeting and felt underlay were removed, replaced and renewed. In addition approximately 900m² (10,000 sq ft) of teak decking was renewed, approximately 1,100m² (12,000 sq ft) was refurbished and 3,000 pieces of furniture and other items had to be purchased or re-upholstered.

The very popular Computer Learning Centre was relocated from Boat Deck to a windowless, but perfectly adequate, area adjacent to the Forward Lobby replacing the Duty Free Liquor Shop and seating area.

## Eight Penthouse Suites

On Signal Deck, a further eight category 'A' penthouse suites were built in the last gap between the funnel and the existing penthouse block – aesthetically completing the row of suites between the mast and the funnel. This was the third penthouse addition in the area over a period of 15 years, featuring work in three different countries. The new unit's aluminium structure was designed by the shipyard, made up in prefabricated sections and incorporated into the ship's existing superstructure. The most sophisticated sound insulation was installed. The eight new 35m² (355 sq ft) suites were luxuriously outfitted with private verandahs, electronically adjustable beds, TV and video, and gold and marble bathroom fittings.

A team of 150 workmen went through the ship renovating cabins to a new, higher standard. Some cabins were lavishly redecorated and fitted with new soft furnishings. All received new 20-channel colour satellite televisions, a new direct-dial satellite telephone enabling passengers to call or be called anywhere in the world and a new multi-lingual clock. All First Class cabins were equipped with a video recorder and personal safe for passenger valuables.

Up to £4 million was spent on upgrading areas such as crew accommodation, galleys and laundry facilities. Crew areas on One Deck forward were completely renewed. The Crew Mess, the Servery, Recreation Room, Shop, Library, Barber Shop, Gymnasium and Club Room were fitted out in an up-to-date style and provided with TV sets and video units. The three galleys underwent conversion and new equipment was installed. A new layout was devised to ensure a smooth flow and speedy distribution of the meals. Due considerations were given to the latest hygiene regulations of United States Public Health and the World Health Organisation. A new computer-supported telephone system was installed as well as a new television system. A huge new Laundry Room was built on Seven Deck and the various launderettes around *QE2* were modernised and brought up to a more modern standard with new equipment.

*QE2* stuck in the ice at Bremerhaven while preparations are made to install the new engines

# Re-engining *QE2*

One of the first jobs undertaken after *QE2* had entered the Kaiserdock II dry-dock was the removal of the ship's funnel. This permitted access to the shaft that led down to the ship machinery spaces to allow for the removal of the existing steam turbine plant and the installation of the new diesel electric plant.

The most noticeable change to the exterior of *QE2* was the new, far more substantial funnel. The new diesel engines required the old funnel to be modified and expanded. Instead of needing only two exhaust vents from the original three boilers, nine uptakes had to be squeezed into the enlarged funnel, plus air intakes capable of supplying 650,000m³ (18,000,000 cu ft) of air per hour to the new diesels and engine spaces. Clearly evident from above, the new funnel gave *QE2* 'a more robust and purposeful look'.

Another aspect of the re-engining was the installation of two new five-bladed 5.8m (22ft) diameter controllable pitch propellers each weighing 42 tonnes. An innovation in the form of 'vane wheels' was introduced at the same time. These seven-bladed wheels of 6.7m (24ft) diameter (each of 15.5 tonnes) were installed behind the main propellers in order to reclaim part of the energy that was normally lost in the propeller slip stream and convert it into additional thrust.

When re-delivered Cunard's 'tomorrow's superliner today' was ready for a third decade.

## Crowning Glory

*On 20 February 1987 the new QE2 was 'crowned' when the new funnel, at 21.2m (69ft 6in) tall, the same height as the previous structure, was hoisted on board by 750-tonne capacity floating crane Hebe 2.*

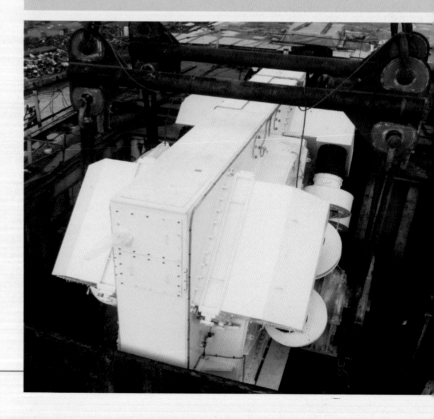

## Stripping Down

In total 4,700 tonnes of redundant equipment were stripped out and removed from the machinery spaces, and deposited on the quayside for scrapping, in an operation the shipyard managing director, Eckart Knoth, described as being 'like hell'. This photograph shows the old double bottom structure in the ship's lower-most deck. The first of the 220-tonne weight MAN and B&W engines have just been placed into position. Slide bars were installed to slide hydraulically the new engines into position.

## Mighty Engines

One of the 400-tonne GEC propulsion motors being lowered into the engine room. These two electric motors, one on each propeller shaft, were rated at a maximum of 44 megawatts each at 144 rpm and were the largest marine motors ever built. The new diesel electric system produced 130,000hp, which was the most powerful propulsion plant of any merchant ship in the world.

# Chapter 7
# *Coming of Age*

After 179 days and 1.7 million man hours, making the re-engining the biggest merchant ship conversion ever undertaken, Lloyd Werft handed back to Cunard its revitalised flagship. On 25 April 1987 a special Handover Ceremony, attended by over 500 guests, took place in the new Grand Lounge. Cunard chairman Alan Kennedy claimed '*QE2* can now carry more passengers in greater comfort than the original vessel, she is faster, more fuel efficient and quieter than before and justifies Trafalgar House agreeing to spend over £100 million to create tomorrow's superliner today.'

---

'*QE2* can now carry more passengers in greater comfort than the original vessel, she is faster, more fuel efficient and quieter than before...'
*Cunard chairman Alan Kennedy*

---

It was time for *QE2* to head home. During the voyage to Southampton she achieved a remarkable 33.8 knots. But the voyage was not without its problems because, unknown to those on board, several of the blades on the new vane wheels mounted behind the propellers snapped off. While this would not affect future speeds it did cancel out the anticipated £1,000-per-day savings in fuel costs, and would affect the comfort of passengers and crew in terms of increased levels of vibration – a problem that would not be sorted out for over a year.

*QE2* arrived back in Southampton on 28 April 1987, and was immediately made ready to welcome on board HRH The Princess of Wales, due to visit the following day. She wasn't coming alone – she was being joined by 500 children from the Southampton area, who had been invited by Cunard to celebrate the ship's return-to-service at the 'biggest children's party afloat!' The children boarded the ship early in the morning, completely unaware that they were to be joined by a surprise guest, and while they tucked into breakfast – possibly the messiest ever served on board – the ship set sail. She anchored just off Cowes on the

*Captain Lawrence Portet and HRH The Princess of Wales in the Grand Lounge*

# 'Maiden Voyage' to New York after Re-engining

Disembarking passengers were questioned by the assembled press on arrival in New York in May 1987.
Their reactions to the new engines and crew were mixed:

'She is still the best ship in the world.'

'Not very satisfactory coming over. Hope it's going to be better going back.'

'My cabin was about 120 degrees. You could fry an egg in there.'

'It was absolutely fantastic, the food has improved tremendously. It's been great.'

'Beautiful, I always enjoy it.'

'It's all been exaggerated.'

'If I wanted to sleep in a cesspool, I would have brought my own.'

'I don't know what all the fuss is about. I hit the Casino on the first night out and by the end of the voyage, I'd won a thousand dollars.'

Isle of Wight, and at 1100 hours Captain Portet welcomed on board the Princess of Wales who arrived by launch.

Meanwhile, in the Grand Lounge, Keith Harris and Orville were keeping the children entertained – until Princess Diana appeared at the top of the new curving staircase behind, and the audience erupted. The Princess joined the audience for the rest of the performance – and the ship returned slowly to her berth. At noon the Princess sounded the whistle, and this was followed by a display of Harrier jump jets and a fly-past by Concorde. A really good time was had by all!

The 'new' *QE2* was re-introduced to service with a second 'maiden voyage' and the Cunard flagship left Southampton on 29 April for Cunard's first diesel-electric crossing of the Atlantic, scheduled to arrive in New York on 4 May. However, things did not go according to plan. Certain work on her interiors had not been completed in time, necessitating workmen sailing with the ship to New York. And a pipe burst, making several cabins uninhabitable.

*QE2* also had a new crew, which resulted in less efficient service than normal. While the diesel engines would reduce their flagship's costs when it came to her annual fuel bill, Cunard intended to reduce costs further and had offered 800 hotel and catering staff on the ship generous redundancy terms in return for re-employment by an outside contractor on lower pay scales. Three-quarters of the staff accepted the deal, which was eventually pushed through despite trade union objections.

As *QE2* crossed the Atlantic she was attracting unfavourable headlines.

Cunard chairman Alan Kennedy had previously been a submarine commander – a fact that led to many jokes. He was on board for the crossing –

along with a press party that included at least one Fleet Street editor. But Kennedy's direct and honest approach won them over, and the headlines – though critical – could have been much, much worse. One well-known Fleet Street commentator, concerned that the ship was listing to starboard slightly as a result of ballast problems, protested loudly that she would be coming to dinner in a lifejacket unless something was done. On hearing this, Commodore Doug Ridley – at that time on board as general manager – rang the engine room. 'Can you get this bloody ship upright?' he bellowed and slammed the phone down. And get it upright they did – only for the ship to take on a gentle list to port.

---

'I can't believe the *QE2* is 40. Mind you, I can't believe I am 60. The difference is that this wonderful ship has matured; I have merely aged. …We all have our favourite bits of the ship, the little bar that's the best place for an apéritif, the quiet corner where you can read in the sunshine, the Queen's Grill, an old-fashioned definition of First Class, and the better for it.'

*Michael Buerk*

---

She was welcomed in New York by fireboats spraying red, white and blue, and New York's mayor, Ed Koch, welcomed her back during a gala lunch in the *Mauretania* Restaurant.

When she departed for Southampton later that day she was escorted by Malcolm Forbes in his yacht *Highlander*, a Coast Guard siren salute, a fireboat water display, a 22m (70ft) sailing yawl and a turn-of-the-century schooner, *Richard Robbins*, while four red Decathlon planes formed an aerial escort. The return crossing, 4–9 May, was better, but there were still difficulties on board. Her next cruise, a seven-day trip to Tenerife and Madeira, was also beset by problems. Around 200 passengers were advised days before the cruise that their trip had been cancelled as the ship still had incomplete cabins. Workmen were still on board rectifying the problems. The compensation paid by Cunard would total £100,000.

## Unscheduled Dry-docking

After *QE2* had been back in service for two months with broken and missing vane wheels Cunard decided to have the remainder removed during an unscheduled dry-docking. Earlier in May Alan Kennedy announced that *QE2's* schedule was being studied to find a suitable slot for the work to be done. Cunard was concerned that the remaining vane wheels would damage the main propellers.

It was decided to take advantage of an overnight mooring in Southampton in order to perform the necessary work. *QE2* was scheduled to arrive in

Southampton at 1630 hours on 9 July and sail at 1130 hours the next day. The schedule was to be amended to give a 1230 hours arrival on 9 July and a 2030 departure on 10 July – with *QE2* embarking passengers while still in the dry-dock and sailing direct for New York. The scheduled call at Cherbourg en route was cancelled and the 400 passengers due to embark there would now join the ship in Southampton.

After disembarking 1,500 passengers and 28 vintage cars from the USA, *QE2* headed for her first Southampton dry-docking in five years. About 100 men from Thew Engineering (who operated the dock after Vosper Thornycroft went into receivership in February 1987) were to work on the vessel.

The one-tonne hubs were removed and replaced with new permanent bronze cone caps. The oil line was also sealed off. The fairing plates were renewed and the leading edges of the propeller blades were ground. Viewing positions were cut into the bottom of the ship so that strobe lights and video cameras could be installed in order to monitor water turbulence from the main propellers. This was to assist the

manufacturers, Lips of the Netherlands, in determining why the vane wheels had snapped off.

During her 20–26 July cruise to Portugal and Gibraltar *QE2* experienced engine problems, which resulted in her call at Praia de Rocha being cancelled and her stay in Gibraltar being extended by a day in order to carry out repairs. *QE2* arrived in Southampton late in the evening on 26 July so passengers were kept on board overnight. Those expecting to board for New York that day were accommodated that night in hotels. *QE2* sailed 24 hours late.

'She was a thing of beauty and joy…. The *QE2* was my last ship and the best.'
*John Rannie*

At 0700 hours on Sunday 23 August Captain Lawrence Portet brought *QE2* into Southampton for the last time after a 41-year career with Cunard.

The 20 September 1987 marked the 20th anniversary of the ship's launch. An 84-year-old

John Rannie recalled: '20 September 1967 was the best day of my life. She was a thing of beauty and joy…. The *QE2* was my last ship and the best.'

1988 began with *QE2's* first long voyage as a motorship: a three-month 'Voyage of the Southern Crown' that would see the liner circle the Pacific, calling at 33 ports along the way. When stock market prices collapsed in October 1987 Cunard reported that they had received cancellations worth $1 million for the voyage in one day. But the voyage was a success and her visit to Sydney on 15 February was declared an official Australian Bicentennial Event. A gala ball attended by the prime minister, Bob Hawke, and Dame Joan Sutherland was held on board.

*QE2* was well on the way to justifying the expenditure Trafalgar House had made on the ship for the re-engining. Cunard's parent company reported in May that her return to service had helped Trafalgar's shipping and hotels division double its contribution to Trafalgar's 58 per cent rise in profits – to £85 million.

## Replacing the Propellers

The problems *QE2* had experienced with her propellers since her re-engining was a situation that could not be allowed to continue. Cunard acted by cancelling the ten-day round-trip to New York. *QE2* instead returned to Lloyd Werft for dry-docking. Lloyd Werft was responsible for the costs incurred, which, according to Cunard, 'were not for publication'. On 22 July, *QE2* left Southampton, after an incredibly short four-and-a-half hour turnaround, for West Germany, where work began the next day. Over 700 men were involved. Cunard stressed that there would be no work done to the exterior of the ship, the passenger areas and accommodation or any other mechanical areas on board apart from the propellers.

After *QE2* had run for almost a year with bare wheel bosses, Cunard decided not to re-fit the vane wheels to the ship. Instead, they decided to replace the five-bladed propellers of 5.8m (19ft) diameter – fitted during the 1986/87 re-engining – with a 6.1m (20ft) diameter set. It was hoped that the new, larger, propellers would rid the ship of the vibration problem she had experienced since the re-engining a little over a year earlier. As the replaced propellers were still under guarantee, they reverted to the ownership of the manufacturer, Lips, and were returned to the Netherlands for tests and disposal. Lips provided the new set of propellers.

September 1988 saw *QE2* complete two million nautical miles, a feat she achieved in less than half the time that *Queen Elizabeth* had taken.

---

'With the new engines fitted you have immediate power at your fingertips...'
*Captain Alan Bennell*

---

Later that month *QE2* was battered by Force 10 winds and 15m (50ft) waves during an Atlantic crossing from New York, which resulted in her arriving in Southampton nearly 24 hours late. Furniture and crockery were smashed and a piano broke loose. The crossing was also notable for the spotting of an iceberg – the first one Captain Bennell had encountered in over 30 years; *QE2* sailed within half a mile of the ice.

In October *QE2* was nearly blown aground when leaving Southampton as high winds, some gusting up to 112km/h (70mph), caught the ship as she was making a sharp turn to port off Cowes. Captain Alan Bennell had to implement a full emergency astern to prevent the liner being swept onto the Isle of Wight. The situation was compounded by the fact that the 50,000grt container ship *Benavon* was coming up the Solent ready to enter Southampton Water at the same time. Captain Bennell was praised for his actions and he later said: 'She responded magnificently. With the new engines fitted you have immediate power at your fingertips and we were able to do 8 knots astern straight away.'

## Nine Cunard Captains

On 14 December 1988 HM Queen Elizabeth The Queen Mother paid a visit to *QE2* to celebrate the 50th anniversary of her launching of *Queen Elizabeth* in 1938. Before lunch, attended by 300 guests, Her Majesty toured several of the public rooms and then met with nine former Cunard captains and commodores and posed with them for a group photograph. At lunch the chairman of parent company, Trafalgar House, presented the Queen Mother with what everyone agreed was a magnificent silver model of the original *Queen Elizabeth*. But what everyone did not know was that the model was in fact a fairly cheap plastic Airfix kit, which a schoolboy had been paid £10 to assemble, which was then expertly 'dipped' by a silversmith.

'We are proud to be a part of the tradition forged by this great ship – of service to Great Britain in war and in peace.'
*Captain Alan Bennell*

Earlier that year, on the actual anniversary of the launch, 27 September 1938, Captain Alan Bennell sent the following message to Her Majesty:

We are proud to be a part of the tradition forged by this great ship – of service to Great Britain in war and in peace. The RMS *Queen Elizabeth* sailed for 28 years and completed 907 Atlantic crossings in peacetime.

May we thank you for the continuing interest you have shown in our maritime history.

Her Majesty replied:

I am most touched by your kind message, which I greatly appreciated.

It was a source of much happiness to me to launch the RMS *Queen Elizabeth* some 50 years ago, and the achievements of this fine ship are remembered with pride and admiration.

I am delighted to be closely associated with her successor, which is so worthily upholding the high traditions of the name she bears.

To celebrate the 130th anniversary of the city of Yokohama, a consortium of Japanese companies chartered *QE2* for 72 days, from 27 March to 7 June 1989. This was the longest charter in the vessel's history and was worth £15–£18 million to Cunard. The celebrations in Yokohama were to continue until September 1989 and *QE2* was chosen to add prestige to the event.

At the same time Cunard also secured a longer Japanese charter for 1990, although plans for a third long-term charter in 1991, resulting in rumours that Cunard was to abandon the North Atlantic, never materialised. The Japanese saw *QE2* as the ultimate in luxury and quality, displaying the best of European traditions that the Japanese found so appealing – 99 per cent of Japanese questioned had heard of *QE2*.

*HM Queen Elizabeth The Queen Mother addresses the lunch guests in the* Columbia *Restaurant, December 1988*

Cunard was jubilant to secure the deal after five months of intense negotiations. A team was assembled to organise all aspects of the charter and was headed by Captain Harvey Smith. 'Port Yokohama 130' saw five roles for *QE2*: a hotel for visitors, a floating restaurant, a wedding ceremony location, a retail shop complex and a commercial advertising and public relations centre.

While her traditional World Cruise was now cancelled, *QE2* undertook two extended voyages in order to arrive in Yokohama on Monday 27 March: New York to Los Angeles (38 days, leaving New York on 13 January and arriving in Los Angeles on 19 February) and Los Angeles to Yokohama via Australia (38 days departing 19 February). The voyages were not without their problems. *QE2* received a great deal of press attention when she failed a health inspection in Los Angeles and she encountered a severe storm while in the South Pacific about 700 nautical miles from New Zealand, which resulted in 30 injuries.

The charter commenced immediately after her arrival on 27 March 1989. The ship docked alongside the passenger terminal in the port as a central attraction. Although she did not go to sea, she maintained her status as an ocean liner throughout her stay – this was important in order to allow visitors to take advantage of the tax-free items available in the ship's shops.

The consortium had chartered *QE2* for £250,000 a day, and to recoup this *QE2* was used as a hotel, with prices up to £1,690 a night for a suite, as well as a venue for companies to undertake corporate entertaining at £600,000 per day. Every day visitors would arrive for the evening on board or just spend a few hours having lunch, looking around or shopping. For those 'passengers' all the ship's facilities were opened and a full programme of entertainment was offered; even wedding ceremonies were available. While the on-board atmosphere was kept Western, extra Japanese staff were employed and additional signage in Japanese was placed throughout.

Despite 69,000 people staying overnight and a further 180,000 visiting for the day, the consortium still made a loss. July 1989 brought further unwelcome headlines when it was claimed *QE2* had broken pollution laws and had illegally dumped rubbish into the sea, resulting in the death of wildlife and pollution on beaches. Two crew members had been so appalled at the practices on board that they secretly filmed colleagues hurling sacks containing cans, bottles and kitchen waste over the side of the vessel under cover of darkness. They sent the tape to a national newspaper, which resulted in unwelcome headlines. But the publicity did have a beneficial effect, and waste disposal on board was significantly improved.

## A New Transatlantic Liner

By the end of the 1980s Cunard was actively looking at constructing a new transatlantic liner – Q5. Market research was undertaken among past passengers as to what they wanted to see on board in terms of facilities. A specification was drawn up and the plans detailed an extremely fast vessel (capable of up to 40 knots) of approximately 90,000grt, with two funnels. Q5 would be 300m (975ft) long and have a passenger capacity of 2,500 in 1,178 cabins. Draft itineraries saw Q5 placed in Atlantic service while QE2 would be despatched to the Far East and Alaska. The project continued into the early 1990s but by this time Trafalgar House seemed to have lost serious interest in Cunard and the plans never left the drawing board.

Prior to her second, longer, Japanese charter, QE2 was given a short refit in Southampton. This time the charter was for six months, for the World Exposition in Osaka. The group behind the charter was the newly formed Marine Leisure Development Company, a joint undertaking of 19 large Japanese companies including the Marubeni Corporation and Sapporo Breweries. The group planned to use QE2 to introduce the Japanese to the world of luxury cruising.

'No matter what bigger or faster ships may be launched, the QE2 holds a unique place in the affections of those of us fortunate enough to have sailed on her. My own journeys have been the Southampton–New York crossings, voyages which gave an unrivalled opportunity to experience the unostentatious elegance, the superb facilities, the spacious cabins and the wonderful service on what for so many will always remain the most gracious queen of the ocean liners.'
*Baroness (PD) James of Holland Park*

QE2 was passed to the charter group just before Christmas 1989 and arrived in Osaka on 28 December at the outset of a 180-day stay. She was to undertake ten short cruises to Hong Kong and other nearby ports. A similar fee to that received in Yokohama, £250,000 a day, was being paid by the charterer, netting nearly £50 million for Cunard.

QE2 was handed back to Cunard in Honolulu. From there she made a five-day cruise in the Hawaiian Islands before heading for New York via the Panama Canal, where she arrived on 7 July.

*HM The Queen, followed by HRH The Duke of Edinburgh, is greeted by QE2's Hotel Manager, John Duffy, July 1990*

On 17 July *QE2* left New York on the first of four special voyages to commemorate the 150th anniversary of the sailing of Cunard's first ship *Britannia* from Liverpool to Halifax. She sailed her fastest-ever eastbound crossing and arrived in Southampton in four days, six hours and 57 minutes, making an average of 30.16 knots. That day, 22 July, Captain Woodall received, on behalf of all the officers and crew, the Freedom of the City of Southampton.

That afternoon *QE2* left her home port for a five-day cruise – voyage 749 – to Cobh, Liverpool, Greenock and Cherbourg; it was perhaps her most emotional cruise ever.

*QE2* was greeted by 60,000 people and units of the Irish Navy on her maiden arrival at Cobh, in the Irish Republic, the next day. Her arrival also coincided with the opening of the new cargo terminal at Ringaskiddy (where she berthed) and the Irish Taoiseach, Charles Haughey, was entertained to lunch to mark the event. Her departure that evening was again greeted with huge crowds, especially as she passed Cobh itself, where every square foot of the town overlooking the water was jammed with sightseers.

An estimated one million spectators greeted her maiden arrival in Liverpool the next day. As she made her stately progress up the River Mersey she became the first *Queen* liner to visit what had been Cunard's home from 1839 to 1967 and the first Cunard passenger ship to do so for over 25 years. *QE2* anchored opposite the Cunard Building on the Pierhead and 10,000 red and blue balloons were released from the ship. The ship's crew had spent much of the night inflating the balloons which were then released under the Magrodome roof; when it was time for the balloons to go, the retractable roof was simply opened. Captain Woodall had to stay on board his ship for the day as the prevailing weather meant the anchor started to drag, so Staff Captain Ron Bolton represented him at the ceremonies ashore. These included the unveiling of a bust of Sir Samuel Cunard and a service at St Nicholas's Church. *QE2* sailed that night after a magnificent firework display and played traditional Liverpudlian and Beatles' songs from her loudspeakers as she departed.

## A Return to the Clyde

The next day saw *QE2* make an emotional visit to the Clyde for the first time since 1968. She berthed at Greenock – the furthest up the river she could travel. She was greeted by bagpipes, a group of pensioners from John Brown's was hosted on board for lunch and she was escorted by a flotilla of hundreds of vessels of all types when she sailed.

*QE2* made a quick call at Cherbourg on 26 July. The weather throughout the cruise had been glorious sunshine but this spell broke just before the highlight of the cruise. At this time Captain

*Previous page: The freshly repainted 7.5-tonne aft anchor during one of QE2's regular dry-dockings*

portsides of the anchored Cunarders. *QE2* and *Vistafjord* passengers lined the boat decks and cheered as the *Britannia* passed. A Concorde, a 767 and 747 then made a fly-past before *Britannia* anchored and a second fly-past, consisting of a Sea King, Lynx and Dauphin helicopters and a Harrier jump jet, took place.

Woodall also handed over command to Captain Ron Warwick and history was made when Captain Warwick assumed command of the same ship as his father – Captain Bil Warwick, *QE2's* first master. The change in command was necessary because Captain Woodall would be required to entertain two VIPs the next day.

On 27 July 1990 *QE2* arrived and anchored in her allocated position. Shortly afterwards she was joined by the Cunarders *Vistafjord* and *Atlantic Conveyor*, which both also took up their designated positions. The three vessels were joined by dozens of private yachts, motor boats and excursion vessels all keen to take part in the planned royal review of Cunard and Royal Navy ships at Spithead by HM The Queen and HRH The Duke of Edinburgh on board the Royal Yacht *Britannia*.

The royal yacht left Portsmouth, led by the Trinity House vessel *Patricia* and followed by *HMS Broadsword*, at 0925 hours and passed the

The Queen and Duke of Edinburgh then transferred to *QE2* by royal barge. Receptions were held in the Queen's Room and Grand Lounge, with the Queen unveiling a plaque in the latter, prior to lunch. The assembled ships dispersed and *QE2* left her anchorage at 1345 hours and proceeded to her berth in Southampton. This was the first time the Queen had sailed on the ship she had launched 23 years earlier. As *QE2* was berthing, the royal party were on the Bridge where they were introduced to Captain Warwick. *QE2* berthed ahead of the *Vistafjord* and later that evening both ships were serenaded with a firework finale. The next day *QE2* sailed for New York on the third of Cunard's anniversary voyages.

On 20 August, while *QE2* was at the start of a Northern European cruise sailing in a Force 9, a Mayday message was received from the Norwegian oil-drilling platform *West Gamma* saying that the

rig was adrift with 49 persons on board and requesting assistance. *QE2* altered course and proceeded at full speed to the distress area 47 nautical miles away. Captain Warwick made a broadcast to passengers informing them of the situation. As *QE2* proceeded to the scene the crew on the rig advised that they did not wish to leave *West Gamma* and, shortly after arrival, *QE2* was dismissed and continued on her passage to Bergen. But shortly after *QE2* had left, *West Gamma* capsized. Fortunately, all the crew members were eventually rescued from the sea.

On 9 August 1990 *QE2* completed her 500th scheduled crossing of the Atlantic.

## Anti-apartheid Demonstration

Anti-apartheid campaigners mounted an early morning demonstration upon *QE2's* 14 October arrival in Southampton because South African

president F W de Klerk was on board as part of the Young Presidents' Association. Mr de Klerk left the docks by helicopter for lunch at Chequers with the prime minister.

Instead of the Lloyd Werft Shipyard in Bremerhaven for her annual refit in December 1990, Cunard chose, for the first time, the Blohm & Voss shipyard in Hamburg.

Graham Fahye of Fahye Design consultants was responsible for the refurbishment and new designs. A fifth main restaurant and third Grill Room, the Princess Grill II, was constructed in space formerly occupied by a *Columbia* Restaurant annexe on the starboard side of Quarter Deck directly opposite the existing Princess Grill. This was the fourth First Class restaurant on board and could accommodate 106 diners. A new staircase entrance to the Grill was built leading down from a new lounge built on Upper Deck above. A 44-seat Cocktail Lounge and Bar was constructed on Upper Deck above the new Grill in space that had been the starboard annexe and entrance area to the *Mauretania* Restaurant.

The Casino was totally re-designed in a 1930s style; the Club Lido was refurbished with new carpeting and chairs installed and, in its 150th anniversary year, Cunard finally took the opportunity to emphasise its heritage by hanging paintings, line drawings and deck plans for some of its former ships.

With the exception of the penthouses numbered 8011 to 8019, which were added during the re-engining, all penthouses on Signal and Sports Decks were rebuilt and totally refurbished in a new décor of natural wood with walk-in wardrobes and soundproofed windows to eliminate the noise of whistling wind.

*QE2's* 1991 World Cruise was originally scheduled to pass through the Suez Canal but the conflict in the Gulf resulted in the itinerary being re-routed around the Cape of Good Hope.

On 15 June 1991 HRH Prince Edward and HRH The Duke of Edinburgh hosted a royal ball on board, attended by 800 partygoers who had paid £280 for a pair of tickets, to mark the 35th anniversary and raise funds for the Duke of Edinburgh's Award Scheme. Two receptions began at 1930 hours with The Duke of Edinburgh presiding over the Queen's Room while the Prince presided over the Grand Lounge. These receptions were followed by a seven-course dinner in the *Columbia* and *Mauretania* Restaurants. After a spectacular mid-river fireworks display just before midnight, guests then pitched into four hours of entertainment featuring artistes including Petula Clark, Paul Daniels and the Jools Holland Big Band Sound, with breakfast being served at 0400 hours.

## Contract Labour

In August 1991 Cunard sparked a major political row. The unions threatened major action against *QE2* when it emerged that the company was planning to end direct employment of British ratings by introducing contract labour in place of 140 British deck and engine crew who worked on board on a rota basis. The move by Cunard was to counteract reduced profits due to the Gulf War and problems being experienced by other Trafalgar House subsidiaries. John Prescott, Labour's transport spokesman, accused Cunard of showing 'contempt for taxpayers who subsidised its vessels' and called upon Prime Minister John Major to intervene. Mr Prescott said that the removal of the British seafarers from *QE2* would be 'the final nail

*HRH Prince Edward unveils a plaque to mark his overnight stay on board, June 1991*

of the merchant navy and the armed forces also attended the lunch including Captain Peter Jackson (who commanded *QE2* on her voyage to South Georgia), Major General Sir Jeremy Moore, Air Marshal Sir John Curtiss, Commodore C J S Craig (*Alacrity*), Captain Tobin (*Coventry*), Captain West (*Ardent*), Rear Admiral Salt (*Sheffield*), Captain Barker (*Endurance*), Rear Admiral Dingemans (*Intrepid*), Commodore Dunlop (*Fort Austin*), Captain Roberts (*Sir Galahad*) and Captain Pitt (*Sir Percival*). Other guests included merchant seamen who served aboard *QE2* and *Atlantic Conveyor* during the conflict.

In her speech Margaret Thatcher praised the role of *QE2* in the Falklands and reflected that the only sleepless night she had had throughout the conflict was as *QE2* entered the war zone.

On 11 June 1992 one of the pistons in 'Echo' engine overheated, which caused it to seize. This resulted in the con-rod failing quite dramatically by shearing and breaking through the side of the engine. The failure physically shook the whole ship and the debris was extensive. Fortunately there were no injuries but the whole engine had to be taken apart and stored in crew corridors on the deck above the Control Room. Later the destroyed engine was laid out in the terminal area in Southampton.

*QE2* was scheduled to make a Bermuda cruise in early August but the cruise had to be cancelled

in the coffin of British merchant shipping'. The dismissed crew members were given packages that included a year's salary and an additional £1,500 for each year served. A subsequent deal was struck between Cunard and the National Union of Seamen whereby the shipping line would pay the union £80,000 a year in return for a guarantee that the running of the company's vessels would not be interrupted by industrial action.

The following year, on 10 May 1992, The Rt Hon Margaret Thatcher lunched on board in Southampton to mark the 10th anniversary of the Falkland Islands Campaign. Senior representatives

when Cunard did not receive from the Bermudan authorities the necessary licences for *QE2* to visit. Instead *QE2* was rescheduled to undertake a short cruise from New York to Newfoundland, Nova Scotia and Martha's Vineyard. So on 3 August *QE2* left New York with 1,824 passengers and 1,003 crew. No one was to know just how fateful the failure to obtain licences to visit Bermuda would prove to be.

## Martha's Vineyard

Having spent the day of 7 August off the northeast tip of the island of Martha's Vineyard, *QE2* weighed anchor just after 2030 hours and headed southwest. On the Bridge were Captain Robin Woodall, the staff captain, the first officer, two deck ratings and an experienced US pilot, Captain John F Hadley. The pilot was going to follow the same route to exit the Sound as he had used when he took the ship in earlier that day – but he changed his mind.

There was much small boat traffic around *QE2* and ferries were frequently travelling between Oak Bluffs, Vineyard Haven and Woods Hole. Later the density of the traffic had reduced, so at 2120 hours the speed was gradually increased to 25 knots from 17 knots.

After making a projected plot from the course, the second officer realised that the ship would be sailing over the Sow and Pigs Reef that extended out from Cuttyhunk Island. The captain was advised of this and discussed the situation with the pilot. The pilot agreed and *QE2* was turned to the southwest.

At 2158 hours *QE2* had reached a point approximately 3.5 nautical miles south-southwest of Cuttyhunk Island. She was about to pass over the southern tip of the shoaling seabed as she prepared to skirt the main areas of the reefs when she experienced two periods of heavy vibration in quick succession.

The engines began to slow and *QE2* began to lose speed. Captain Woodall contacted the staff chief engineer in the engine Control Room who reported that the propeller shafts were still turning at 144 rpm and that he was instructing his staff to check for possible damage. Thus mechanical breakdown was quickly ruled out and the first officer confirmed that *QE2* had not been involved in a collision with another vessel.

---

'My first thought was that this was a catastrophic machinery failure; an engine broken loose or a propeller had come off!'
*Captain Woodall*

---

Captain Woodall later said: 'My first thought was that this was a catastrophic machinery failure; an engine broken loose or a propeller had come off!'

The second officer reported to the captain that *QE2* was in an area where the chart indicated a sounding of six and a half fathoms (12m/39ft).

Other personnel, including the chief officer and the senior first officer arrived on the Bridge. The pilot checked the charted position of the vessel with his own observation of the after radar display.

The pilot and captain soon concurred that QE2 had probably passed through an area where the water was not as deep as the charts indicated. The chief officer was instructed to undertake internal soundings in order to determine the extent of the damage. Hold spaces, dry tanks and void spaces and the tanks were all checked, and it was soon ascertained that there was water in what should have been empty ballast and oil overflow tanks.

The captain made a general announcement throughout the ship to the effect that QE2 appeared to have struck an underwater object but that she was quite safe and the matter was being investigated. At 2236 hours the pilot reported the incident to the United States Coast Guard (USCG) at Point Judith.

Further damage assessments concluded that the No.15 Freshwater Double-Bottom Tank, which had previously been slack, was now full and pressurised; a cofferdam located between No.13, 14 and 15 Freshwater Double-Bottom Tanks and No.8, 9 and 10 Fuel Oil Double-Bottom Tanks, was also found to be full, and some buckling was found in the tank top of No.3 Hold.

A possible sighting of oil in the water around the liner was reported to the captain and, at 2252

hours, the pilot informed the USCG of this. At 2255 hours, the vessel was instructed to anchor and wait for the arrival of the USCG boarding party.

There was no panic among the passengers and the evening entertainment continued as scheduled with many passengers taking advantage of free drinks now being offered in the bars.

## Possible Oil Pollution

At 2232 hours QE2 was anchored near Buzzards Lighthouse and shortly afterwards Lifeboat 11 was lowered to the water to search for signs of oil pollution. The chief officer reported a light sheen on the water surface in the area below the port Bridge wing and he also reported the draughts of the vessel which were noted to equate to those calculated by the stability officer; no visible damage was reported.

At 2400 hours ballast pumping operations from No.1 Saltwater Double-Bottom Ballast Tank were terminated. At the same time No.14 Freshwater Double-Bottom Tank was found to be pressurised and the contents of No.14 and No.15 Freshwater Double-Bottom Tanks were sampled and found to contain salt water.

At 0215 hours USCG vessel *Bittersweet* arrived on site and Coastguards boarded QE2. The Forward Engine Room Void Space was taking in water.

QE2 was carrying 4.2 million litres (925,000 gallons) of fuel oil, of which there was a danger of

*QE2 in the Blohm & Voss Dry-dock for repairs, September and October 1992*

about 180,000 litres (40,000 gallons) leaking, so the USCG ordered an oil containment boom to be placed from amidships on one side of the *QE2*, around her stern to amidships on the other side, and this was in place by 0650 hours.

In accordance with regulations a nurse boarded *QE2* in order to perform drug and alcohol tests on the captain, first officer and pilot. These tests would later report that only low levels of caffeine had been found.

From 0700 to 0725 hours floodwater from the Forward Engine Room Void Space was pumped directly overboard under USCG observation followed by water being pumped overboard from No.12 Saltwater Double-Bottom Tank. In order to assess the extent of hull damage divers were sent down.

It had been decided that the passengers would have to be disembarked. At 1405 hours the passenger launch *Schamonchi* arrived alongside. Initially 555 passengers were taken ashore at 1500 hours.

At 1730 hours permission was granted for *QE2* to proceed towards Newport where she anchored at 2006 hours. This would make disembarking the remainder of the passengers easier and that operation was commenced again at 2040 hours using the ship's own lifeboats and two shore tenders, *Viking Queen* and *Spirit of Newport*. The disembarkation of all passengers was complete by 0220 hours on 9 August. Passengers were then taken by train and bus to their intended destination, New York.

In the event only 136 litres (30 gallons) of fuel leaked from *QE2* so the oil protection boom was removed.

*QE2* then proceeded, accompanied by a USCG cutter and two tugs, to Boston at around 8 knots.

She arrived there after a nine-and-a-half-hour journey to be dry-docked for survey and temporary repairs. *QE2* was dry-docked at the General Ship Corporation and the previously surveyed damage to her hull was confirmed once the dock was pumped dry.

## Severe Damage

It was only after *QE2* had been placed in the dry-dock that the true extent of the damage to the underwater hull became known. In all, the damage covered a width of 25m (80ft) over the keel and either side of it and extended over a length of 125m (400ft) aft from the bulbous bow. The keel was covered in dents – some up to 74m (240ft) in length and 35cm (14in) deep – gouges and fractures, and plates were buckled in places. In total 20 double-bottom tanks had sustained damage and the port bilge keel had been severely damaged.

It soon became clear that full repairs would not be able to be carried out in Boston as the yard did not have the staff, the resources or the correct grade of steel to complete the job. After initial repairs *QE2* would have to proceed elsewhere for final repairs. The Hamburg shipyard of Blohm & Voss was successful in its bid and *QE2* left Boston on 1 September and headed for Germany. On arrival in Hamburg the liner was lifted in a floating dock and full repairs were undertaken.

In total, nine Atlantic crossings and two cruises were cancelled while *QE2* was undergoing repairs.

There was intense speculation in the press that the repairs, lost revenue and compensation payments would cost Cunard up to £50 million, but the company never revealed the actual cost. *QE2's* return to Southampton on 3 October was jubilant, with three fireboats escorting her up the Solent. She returned to service the next day.

Despite having already been dry-docked twice in 1992 for repairs QE2 still had to be dry-docked on 20 November for her scheduled overhaul which again took place in Hamburg. The refurbishments undertaken in 1990 and 1992 were part of a five-year plan by Cunard to change QE2's interiors to reflect the ocean liner style of the 1930s. Research had shown that this is what passengers expected to find, but, because the ship was built in the 1960s and blatantly reflected the cutting-edge design of that period, they were sometimes disappointed. The refurbishment of some of the public spaces brought more art deco styling to the ship.

## New Spa Facilities

Throughout the 1980s, health spas on cruise ships became the norm, prompting Cunard to go one step further. The company decided to completely renovate the spa and fitness facilities with a state-of-the-art design.

In all, £2 million was spent on a major rebuilding of the Golden Door Health Spa facilities – notably the Six and Seven Deck swimming pool and gymnasium areas. The plan was for work to

# QE2 Runs Aground – The Inquiry

Investigations into the cause of the grounding were undertaken by both the National Transportation Safety Board in the USA and the UK Marine Accident Investigation Branch (MAIB). The actual grounding site on Sow and Pigs Reef was located and surveyed. Both investigations came to similar conclusions. There could be no doubt that the cause of the grounding was that the charts for the area were wrong and there was significantly less water than charted. In fact it was discovered that the area was last surveyed in 1939 by dropping a line at regular intervals; this method, of course, can miss significant peaks. It was noted that prior to the grounding QE2 had passed over an area with a 12m (40ft) sounding without mishap or any indication of shallow water effect.

QE2 grounded twice in quick succession; at the time of the initial grounding the depth of water was 10.67m (35ft) while the depth of water at the second grounding was 10.42m (34.2ft). The stationary forward and after draughts of the vessel were 9.85m (32.3ft) and 9.54m (31.3ft) respectively. On the assumption that no change in draught

was caused by the effect of the prevailing weather conditions, it was apparent that the effect of 'squat' on the vessel caused the bow to sink by at least 82cm (32in). 'Squat' is a phenomenon whereby ships travelling at speed in shallow water settle lower in the water than they would normally – but the degree to which they do so is not easy to calculate. The extent of the damage suggested that, on grounding, the vessel was trimmed by the head. The master had expected squat of 30–45cm (12–18in), with change of trim by the stern. It was clear that Captain Woodall had underestimated the magnitude of 'squat' effect upon his vessel in the prevailing circumstances – a factor magnified with the increase of speed to 25 knots. But the fact remains that, had the US chart been correct, the accident would not have happened.

Divers found traces of QE2's red anti-fouling paint and shavings of steel on several rocks that had either been moved horizontally, compressed into the seafloor or partially pulled out of the seabed. It was generally agreed that if a lesser vessel had sustained the damage QE2 had, then it would probably have been lost.

commence at the yard and continue into the New Year. Steiners of London would be responsible for the concession after opening, taking over from Golden Door, and so they were responsible for the design of the new spas. The design offered facilities both for those who took health and exercise seriously and for those who simply wanted to wallow while being pampered. The two areas, while both being complementary parts of the Spa complex, were each given a different emphasis.

The exercise facilities on Six Deck became the Spa proper. The whole area was rebuilt, involving the removal of the traditional swimming pool.

Facilities included separate saunas for men and women, a steam room, a whirlpool spa bath, an 'inhalation room' and a thalassotherapy pool. The latter was designed with strategically placed, high-powered jets to encourage relaxation, boost circulation and relieve aches and pains. The 'inhalation room' was an area where moist negatively ionised sea water or herbal mist was released into the air – a therapy to relieve asthma and sinusitis. A relaxation area, spacious changing rooms and lockers as well as three French hydrotherapy bath treatment rooms and seven further treatment rooms were built.

It had been planned to replace the Seven Deck swimming pool with a total exercise facility. However, the pool was retained because an indoor pool was seen by Cunard as being a basic *QE2* facility, so a new fitness suite was built around it. The Fitness Deck received new equipment and exercise class facilities. The new gymnasium and aerobic studio featured the latest exercise machines. A shop selling a full range of fitness wear was also built.

All of the restaurants were refurbished and the shopping promenade was remodelled at a cost of over £1 million, while the Midships Lobby on Two Deck was totally redecorated in the 1930s art deco style with a further £130,000 being spent on a much-needed refurbishment of the Cinema. A new suite, the 46m² (500 sq ft) Midships Suite, was constructed at a cost of £72,000 adjacent to the starboard Midships Lobby entrance in the space previously occupied by the Doctors' Office and a storeroom.

## Engine Replacement

The rebuilding of 'Echo' started in November in Hamburg. Cunard described this as 'substantial technical work normally performed during an overhaul' but was more than Cunard admitted to publicly as it involved the complete replacement of one of the engines. The work required the hull to be cut open and the engine frame and crankshaft to be replaced. The engine was then rebuilt while *QE2* was in service and was finally commissioned in January 1993.

One of the engine's cylinder 'lids' was put on display in the Officer's Wardroom on board. Also in the Wardroom, at the outboard side of the bar, there is an engine part from that failure mounted on a piece of wood – 'in commemoration'. The brass plate mounted on the piece says 'Echo Engine – R.I.P. (Ripped Itself to Pieces)'.

In a move that had no immediate effect on Cunard, but which did have longer-term implications, Sir Nigel Broackes was ousted as chairman of Trafalgar House at the start of 1993 and was replaced by Alan Clements of HongKong Land just before that company won their fight for control of Trafalgar House.

## Three Cruises in One

Unusually *QE2's* 108-day World Cruise in 1993 was three extended voyages combined. The first, New York to Los Angeles, circled South America before the second, Los Angeles to Los Angeles, circled the Pacific. The third voyage took *QE2* from Los Angeles to New York around the Mediterranean.

On 12 June 1993 HRH Prince Edward was Guest of Honour at a special lunch held in Southampton to celebrate the 40th anniversary of the Queen's accession to the throne. The Prince arrived in the port by helicopter and toured *QE2* prior to the lunch in the *Columbia* Restaurant. To allow as many passengers to meet the Prince as possible half were invited to attend a reception in the Queen's Room while the other half dined in the restaurant. Prince Edward was taken off *QE2* by helicopter off the coast of Kent as the ship was en route on a seven-day Northern Capitals cruise, which saw her make her first call at Edinburgh. A special hour-long episode of the BBC's hit show *Keeping Up Appearances* was filmed on board.

When *QE2* left New York for Southampton on 22 September 1993 the captain advised those on board that the ship would run into bad weather in the eastern Atlantic. By 0400 hours on 1 October *QE2* had run into a Force 8 blowing in from the northwest by west. Although the seas were rough *QE2* was riding them easily at 28.5 knots but by 0800 hours the wind had increased slightly to Force 9 and was now from the northwest. As the day was actually fine and sunny some passengers were on deck videoing the dramatic seas with waves 7–9m (25–30ft) high. At around mid-morning, *QE2* suddenly rolled 19 degrees to starboard but there was no damage and not even one passenger fell over. The ship continued to roll easily until lunchtime when, without any warning, *QE2* heeled over 21 degrees to starboard. Despite this being only two degrees more than the earlier roll, the effects this time were more serious as people and loose items, including china, tables and chairs, and gaming equipment in the Casino, slid across the floor. After the roll the liner

recovered sharply and the resultant whip action caused most of the damage. Fifty people received treatment for cuts and bruises with two people suffering broken limbs. *QE2* continued her passage at 28.5 knots and arrived on time in Southampton where some of the injured were taken to hospital.

In the same year *QE2's* usual Christmas festivities were nearly scuppered when thieves stole food worth $45,000 from the dockside as the ship was being provisioned for her Christmas cruise.

To celebrate the 25th anniversary of her maiden voyage, Cunard launched a search for those who sailed on the 1969 trip. Cunard offered those who responded the chance to sail on a special

*HRH Prince Edward, accompanied by Rosemarie Burton-Hall (wife of Commodore John Burton-Hall), in the Grand Lounge, June 1993*

'Commemorative Crossing' leaving Southampton on 8 May 1994 at a 25% discount on brochure prices. On 11 May a fly-past by the Red Arrows took place over the ship while it was berthed in Southampton.

A separate 'Silver Anniversary' cruise around the UK also took place between 26 August and 4 September. This included *QE2's* second-ever call into Liverpool and a return to Greenock.

On 22 May Albert Reynolds, the Irish Taoiseach, made a private visit while *QE2* was berthed in Cobh. He was a guest of the Irish National Petroleum Corporation and lunched on board.

## D-Day Anniversary

The 50th anniversary of D-Day was marked on 5 June 1994 with a series of special events both on and off the French coast. *QE2* took the lead role in the planned review and she joined other vessels including *Vistafjord*, *Canberra*, *Sea Princess*, the *USS George Washington*, the restored Liberty-ship *Jeremiah O'Brien* and the *USS Guam*. As the vessels took up their positions the beaches overlooking Spithead and the Solent were packed with thousands of spectators. The Royal Yacht *Britannia*, with the Queen, the Duke of Edinburgh, Queen Elizabeth the Queen Mother, Diana, Princess of Wales, President Clinton and Prime Minister John Major plus a host of other world leaders on board, proceeded to review the assembled fleet. The Royal Yacht sailed round the outer perimeter of the fleet using *QE2* as a marker to make her turn.

After the review *QE2* made her way to Cherbourg where a special live BBC programme, featuring Bob Hope, Chris de Burgh and Dame Vera Lynn, was to have been broadcast from the ship. Satellite problems meant the broadcast was cancelled and replaced by a nature programme about…racoons. The *QE2* programme was shown several weeks later.

## Urgent Action

Years of refurbishment had, by the 1990s, given *QE2* a piecemeal interior, with styles ranging from the 1930s to the 1980s. The 1990 and 1992 refits had gone some way to giving the ship an art deco 1930s style in several key areas but a great deal of work was necessary on her public areas. Increasing competition in the cruise industry prompted Cunard to take urgent action.

In all £45 million was spent on 'Project Lifestyle', the brainchild of the Cunard chairman, John Olsen. It attempted to emphasise *QE2's* uniqueness, give the ship a coherent and traditional style, meet the needs of changing lifestyles, allow passengers to move around the ship more freely, clearly define decks, bring 'the outside in' to make passengers more aware of the sea, display the Cunard heritage, restore the ship's original identity and bring her up-to-date in areas

QE2 *as she was before the 'Project Lifestyle' refit of 1994*

such as catering, service and on-board revenue-earning opportunities.

Cunard appointed the British MET Studio and John McNeece Ltd to design the new interiors and oversee the project in its development. The new designs would emphasise style, tradition and Cunard pedigree, while at the same time providing standards of passenger comfort and facilities that would be among the best and most modern afloat. This refit would maintain *QE2's* position of being ahead of the rest.

*QE2's* scheduled annual dry-docking (26 November–10 December) was used and further time was gained with the cancellation of the two seven-day cruises either side of the original overhaul (scheduled to depart 19 November and 10 December). The refit contract was awarded to Blohm & Voss of Hamburg and was the biggest 'short timescale' project in its 140-year history.

As Project Lifestyle developed, several grand proposals were cancelled, but this was still the largest public room and passenger accommodation refit ever undertaken in such a short period of time; it resulted in the reconfiguration or renovation of 75% of *QE2's* infrastructure.

*Continued on page 210*

# The 1994 Refit: 'Project Lifestyle'

QE2 left New York on 13 November 1994 with a team of contractors on board, arriving at Blohm & Voss on 20 November. A total of 32 days of rebuilding lay ahead and a workforce of 2,000 from 20 countries (and 400 QE2 crew) would work 24 hours a day in order to complete the ambitious project.

In total £32 million, more than QE2 cost to build, was spent. Almost 93,000m² (1 million sq ft) of public area space was affected. Every passenger area on board – with the exception of the Casino (redone in 1990), the Royal Promenade (rebuilt in 1992) and the Boardroom – was replaced, re-designed or re-decorated.

Many public areas were renamed during their re-design, with the Princess Grill Starboard becoming the Britannia Grill, the Midships Lounge becoming the revamped Chart Room and the former First Class Columbia Restaurant being moved up to Upper Deck and being renamed the Caronia Restaurant, while the Mauretania Restaurant took its place on Quarter Deck.

Among the dramatic new areas was the building of the Lido for informal dining on Quarter Deck, which involved the removal of the swimming pool and Magrodome; a new enlarged Yacht Club; and the new Crystal Bar and the new Golden Lion Pub both on Upper Deck.

To compensate for the loss of the staircase in the Grand Lounge, 'G' Stairway was extended up from Upper Deck to Boat Deck with a new U-shaped staircase. All the signage throughout was replaced.

The designers paid careful attention to traditional colours and leaned towards dusky reds and pinks, dark blue, deep burgundies, gold, black and biscuit with accents of taupes and mauves. Woods, granite and marble were used extensively, while carpeting and upholstery were replaced throughout.

Materials used in the refit work including 300 tonnes of steel, aluminium, ceramics and wood; 2,252 new light fixtures; 62,000m² (74,000 sq yd) of fabric for chairs and curtains; 38,000m² (45,000 sq yd) of new carpet in 25 separate carpet designs; 12 pieces of commissioned artwork and 12,000 litres (2,640 gallons) of paint.

## Cunard Heritage Trail

A key element of the new design scheme was the introduction of the Cunard Heritage Trail, a historical exhibition of nautical memorabilia. In strategic locations throughout the ship, exhibits including original charts, flags, pennants, paintings and ship models were placed in showcases of burr oak veneer.

The lighting of the public spaces on board was completely re-designed. In order to vary the mood around the ship and establish boundaries around spaces, most of the new lighting was dimmable tungsten.

The cabin refurbishment programme accounted for 30 per cent of the total interior redesign cost. John McNeece Ltd was given the task of updating all passenger cabins, but with structural modifications limited to the cabin bathrooms. All cabins received new soft furnishings: bedspreads, carpets, curtains, upholstery etc. New chairs and/or stools were installed and all settees were re-covered. The majority of cabins received a brand-new bathroom.

Four staterooms were redesigned for use as disabled accommodation using the latest technology. In these, the pneumatically operated outer doors and sliding bathroom doors could be controlled from a special transmitter carried by the passenger. This transmitter also controlled lighting, curtains and television.

Extensive technical overhaul work was undertaken on the hull and machinery spaces of *QE2* at a cost of around £13 million. The existing automatic sprinkler system was modified and extended to comprise 8,700 heads controlled by 68 sets of section valves. Additional fire doors and control systems and new fan rooms for additional air-conditioning units were supplied and fitted. For the ship's waste-disposal system a new garbage grinder plant was supplied.

The heaviest work arose from the scheduled inspection of the propellers – the starboard tail shaft was the subject of a full survey, necessitating its wholesale removal, while the portside tailshaft was partially withdrawn. The stern tube bearings were scrutinised on the starboard side, while the propeller shaft seals and propeller hub seals were renewed and the propeller blades were reconditioned where necessary.

The main change to the exterior profile of the ship was the new silhouette at the aft end. An additional 465m² (5,000 sq ft) of open deck space aft of the new Yacht Club was reclaimed with the removal of the Magrodome sliding glass roof and the Alpha and Beta tenders.

MET Studio was responsible for the new livery. *QE2* exchanged her trademark black, red and white for Cunard's new corporate colours of blue, red, white and gold. The white superstructure was given a stripe of the new Cunard tricolour – red, gold and blue – running along the lower section of the structure, stretching for 200m (660ft) along each flank (with a width of 500mm/20in). The

stripe took the unusual form of a decal, applied with fierce adhesive. It took six days to apply this, the longest 'speed-stripe' in the world!

The Cunard name in red was moved further forward underneath the Bridge on each side and, above the name, the golden Cunard symbol – a lion rampant – was placed, standing 4m (13ft) high. *QE2*'s hull was painted royal blue with a thin gold stripe before the red boot-topping, which continued right across the underside of the ship.

The Alpha and Beta tenders were replaced by two new 112-seat Harding catamaran-type launches. These were installed on new davits on the Boat Deck, midships, Nos 13 and 14. A speed in excess of 12 knots made transfer between ship and shore very quick. As partially enclosed lifeboats, each tender could accommodate 150 passengers. Propulsion was by twin 290 bhp diesel engines driving 600mm (24in) diameter alloy bronze propellers.

*The new* Caronia *Restaurant on the Upper Deck*

One of Chairman John Olsen's oft-repeated messages to his staff was that he wanted 'everyone in Britain' to know that *QE2* had had the biggest refit ever. He certainly got his wish.

> 'I think you are very brave going to sea this week.'
> *Prince Andrew after 1994 refit*

The first move to achieve this was a visit by Prince Andrew on the day she was due to sail for New York (17 December). The carefully devised tour route planned for the royal visit had to be abandoned on the day as several of her decks still looked as if they were under construction; whole blocks of cabins had no fittings whatsoever, and the ship's corridors were carpetless and littered with pipes and wiring. Workmen were everywhere. Even the sanitised route involved the royal party stepping over workmen laying carpet, and the Prince wryly remarked that his experience at sea had taught him to always expect refits to overrun. He remarked to crew: 'I think you are very brave going to sea this week.'

But worse was to come. Cunard had 'repossessed' two large paintings that had been on board *Caronia* and *Queen Elizabeth*, and which, since those ships left service, had been on loan to the City of Southampton to grace the Mayor's Parlour. One, depicting Prince Andrew's grandmother, the Queen Mother, had been commissioned by Cunard for the ship that bore her name; the other, showing the Prince's mother and

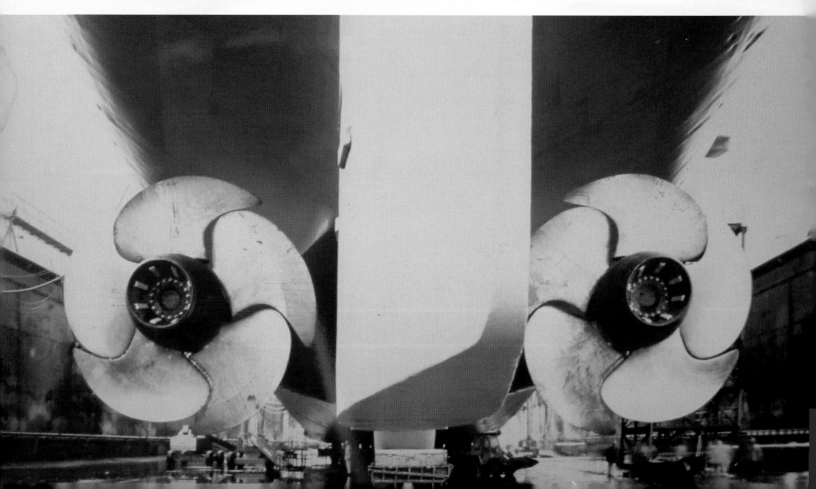

father on honeymoon at Broadlands, had been on board *Caronia* – which the Queen, as Princess Elizabeth, had launched just before her marriage. It was deemed appropriate that Prince Andrew should unveil these royal portraits in the Queen's Room, before they were finally hung on D Stairway Boat Deck.

It cannot be said he didn't try; he tugged and tugged at the cord that should have drawn back the curtain in front of the two pictures – but nothing happened. Until, that is, the curtain rail collapsed dramatically, revealing the pictures in a partial and undignified way. It was a sign of what was to come.

## Angry Passengers

Once the royal visit had finished Cunard personnel had to turn their attention to the passengers in the terminal building who were waiting to board and who were becoming angrier by the hour. The company had managed to contact around 300 people prior to their leaving home to advise that their cabins would not be ready and so not to travel to Southampton. However, several hundred more had arrived at the terminal expecting their cabins to be available and a further 160 had to be informed at the terminal that they could not sail with the ship. All cancelled passengers were given a full refund and a guarantee of a future free cruise as compensation, which was generous to a level previously unheard-of in the travel business.

The unfinished state of the ship had resulted in the Inspector from the Marine Safety Office placing a restriction of 1,000 passengers being carried. To exacerbate the problem further this number also included the workmen who would have to sail in order to complete the unfinished areas. In all 600 passengers were allowed to board.

*QE2* eventually sailed several hours late, leaving many angry passengers behind, and headed straight into a Force 8 storm that resulted in many of the workers being seasick – thus delaying the work even further.

The aft ends of Quarter and Upper Decks were unfinished and workers busied themselves to complete the new Lido and Yacht Club. Staircases and corridors remained uncarpeted and blocked with furniture piled high. Some passengers had to endure constant flooding and toilet and washing facilities that ran with rusty brown water. But most passengers were mollified by the news that the entire voyage was to be free – and that they were to receive a further free voyage as recompense for discomfort.

## Modern Communications

But the ship's progress across the Atlantic wasn't a private matter as it might have been in earlier years. Modern communications – including direct-dial phones installed in every cabin during a previous refit – meant that before long the whole saga was unfolding on the front pages of national

*QE2's two 6.1m (19ft 8in) diameter propellers seen during her 1994 dry-docking*

newspapers around the world. It was a gift for the tabloid press, especially in the quiet week leading up to Christmas, and they exploited the opportunity to the full – making use of pictures taken at the yard during the refit, but which bore no relation to the current situation on the ship.

## An Eye to Compensation

A coterie of disgruntled passengers stoked the fires, often with an eye to compensation in addition to the free sailing they were already on and the further free trip promised. First they demanded to be taken off the ship (even though she was in mid-Atlantic) and on arrival in New York they threatened to refuse to get off. The absurd over-reaction to the incident was best exemplified by the fact that on the same day that a plane crashed in Coventry killing five people, tabloid newspapers' front pages led on a *QE2* passenger complaint that her toilet had 'exploded'.

---

'This is a unique maritime disaster; only the staff, including those ashore, are in danger of drowning.' *Cunard press officer*

---

As one of Cunard's weary press officers remarked at the time: 'This is a unique maritime disaster; only the staff, including those ashore, are in danger of drowning.'

Matters were not helped by the perverse attitude of parent company, Trafalgar House, which was so concerned to protect its share price that it suppressed information rather than putting its efforts into informing the press. It thus allowed speculation to fester.

## Dangerous Condition

When *QE2* finally arrived in New York 12 hours late on 23 December, the United States Coast Guard boarded the ship earlier than expected for an inspection. It issued a certificate of 'Control Verification for a Foreign Vessel' having become convinced that 'the ship was in a dangerous condition'. It advised that a certificate to sail would only be issued if the huge pile of rubbish that had accumulated was cleared and if the crew could prove that the fire doors were in working order. Cunard had also to guarantee that the outstanding building work, mainly in the Lido, was to be completed as soon as possible. In all the USCG issued a number of requests that totalled six pages.

Cunard's chairman, John Olsen, also boarded to negotiate with the passengers who were refusing to leave the ship until their grievances had been aired. This led not just to angry scenes, but also to Olsen being filmed beneath an 'Exit' sign – an omen for his future as chairman.

Matters worsened when it became clear that the USCG would actually detain the ship and prevent her from sailing until the problems had been rectified. *QE2* became the first vessel to be detained this way in New York for many years.

*QE2 in New York after her 1994 refit*

A series of meetings was hurriedly convened in Washington and New York to sort out the mess.

QE2 was eventually permitted to sail – 24 hours late. She sailed straight into another storm, resulting in the cancellation of the call at Fort Lauderdale, which disappointed even more passengers.

After getting over the problems associated with the refit, 1995 would prove to be a busy year for the Cunard flagship. Even though the publicity John Olsen got was not the kind he had in mind, it did result in bookings for QE2 soaring by 15 per cent –

presumably because, despite the welter of criticism, the message had got through that QE2 was virtually a new ship.

---

'There may be pretenders to the throne, but there is only one *Queen*.'
*Cunard press release*

---

P&O had been busily promoting their forthcoming *Oriana* as the new superliner for Britain but the re-measured QE2 was now almost 1,200grt greater than the P&O vessel. A Cunard

press release simply stated: 'There may be pretenders to the throne, but there is only one *Queen*.'

On 8 May *QE2* made her first-ever visit to Plymouth, where she anchored for the day to commemorate the 50th anniversary of VE Day. A 'victory' sail past of more than 80 yachts and power boats, led by the square-rigger *Lord Nelson*, preceded a magnificent firework display that evening. The next day *QE2* anchored off Guernsey to mark the island's Liberation Day celebrations.

Another milestone for *QE2* occurred on 14 June when she left New York on her 1,000th voyage – appropriately a transatlantic crossing for Southampton. She had sailed 3.8 million nautical miles and carried over 1.7 million passengers. When she arrived in Southampton all the ships in port sounded their whistles in salute, the local Red Funnel ferries were dressed in bunting and a congratulatory banner was hung from the Queen Elizabeth II Terminal. That night senior personnel from Associated British Ports boarded to make a presentation to Commodore John Burton-Hall. The next day when *QE2* set off for her 1,001st voyage – a cruise to Stockholm, Oslo and Copenhagen – a military band played and she was escorted downriver by fireboats while 1,001 red, blue and gold balloons were released from the aft decks of the liner. During the voyage passengers were entertained by Edmund Hockridge who had entertained on *QE2's* maiden voyage and was back on board 1,000 voyages later.

A further royal visit took place in Edinburgh on 17 July 1995 when HRH Princess Anne lunched on board to present the Scottish Business Achievement Awards. A Sea King helicopter lifted off a Jaguar XJS coupé that had been carried on the aft decks of *QE2* and which was later auctioned. *QE2* later that day provided the backdrop for the departure of 100 historic sailing ships on the first leg of the Cutty Sark Tall Ships Race, watched by 500,000 people.

Between 30 August and 7 September *QE2* made her first-ever complete circumnavigation of the UK. The calls at Liverpool and Greenock proceeded without problem before a maiden call at Invergordon but heavy weather led to the cancellation of the planned maiden call to the Tyne. As *QE2* headed for her final port of Le Havre she sailed down the east coast of England and thousands turned out to see her sail past the bay at Scarborough.

## Hurricane Luis

On 7 September 1995 *QE2* left Southampton on Voyage 1,014 under the command of Captain Ron Warwick for New York via Cherbourg. Among the passengers were magician Paul Daniels and *Coronation Street* star Johnny Briggs. During the course of the voyage *QE2's* officers closely monitored the progress of Hurricane Luis from the

Caribbean. It soon became clear that it would pass close to the current course of *QE2*, which was already experiencing heavy weather. On 10 September, *QE2's* course was changed to the southwest in an attempt to avoid the worst of the storm. Captain Warwick reckoned that Luis would pass ahead of *QE2* at 2300 hours and had accordingly taken the necessary precautions and advised the passengers and crew that the effects of the storm would be increasingly felt after dinner.

As the Sunday evening progressed, *QE2* was experiencing winds of more than 50 knots, greater than forecast, and average wave heights of 12m (40ft). The weather deteriorated further by the early morning of 11 September with the 'eye' of Luis around 130 nautical miles away; the wind speed had increased from 50 to 130 knots, giving *QE2* a heel of 7 degrees to starboard. Luis was heading in a northeasterly direction and making a forward speed estimated to be between 40 and 50 knots.

Captain Warwick, on the Bridge throughout with three other crew members, reduced *QE2's* speed to 5 knots and by 0145 hours *QE2* was hove-to, riding 10–12m (30–40ft) waves. It was a dark night and visibility was affected by the storm conditions. The sea was nearly white, with foam and driving spray lashing the ship and submerging the bow.

Then at 0210 hours a rogue wave was sighted right ahead looming out of the darkness. Hundreds of tons of water broke over *QE2's* bow, sending a

shudder throughout the ship. The weight of water landing on the foredeck bent a few of the railings and dented the deck plating to such an extent that the tip of the foredeck was buckled downwards to show the lines of the beams underneath.

---

'The wave seemed to take ages to reach us, but it was probably less than a minute before it broke with tremendous force over the bow of *QE2*.'
*Captain Ron Warwick*

---

*The imposing shape of QE2 bows-on, as she looked in 2005*

Captain Warwick, confirming it was the biggest wave he had ever seen during 38 years at sea, said:

The wave seemed to take ages to reach us, but it was probably less than a minute before it broke with tremendous force over the bow of *QE2*. An incredible shudder went through the ship followed a few moments later by two smaller shudders. At the same time the sea was cascading all over the fore part of the ship, including the Bridge, and it was several seconds before the water had drained away from the wheelhouse windows and vision ahead was restored.

The captain would later add: 'It looked as if we were going straight into the White Cliffs of Dover! The fact that *QE2* handled it so well is a tribute to her. She withstood it marvellously. I think British people should take pride in such marvellous engineering.'

Captain Warwick reported that the wave had been more or less level with the line of sight on the Bridge which is 30m (95ft) above the surface of the water. His claim was later supported by data taken from Canadian weather monitors in the area which showed the wave had been around 30m (95ft) in height and around 370m (1,200ft) wide.

The amazing thing was that most of the passengers slept through the rogue wave and only became aware the next morning when presented with a Storm Certificate as a memento. *QE2* docked in New York 12 hours late.

A special feature-length episode of *Coronation Street* was filmed on board between 13 and 25 October 1995 with several of the major stars travelling. The subsequent video became the biggest-selling UK video of all time!

---

'I first discovered her when we filmed a *Coronation Street* special. I, as Alec Gilroy, was playing her hapless Cruise Director. We had such a wonderful time – she is rather like a stately home – steeped in history and staffed by the most caring and talented people. But most of all, unlike many more modern vessels, she is very much a ship.' *Roy Barraclough*

---

Just prior to *QE2's* 1996 'Voyage to Distant Empires' World Cruise, on 2 January, the liner clocked up her four-millionth mile at 2100 GMT. The World Cruise would see her sail 53,000 nautical miles and call at 38 ports on four continents.

Apart from that, 1996 did not start particularly well for Cunard. The company made history by sending three ships off on a World Cruise: *QE2*, *Sagafjord* and *Royal Viking Sun*. But only *QE2* returned as *Sagafjord* caught fire in the South China Sea and *Royal Viking Sun* was badly damaged after hitting rocks in Egypt.

**Cunard Line**

# Queen Elizabeth 2

Trans Atlantic Voyage
No. 1014

*Westbound from Southampton and Cherbourg
to New York City.
7th September - 12th September, 1995.*

Record of contact with

## *Hurricane Luis*

on
10th and 11th September, 1995.

The following information was
recorded in the ship's log:

*Highest winds - 130 miles per hour.
Average wave height - 40 feet*
with one specific wave at 0205 hrs (11 Sep) estimated at 90 feet.
*Nearest position to the "eye" - 130 miles.
Ship's speed reduced to 5 knots.*

*Captain R. W. Warwick*

*The Storm Certificate presented to the
passengers on the September 1995 crossing*

and turned by means of a bow thrust. There were no problems and most passengers didn't even notice. Power to the shaft was quickly restored.

On 15 September 1996 *QE2* hit an 18m (60ft) whale, which then became lodged on the bulbous bow as the ship entered Lisbon. As the whale was pinned by the tide the rescue workers had to wait for the direction of the current to change before they could tow it away. A crane was used to remove the whale, by which time it was dead.

Two weeks later, on 28 September 1996, HRH Prince Edward hosted a second royal ball on board in Southampton in honour of the Duke of Edinburgh's Special Awards Projects Group.

## The 1996 Refit

Earlier in the year, on 14 May 1996, Cunard announced in London that the A&P Shipyard in Southampton had won the contract for *QE2's* 1996 refit, scheduled to take place in November and December. This was a major coup for the UK yard as it would be the first time *QE2* had been dry-docked in Britain since 1982. The contract, worth £7 million to the yard itself, would provide employment for 1,000 workers on site, including a large number of specialist sub-contractors.

Cunard was determined not to have a repeat of the 1994 fiasco so a 'Refit Project Office' was established in Southampton. This consisted of four individuals including a Project Planning Specialist

On 4 March the Norwegian conglomerate Kvaerner acquired Trafalgar House for £904 million and assumed control of Cunard. It became clear that Cunard did not feature in Kvaerner's long-term plans and the company, including *QE2*, was effectively for sale.

While *QE2* was being pulled out of Copenhagen harbour on 5 August 1996, strong winds pushed the ship on to the quay when the two tugs were unable to hold her. She sustained a 50m (160ft) scrape and the lines from the tugs snapped, damaging the steering. The steering was repaired during *QE2's* 1996 refit in Southampton.

While off Cowes later that month *QE2* lost temporary use of her starboard propeller shaft and could not make a left turn. The ship was slowed

on loan from Kvaerner John Brown. This was despite only 10–15 per cent of what was done in 1994 being planned for 1996 and 24 days being allowed as opposed to 20.

*QE2* was originally scheduled to arrive at Southampton from a Mediterranean cruise on 21 November and go into dry-dock later that day but she arrived in Southampton 20 hours late as she had to be diverted into Lisbon to offload an ill crewman. She arrived late on 21 November and passengers were disembarked on the morning of 22 November. The ship then made her way to the King George V dry-dock.

MET Studio was re-appointed for the 1996 refurbishment to ensure continuity and consistency in the style of the public areas created in 1994. All the restaurants were refurbished but the two-sitting *Mauretania* Restaurant on Quarter Deck was totally re-designed and refurbished at a cost of £300,000. The whole area was stripped right back to the metal before refitting began. The new look reflected the age of classic cruising with an art deco atmosphere. The room was further differentiated from the other dining areas on board by the introduction of a rich colour palette of deep blues, amber-golds and bronze metals. The walls were covered with a gold fabric; lavish gold curtains were hung; new blue carpeting was fitted and all seating was re-upholstered in a purple and pink velour.

In total, £2 million was spent on cabin work during the refit. In order to enhance *QE2's* reputation for providing the best accommodation at sea, Cunard built two ultra-luxurious 75m$^2$ (800 sq ft) 'Grand Suites', which would be among the largest and most lavish accommodation afloat. The two existing top suites, *Queen Mary* (8082) and *Queen Elizabeth* (8081) were amalgamated with the two penthouses adjacent. Each Grand Suite was decorated in creams, beiges, light woods, chrome and flowing lines. Bathrooms in each were totally rebuilt, decorated with marble and featured twin washbasins.

## Five-star Status

Cunard's plan to upgrade all vessels in the fleet to five-star status saw a determined effort being made with *QE2*. It was important that the vessel offer single-sitting dining throughout, which would only be achieved by reducing the passenger capacity by closing many of the lower-grade cabins.

The closure of cabins left *QE2* with 781, divided as 719 doubles (1,438 beds) and 62 singles (62 beds). This reduced *QE2's* passenger capacity from 1,720 to 1,500. *QE2* now had the highest space-per-passenger ratio of any cruise ship in the world.

£1.4 million was spent on new bathrooms in 55 staterooms including all penthouses on Signal and Sun Decks and the Midships Suite on Two Deck. A total of 160 cabins received refurbishment work.

Around 75 per cent of the 1996 refit was behind-the-scenes and technical work mainly involved with bringing *QE2* up to SOLAS (Safety of Life at Sea) standards. New SOLAS regulations were to come into effect on 1 October 1997 and all cruise ships worldwide had to be refitted to comply. Such was the foresight of her designers in the 1960s that *QE2* already met some of the standards, such as her sprinkler system and the fact that passenger cabins did not open directly onto stairwells.

## Fire Detection

£300,000 was spent on improving the fire-detection system on board. *QE2* already had a state-of-the-art system but now detectors and sprinklers had to be installed in storage lockers, cabins, certain public areas and other operational areas. Over 4,000 detectors/controllers and call points were installed by Thorn Security. A main control was placed on the Bridge and in the Safety Control Room on Three Deck.

A new foredeck was installed, replacing the damaged area caused as a result of Hurricane Luis and the 30m (95ft) wave in September 1995. The hull in the hospital area was also repaired, having sustained damage by tug contact in Trondheim on 22 July 1996.

The whole of the exterior was repainted, using 20 tonnes of paint. Other external changes included the gold stripe above the boot-topping being repainted white and the Cunard lion (port and starboard) underneath the Bridge wings being removed. Despite the delay in arrival, A&P completed the contract on time and on budget with *QE2* putting to sea again on 12 December 1996 for overnight trials.

And so she entered her fourth decade ship-shape and in fine form.

# Chapter 8
## *Breaking Records*

*QE2's* call at Hong Kong in March during the 1997 World Cruise was her last visit there before mainland China took over the British colony. Sixteen government officials and 17 descendants of British settlers boarded *QE2* to return to the UK.

The end of another era came on 14 April while the ship was heading for New York. The ashes of Commodore Geoffrey Marr, last captain of *Queen Elizabeth*, were committed to the sea in a ceremony held by Captain Roland Hasell and Archdeacon Willing, the ship's chaplain.

Several marketing initiatives and improvements were made in time for the 1997 transatlantic season. These included introducing one-seating dining throughout, changing the on-board currency to the US dollar (up until then the £ sterling had been used on European cruises), á la carte dining in the Queen's Grill and the introduction of informal dinner dining in the Lido. The most important change, though, was the introduction of six-day Atlantic crossings instead of five days. The longer crossing would enable the ship to take a more southerly route across, thus avoiding some of the bad weather on the northerly passage. It would allow the ship to make up lost time should she need to do so, and significantly reduce fuel costs. But a bonus for Cunard would be the increase in revenue resulting from the passengers' extra day on board.

### Capacity Increased

These changes proved so popular throughout the summer of 1997 that in October the ship's capacity was increased to 1,750 in order to cope with the demand.

One of *QE2's* notable passengers on the Atlantic in 1997 was Milvina Dean, one of the last survivors of the *Titanic*. Ms Dean was making her first crossing of the Atlantic since the disaster 85 years earlier.

Throughout the year plans had been made to hold a special function on *QE2* in Southampton on 1 October in aid of the British Red Cross, and Diana, Princess of Wales, had agreed to attend.

*President Nelson Mandela and Graca Machel on board, March 1998*

Despite the death of the princess on 31 August it was decided to continue with the event as a tribute to her work for the Anti-personnel Landmines Campaign for the British Red Cross. The lunch was attended by Cherie Blair, wife of the British prime minister, Elizabeth Dole, president of the American Red Cross, Lord Attenborough, Terry Waite and Lord Deedes, as well as 150 other guests.

The highlight of *QE2's* 1998 World Cruise was 29–31 March 1998 when South African president Nelson Mandela, accompanied by future wife Graca Machel, sailed from Durban to Cape Town. A Gala Dinner for the Nelson Mandela Children's Fund was held on board in Cape Town. Mandela wrote in *QE2's* visitor's book: 'Travelling on *QE2* was an unforgettable honour and pleasure.' Mr Mandela also broadcast a live BBC interview with Sir David Frost from the captain's cabin.

## Carnival Acquires Cunard

On 3 April 1998, after months of speculation about the future of the company, Kvaerner announced that it had sold Cunard to a consortium led by the Carnival Corporation for $500 million.

## The Greenpeace TBT Protest

On arrival at Lloyd Werft Shipyard in Bremerhaven in November for her 1999 refit *QE2* became the target of protest by the environmental group Greenpeace. In common with many hundreds of other ships *QE2's* underwater hull was painted with an anti-fouling paint that had, as a chemical biocide, a high tin content known as tributyltin (TBT). This effectively prevented algae and molluscs from growing on ships' hulls, reducing resistance and reducing fuel bills. The paint also prevented potentially undesirable marine life from being spread from one world location to another. Equally, it was a toxic pollutant, released during hull cleaning as well as by erosion due to its self-polishing attributes. The pollution persisted in water and had become a prime concern as it killed sealife, harmed the environment and possibly entered the food chain.

To make their protest against TBT Greenpeace had chosen their target well. A flotilla of small inflatable craft sped around the ship as she sailed through Bremerhaven harbour and 50 protestors dived into the water to prevent the vessel from moving forward or astern. Two hundred other protestors waved banners that proclaimed 'Stop TBT' and the crew of one inflatable drew up alongside and spray-painted 'God save the Queen from TBT' along her hull just above the waterline. Cunard countered that it had already decided on the removal of all tin-based paints by 2001, seven years ahead of the required IMO date, and confirmed that this commitment could not be completed in the 1999 refit because of the significant hull work planned.

*Sir David Frost talking to Chief Mangosuthu Buthelezi, March 1998*

Erik Tonseth, president and CEO of Kvaerner, said of the deal: 'During the last two years we have worked hard to improve the performance of Cunard and to find a new owner which, we are confident, will continue with those efforts.' In return, Carnival Corporation CEO Micky Arison said: 'The *QE2* is the best known cruise ship in the world and commands a vast customer following.'

---

'Travelling on *QE2* was an unforgettable honour and pleasure.'

**South African president Nelson Mandela**

---

The transaction was completed on 28 May and as if to underline its commitment to its new purchase just one week later, on 8 June, the company unveiled plans for 'Project *Queen Mary*' – the beginning of the design and development of a new class of superliner, a project that would 'lead to the development of the grandest ocean liner ever built'.

Twitchers usually don their anoraks for birds not ships, but in October they turned their attention to *QE2* when a rare grey catbird decided to land on the ship as she headed for Southampton. This would have been the first time this species had ever been seen in Britain. Unfortunately the bird decided to leave *QE2* before her arrival in the UK but that didn't deter about 1,000 birdwatchers descending on Southampton hoping to catch a glimpse. One organisation said: 'The sighting created a life or death situation for birdwatchers. It stirred up a major panic.'

During the final crossing of 1998, 14–20 December, *QE2* experienced severe weather with Force 10 winds and associated heavy seas and swell. The ship was damaged, and hove-to while temporary repairs were made. The door leading to the foredeck was 'blown in 30ft [9m], knocking down an internal fire door' (a temporary plate was welded in place), vent-trunking on the fo'c's'le was damaged with water flooding 75 crew cabins; cracks in the aluminium superstructure opened up and frames in the forward part of the ship were fractured. *QE2* arrived in New York approximately eight hours late on 20 December. Lloyds surveyors visited the ship two days later in Miami and cleared the ship to sail while ongoing temporary repairs were being carried out during her Caribbean Christmas cruise.

On 14 April 1999 a special lunch was held in Southampton to mark the 30th anniversary of *QE2's* first transatlantic crossing and Cunard took the opportunity to unveil plans for a £19.5 million refit of the ship, scheduled for the end of the year. The ship's two masters, Captain Ron Warwick and Captain Roland Hasell, were joined by every surviving former master of *QE2*: Mortimer Hehir, Peter Jackson, Bob Arnott, Doug Ridley, Keith Stanley, Robin Woodall and John Burton-Hall. One former captain, her first master, Bil Warwick, had also accepted the invitation to attend the function but he died on 27 February aged 86. A minute's silence was held in his honour. When *QE2* left port for New York later that day, she was escorted by fireboats and her whistle was blown 30 times in acknowledgement of her 30th birthday. In those 30 years *QE2* had made 1,159 voyages and sailed 4,648,050 nautical miles.

'The QE2 is the best known cruise ship in the world and commands a vast customer following.'
*Carnival Corporation CEO Micky Arison*

A further milestone was passed on 13 June 1999 when, at 1500 hours while en route from Madeira to Southampton, *QE2* exceeded 175,296 hours steaming time. This equates to exactly 20 years (including four leap years).

By the start of 1999, it had been clear that several areas on board *QE2* were in need of refurbishment. The ship had been last refurbished in 1996 (the 1998 refit had been postponed for a year) and the passenger areas and accommodation were showing signs of wear and tear. The Carnival purchase of Cunard and the subsequent major re-branding saw a concerted effort to improve *QE2* and the 1999 refit was a key element in this.

Cunard's president and chief executive, Larry Pimentel, said:

This magnificent vessel, certainly the most famous ship afloat, will sail into the Millennium with new vigour. As the flagship of the British merchant fleet, *QE2* will reflect the essence of Britain. The ship has a long life ahead of her and we are committed to maintaining, and improving even further, the already high standards for which she is known.

*QE2* returned to service after her £30 million refit on 12 December 1999. Before she embarked on the last transatlantic crossing of the 20th century she was joined in Southampton by the 'new' *Caronia* (formerly *Vistafjord*), which had arrived from Liverpool where she had just been renamed. A special lunch was held on board *QE2* to mark her return to service.

Many regulars were pleased with the refit, noting that the ship had never been in better condition. One regular cruise journalist wrote:

Favourite rooms have been refreshed, with the most noticeable changes in the lighting, and in the brighter colours and plush fabrics used in carpeting and furniture. The public rooms have taken on a more contemporary flair in some cases while reflecting a return to the grand era in others. The ship looked much better than I remembered from my first voyage some 28 years ago and my dozen or so subsequent cruises. It's more like a revitalization than a facelift for a lady who admits to being 30-plus.

QE2 spent 31 December 1999 positioned off Barbados to welcome the third Millennium and was joined by Caronia on her inaugural cruise. She began the Millennium on a high note by being

## The 1999 Refit

QE2 arrived at Lloyd Werft Shipyard in Bremerhaven in November 1999 for her £30 million refit. In total, over 3,500 pieces of furniture were removed for refurbishment and re-upholstery. All the restaurants were refurbished but over £1 million alone was spent in the Caronia Restaurant, which was totally redone with rich mahogany panels in the style of an English country house. The Queen's Room was totally refurbished with rich colours of blue and gold and all the major public rooms received work or new furnishings.

In order to obtain greater revenues from QE2's deluxe range of accommodation, three new luxury suites were built. The Radio Room on the portside of Boat Deck was completely removed; advances in technology had rendered the large facility redundant. Equipment was transferred to the new compact Communications Centre on Two Deck and individual department terminals now installed on the navigation bridge. A new 54m² (575 sq ft) suite called the Caledonia was built. The existing Hotel Manager's and Cruise Director's cabins on the starboard side of Two Deck forward of the Midships Lobby were gutted and combined to provide space for the construction of a second suite – the 73m² (777 sq ft) Aquitania Suite. The existing 43m² (463 sq ft) Midships Suite located on the starboard side of Two Deck aft of the Midships Lobby was enlarged by incorporating the small Conference Room and locker facility off the Midships Lobby to become the third new suite: the 65m² (700 sq ft) Carinthia Suite.

All passenger cabins were refurbished. In total, 30,000m (98,000ft) of fabric was required, incorporating 21 special custom textiles including double-sided jacquards for bedspreads, colour-woven jacquards for upholstery, damask jacquards for wallcoverings, and printed curtains and voiles – all produced to exacting maritime standards including the latest IMO fire safety regulations. In total, £500,000 was spent on new carpets in the passenger accommodation.

QE2 received a new, fresh look on the outside too. In the months leading up to the refit, her exterior paintwork was looking tired. Continuous painting over the years had resulted in the hull wearing 57 coats of paint, now 2.5cm (1in) thick. Restoring the exterior involved grit- and hydro-blasting the hull to take it back to the steel (last undertaken during the 1986/87 re-engining at Lloyd Werft) – an operation that took three weeks to complete. In total, some 8,450m² (91,000 sq ft) of hull was blasted prior to the application of new self-polishing anti-fouling paint. In addition, the boot-top was coated as was the hull and topsides. In total, International Coatings supplied about 12,000 litres (3,170 gallons) of paint to cover 61,040m² (657,000 sq ft). Her hull was redone in a matt black that replaced the dark blue she had worn since 1994 and the 'speed-stripe' Cunard tricolour was also removed from her superstructure.

proclaimed a 'British Icon of the 20th Century' in one of the exhibitions at the Millennium Dome.

On 6 January 2000 *QE2* embarked on her first World Cruise of the Millennium – a voyage of 104 nights. Her call at Fremantle on 21 February was memorable because, while manoeuvring within the entrance to Fremantle Harbour at 0650 hours, the tug *Burra* hit her stern on *QE2's* starboard side in the Six Deck area, as a result of which *QE2* sustained some hull damage.

## *QE2* to the Rescue

On 19 June *QE2* was requested by the Royal Canadian Coastguard to investigate the status of a single-handed yacht that had been damaged by rough weather during a transatlantic race. The yacht *Syllogic* had reportedly been knocked down twice by heavy seas and the RCC in Halifax had been unable to contact the boat by radio. Captain Paul Wright altered *QE2's* course just after midnight and at 0418 hours spotted the 12.2m (40ft) *Syllogic* sailing under a staysail only. *QE2* was slowed and the ship's officers tried to attract the sailor's attention by using the ship's signalling lamp and whistle. They finally made contact by VHF radio. The sailor, Pieter Adriaans, advised that he

had sustained severe damage to his mainsail and lost his liferaft but required no assistance. *QE2* reported the status of the yacht back to the RCC and resumed her course for New York where she arrived on time on 19 June.

On 4 July 2000, while docking in New York, *QE2* hit the Japanese warship *Koshima* berthed alongside. It was an extremely busy time in New York with warships from all over the world taking part in a naval display. Captain Paul Wright had earlier met the docking master of the New York Port Authority and had been assured that the warships would be docked well back from the corner of the downsteam pier, giving him the corner to rest on if needed when berthing *QE2*. Captain Wright delayed his arrival on 4 July by about 30 minutes in order to wait for less current and then began to manoeuvre with tugs in place. When he started to enter Pier 92, it was clear that the warships were much farther out than he had been promised, in fact they were very near the end of the pier. There were two warships rafted abreast on the opposite pier with bows outward, making a narrow entry into the slip. However, Captain Wright had no choice but to continue the manoeuvre as to attempt to stop and reverse would have been very dangerous. The aircraft carrier *USS Kennedy*, with 14 or 15 tugs on her, was behind *QE2* waiting to dock after her.

---

### '…it was an honour to be kissed by a Queen!' *Japanese admiral on* Koshima

---

All was going well with *QE2* until one of the tugs at the stern got caught in the current and had to pull away to reposition. At that point, the remaining tug could not hold *QE2* against the current and her stern swung into the bow of *Koshima*. The tug had been on the opposite side of the ship from the captain and pilot who were on the portside wing. *Koshima* was pushed forward into a British warship, *Manchester*. Captain Wright and his officers visited the captains of the warships to apologise but as damage was limited to scratches, lost paintwork and severed lines holding the *Koshima* the naval officers were not concerned. The US Coast Guard considered the whole incident to be very minor. An admiral on *Koshima* stated: '…it was an honour to be kissed by a Queen!'

Days later two pigeons, who had 'stowed away'

on *QE2* while she headed for Southampton were handed back to their owner– an event that was reported live on lunchtime news broadcasts.

On 4 August *QE2* sent a message to Her Majesty The Queen Mother to congratulate her on her 100th birthday, and a special dinner was held on board that night for her passengers. In his message, Captain Warwick, said:

Today the entire company reflects not just on Your Majesty's remarkable and inspirational life, but with particular affection and pride on your long association with Cunard; an association which began on 27 September 1938 when Your Majesty launched the Cunard liner that bore your name, the RMS *Queen Elizabeth*, and which continued through your numerous visits and voyages on that great ship; an association which has prospered as a result of your keen interest in her successor, *Queen Elizabeth 2*.

A week later *QE2's* passage en route to New York took her past the position where *Titanic* sank. The research vessel *Akademik Keldysh* was stationed over the wreck position for a diving expedition. Hundreds of passengers lined *QE2's* decks to observe the research vessel and both ships exchanged the usual courtesies with three long blasts on their whistles.

Before 2000 ended the formal contract for *Queen Mary 2* was signed in Paris. *Queen Mary 2* was to be the largest, longest, tallest, widest and most expensive passenger ship in history and was destined to take over *QE2's* role as a transatlantic liner and flagship of the Cunard fleet.

Cunard history was recreated in 2001. In the 1950s and 1960s it was common for passengers to disembark from either *Queen Mary* or *Queen Elizabeth* in Southampton or New York and then board the famous *Caronia* for a cruise. In 2001 the schedules of *QE2* and *Caronia* were so planned that both would be in Southampton or New York together during the summer months to allow passengers to sail on both ships. This was perfect for those who did not like to fly.

In March 2001 *QE2* officiated at the opening of the new cruise terminal in Dubai during her call there as part of her World Cruise.

## Commemorating *Queen Mary*

The 3 May and 6 June Atlantic crossings were designated as special anniversary crossings to mark the 65th anniversary of *Queen Mary's* maiden voyage. Cunard undertook a search for passengers who travelled on that voyage and invited them to sail on either of these celebratory voyages for the same fare as they paid in 1938 – with Third Class fares on *Queen Mary* starting at £70.4s.0d, former passengers had the opportunity to sail on *QE2* for just £70.20, and several took Cunard up on the offer. Special events on the two crossings included

a *Queen Mary* lecture programme, a *Queen Mary* tea and a special *Queen Mary* dinner and ball with a reproduction of one of the menus from 1936. Cunard also took the opportunity to promote its new transatlantic liner *Queen Mary 2*, scheduled to enter service in 2004.

## Man Overboard

On 23 July 2001 a crew member was reported missing from *QE2* while the vessel was en route from New York to Southampton. The 27-year-old Indian national, who had worked on board for two years as a breakfast chef, was last seen, apparently asleep, in his cabin at 0130 hours. He was due to report for work at 0300 hours but failed to do so. At 0909 hours a full missing person search routine of the ship was carried out, and tannoy messages were relayed to all areas. Neither the search routine, which was completed at 0945 hours, nor the tannoys produced a result. A Bridge conference was held at 1020 hours involving the master, doctor, hotel manager and staff captain. It was decided that if he had gone overboard his chances of survival were poor. The ship was travelling at 25 knots, the sea temperature was 15 degrees Celsius and there was a Force 6 wind with 2m (6ft) waves. The ship had covered a distance of 200 nautical miles from the time it was discovered that the chef was missing. The Falmouth Coastguard was advised at 1045 hours and a search was commenced. An RAF Nimrod was despatched from

RAF Kinloss in Scotland, and an Irish Maritime Patrol aircraft also joined the search. Other merchant shipping in the area was also alerted to join in the search, but no body was ever found.

The 11 September World Trade Center attack resulted in *QE2* being diverted to Boston for the remainder of the year. It was during one of these calls in Boston on 4 October that Captain Warwick conducted the first wedding service on board when he officiated at the wedding of his daughter.

Once again the contract for *QE2's* annual overhaul was awarded to Lloyd Werft. After completing her 2001 Cape Town Line Voyage, *QE2* left Southampton on 20 November for her 21-day

$12 million refit at Bremerhaven. A Ministry of Defence exercise involving Special Forces took place as *QE2* sailed down the Solent. In a rare occurrence, both *QE2* and *Norway* were together in the shipyard for a time, *QE2* entering the dry-dock just vacated by *Norway*.

The Queen's Grill, Queen's Grill Lounge, Pavilion, Yacht Club, Theatre, Midships Lobby, Nursery and Seven Deck Gymnasium were all refurbished, as were the *Queen Mary* and *Queen Elizabeth* Grand Suites. General dry-dock work included replacing the propeller blade foot seals, overhauling the port forward stabiliser and the bowthruster and a new sewage treatment plant. This, together with the

*Continued on page 232*

# QE2 Springs a Leak

On 18 May 2002 QE2 left Southampton for New York with 1,457 passengers and 973 crew. At approximately 0200 hours on 21 May, the senior watch-keeping engineer discovered a large sea-water leak in the aft engine room and raised the alarm. The leak was in the starboard forward corner of the aft engine room. The flooding was caused by the perforation of a 250mm (10in) diameter sea-water inlet pipe serving the starboard sea-water evaporator used for producing fresh water.

Because the position of the failure was between the isolating valve and the vessel's skin the leak could not be stopped by closing the valve. Preparations were made to fabricate a clamp to hold a rubber seal over the leaking pipe. Using the bilge pumping system, water was pumped into the oil-water holding tanks.

The aft engine room 'Hi-Hi' bilge level alarm activated at 0315 hours. Soon afterwards 'Echo' main engine, the port engine in the aft engine room, shut down automatically on 'Governor Fault'. This was attributed to floodwater being picked up by the rotating flywheel and soaking the electronic pickup for speed control.

At 0345 'Hotel' main engine, the starboard inner main engine in the aft engine room, was shut down manually because of the high floodwater level. No main engine remained running in the aft engine room.

At 0400 hours, all oil-water holding tanks were full. With the water level still rising in the aft engine room, the bilge injection valve on the main sea-water circulating pump was partially opened and several hundred tonnes of water were pumped overboard during the course of two hours.

This reduced the water level, allowing work to be carried out on the leaking pipe. A clamp was fitted around the pipe, which reduced the water ingress slightly. To reinforce the pipe, stiffeners were welded between the flange and the surrounding structure.

The bilge injection valve was again partially opened between 1030 and 1230. Several hundred tonnes of water were again pumped overboard. This reduced the water level sufficiently to allow work on the leaking pipe to continue.

The lubricating oil sumps of the aft main engines were checked for water contamination, and their generators were checked for electrical resistance. All results were satisfactory and between 1040 and 1130 hours 'Golf', 'India' and 'Hotel' main engines were started.

At 1200 hours the inboard main engine cooler began to show symptoms of being choked. This was attributed to the effects of bilge water being pumped through when the bilge injection was opened. To maintain engine temperatures, the outboard cooler was opened to operate in parallel with the inboard unit.

## High Bilge-water Levels

'Echo' main engine was prepared for starting at 1400 hours by turning it over on compressed air. Shortly afterwards, the sea-water leak became noticeably worse and the bilge injection valve was opened again. 'Golf', 'India' and 'Hotel' main engines were again stopped because of high bilge-water levels. From 1430 to 1730 hours, an estimated 600m³ (17,000 cu ft) of water was discharged overboard.

Following electrical checks on the generators, all aft main engines were restarted between 1735 and 1739 hours. Using canvas, clamps and various blocking mediums, such as silicone and sawdust,

efforts to restrict the rate of sea-water ingress continued. Meanwhile, work continued on a mechanism that allowed an inflatable bag to be inserted in the leaking pipe. Inflation of this device stemmed the inflow at 2100 hours.

At 0915 hours the following day, the inflatable bag failed and deflated. The rate of water coming in was again at its maximum. Again the aft engine room quickly became flooded and the bilge injection valve was opened between 0930 and 1030 hours; an estimated 200m³ (6,000 cu ft) of sea water was pumped overboard.

Using a repetition of the earlier technique, a second inflatable bag was inserted into the leaking pipe. This bag was longer than the first and, once inflated, stopped the inflow of water at 1015 hours.

At no stage of the incident had the floodwater level risen above the engine room floor plate level, which is about 1m (3ft) above the inner bottom or tank top. Throughout these operations a secondary cofferdam was being fabricated and prepared for fitting once the water flow had been reduced sufficiently to allow it to be welded to the adjacent structure.

During the remainder of 22 May, the cofferdam was welded around the failed pipe and water ingress was totally stopped. If the flange had become detached then the aft engine room would have been free to flood, with serious consequences. Initially, all main engines in the aft engine room would have been disabled, followed by the main sea-water pump being used on the bilge injection. By this stage, the water levels would have been at a depth such that access to the failed pipe would have been impossible.

Loss of the bilge injection would have allowed the water level to rise at an uncontrolled rate. Flooding into the motor room, aft of the engine room, would have followed. In spite of the four main engines in the forward engine room continuing to run, QE2 would have come to a stop.

## Clearly Hazardous

In this state, QE2 would have been disabled and drifting in poor weather conditions with a major compartment flooded. Even in this condition, QE2 would have been stable enough to remain safe for those on board, but it was clearly hazardous.

Steps taken by the engineering staff ensured that the situation did not deteriorate to this extreme. It was a credit to QE2's engineers that they produced such an effective and ingenious solution while under severe pressure.

The ingenious arrangement of a flexible bladder, inserted into the failed pipe and then filled with compressed air, allowed the vessel to reach New York safely on 24 May, where permanent repairs were made. The pipe's failure was found to have been caused by simple sea-water corrosion.

blasting and coating of the ballast tanks, required access openings to be cut into the hull.

On 8 January 2002 *QE2* became the first passenger ship to call again at New York following the 11 September attacks. It was to be the liner's 668th call at the port and as *QE2* approached the approximate site of the Twin Towers her speed was reduced, her flag was lowered in a mark of respect and a wreath was laid in the harbour. She then sounded three long blasts in support of New York. She was escorted up the Hudson by fireboats.

## Book of Condolence

The death of the Queen Mother was marked on 30 March by prayers during the regular church service. A book of condolence was opened and signed by passengers and crew, the flag was flown at half-mast and the captain sent a message to Buckingham Palace. Similar marks of respect were observed on the day of the funeral, together with a minute's silence.

When *QE2* departed Fort Lauderdale on 26 April for Southampton she was carrying in her hold one of *Queen Mary's* original 635kg (1,400lb) whistles. This had been donated by the City of Long Beach for use on *Queen Mary 2*, and is now in service on that ship.

At a press conference on board *Caronia* in Southampton on 13 May 2002 Cunard president Pamela Conover announced that 2003 would be *QE2's* last full season on the Atlantic – the role of Cunard transatlantic carrier would be assumed by *Queen Mary 2* from April 2004. *QE2* was to be reassigned to cruise service out of Southampton and to continuing World Cruise service for the first few months of each year.

---

'Cunard is proud of Her Majesty's long association with our company, beginning in 1938 when she attended the naming of *Queen Elizabeth*…and culminating in her presence at the company's 150th anniversary celebrations on board *QE2* in 1990.'
***Cunard message to Buckingham Palace***

---

In early June the Queen's Golden Jubilee was marked on board with a special dinner and a message was sent to Buckingham Palace:

Cunard is proud of Her Majesty's long association with our company, beginning in 1938 when she attended the naming of *Queen Elizabeth,* continuing with her launching of the *Caronia* in 1949 and *Queen Elizabeth 2* in 1967, and culminating in her presence at the company's 150th anniversary celebrations on board *QE2* in 1990.

On 14 June 2002 Baroness Thatcher was guest of honour on board at a special reception and lunch to mark the 20th anniversary of the Falkland Islands Campaign. The event was also attended by Sir Rex Hunt, governor of the Falkland Islands at

*QE2 on a cruise in the spectacular setting of Geirangerfjord in Norway*

## Baroness Thatcher's memories of QE2

At a splendid lunch aboard *QE2* in Southampton to commemorate the 10th anniversary of the Falkland Island conflict, I said in my speech that I had never had so many sleepless nights as prime minister than during the weeks the liner was journeying to the South Atlantic as a troopship.

I wrote in my memoirs, *The Downing Street Years*, that I do not think I have ever lived so tensely or intensely as during the whole of that time.

When the military chiefs first suggested that *QE2* join the war effort, such was my concern that I queried whether it was truly necessary to involve this great ship.

My family fell in love with Cunard many years before. We used to spend summer holidays in Seaview on the Isle of Wight and watch the old *Queen Elizabeth* and *Queen Mary* steam past on their way into Southampton.

The ecstatic and patriotic welcome *QE2* received on her return from the Falkland Islands cemented her place in British hearts as a greatly cherished national icon.

I remain a devoted fan.

the time of the Argentinian invasion; Captain Peter Jackson, master of *QE2* at the time, and Simon Weston, who went down to South Georgia on board *QE2* and whose resilience and cheerfulness following the attack on *Sir Galahad* are legendary.

On 20 June *QE2* left New York. During the passage the oil-fired boiler was being prepared ready for survey in Southampton. The preparation involved all the boiler mountings being removed and stripped down for inspection. Just as Edgar Villasis (motorman) and Nelson Venzal (wiper) were in the process of cleaning the port boiler main steam stop valve, hot water and steam discharged from the opened valve, covering both men.

The casualties were treated on board *QE2* before being airlifted to hospital as soon as the ship came into helicopter range of land. Edgar Villasis subsequently died on 24 June in Cork University Hospital.

Later inspection and testing revealed that the isolating valve to the engine room steam ring main was leaking at the time of the accident. It was thought that this led to localised heating of trapped condensate in the isolated steam line, which resulted in some of the condensate boiling and escaping through the dismantled steam stop valve.

At approximately 2150 hours ship's time on 29 August 2002 *QE2* completed five million nautical miles – a world record. All passengers on board the transatlantic crossing were presented with a certificate.

Menu signed by Margaret Thatcher, Sir Rex Hunt
(governor of the Falkland Islands during the conflict) and
Captain Peter Jackson

## Queen Elizabeth 2
## Menu

Friday, 14 June 2002

'The *QE2* sails on – a real, beautiful ship with a wonderful history in peace and war. It was a delight to return to her with Margaret Thatcher for the 20th anniversary of the Falklands Campaign. The *QE2* exudes a sense of history, security and good living.'

**Sir Bernard Ingham**

When *QE2* arrived in Singapore on 14 March Captain Warwick left the ship for the last time as master, thus ending the Warwick link with *QE2*. Captain Warwick then went to the shipyard to standby his new command, *Queen Mary 2*, just as his father did with *QE2* over 30 years earlier. He was subsequently promoted to commodore prior to *Queen Mary 2* entering service – a position his father also held.

*QE2* welcomed her most unusual 'passengers' on her 16–22 July Atlantic crossing when the Muppets joined the ship as part of a family themed crossing. Among the featured Muppets were the Great Gonzo, Dr Bunson Honeydrew, Kermit's nephew Robin, Zoot and Floyd Pepper, and Dr Strangepork. Captain Ray Heath posed with them for photographs on the Bridge.

At 0925 hours on 26 July 2003 while on the Atlantic and sailing at 26 knots the rudder suddenly went hard to starboard (30 degrees). The ship commenced swinging to starboard and gradually listed five degrees to port. The officer of the watch immediately switched to non-follow-up hand steering and brought the rudder back to midships. He then counteracted the swing and brought the ship back to its original heading. The steering system was then switched to the port unit and hand steering tested. This was found to be in order and was then utilised.

*Captain Ray Heath*

There were no other ships in the vicinity. The cause of the malfunction was found to be a fault in the rudder server servo amplifier card. The card was replaced and the system tested with positive results.

On their last day in commercial service on 24 October 2003 one of the Concordes passed over *QE2* on the Atlantic for the last time. Captain Ray Heath sent the following message to the captain of Concorde: 'From one British icon to another: *QE2* and Concorde have been an improbable, unique and successful transatlantic partnership for the past 20 years. We are sorry to see you go.'

> 'From one British icon to another: *QE2* and Concorde have been an improbable, unique and successful transatlantic partnership for the past 20 years. We are sorry to see you go.'
> *Message from* QE2 *to Concorde*

*Queen Mary 2* was handed over to Cunard on 22 December 2003. The first Atlantic liner to be completed since *QE2* in 1969 arrived in her home port of Southampton on Boxing Day. She was named in a spectacular ceremony by Her Majesty The Queen on 8 January and sailed on her 14-day maiden voyage to Fort Lauderdale on 12 January. A new era was about to begin – but *QE2* was still Cunard's flagship, for now.

On 19 April 2004 *QE2* left Southampton for the last time as Cunard flagship and headed for New York where, on 25 April, she berthed alongside *Queen Mary 2* for the first time. It was the first time two Cunard Queens had berthed together in New York since *Queen Mary* and *Queen Elizabeth* in 1940. Later that day both ships left New York after a stunning firework display around the Statue of Liberty. They then headed for Southampton together on the first-ever tandem Atlantic crossing. Both ships remained within sight of each other as they crossed the Atlantic and were greeted by a Nimrod and a Harrier Hawk off the Cornish coast on 30 April.

## The Flagship Retires

On 1 May *QE2* escorted *Queen Mary 2* into Southampton. *QE2* then berthed at the Mayflower Terminal while *Queen Mary 2* berthed at the Queen Elizabeth II Terminal. *QE2* had been the Cunard flagship since entering service in 1969; in fact she had served as flagship far longer than any other Cunarder, easily outstripping by 13 years the 22 years *Queen Elizabeth* had served as flagship. A special reception was held on board *QE2* in the Yacht Club with the guest of honour being the deputy prime minister, John Prescott, who gave a moving speech.

Cunard president Pamela Conover read out a message received from Buckingham Palace: 'Her

*The most famous name at sea!*

Majesty and The Duke of Edinburgh remember with pleasure their many visits to the ship and send their best wishes to you all for a memorable event.'

When Samuel Cunard arrived in Boston on board his first ship, *Britannia*, in 1840, the citizens presented him with an enormous silver cup as a mark of their appreciation at the establishment of a scheduled steamship service. Ever since – apart from a brief period when it was 'lost' – the cup has been carried on the company's flagship.

A special ceremony to mark the passing of flagship status to *Queen Mary 2* took place when Captain Ian McNaught handed the Boston Cup to *Queen Mary 2*'s commodore Ron Warwick. As the cup exchanged hands *QE2's* whistle blew one long blast. *QE2's* role as flagship of Cunard was over.

After this the guests transferred by boats from *QE2* to *Queen Mary 2* for lunch. *QE2* sailed past *Queen Mary 2* heading for refit. Both ships

exchanged salutes and *Queen Mary 2* played the Stevie Wonder song 'Isn't She Lovely' as the former flagship suddenly appeared out of the mist and passed the new flagship.

Having completed 35 years, six months and three days in service, *QE2* reached a notable milestone in her life on 5 November when she became the longest-serving Cunard express liner in the company's history. She took the record from *Aquitania*, which served Cunard Line, in peace and war, from May 1914 to December 1949. During her service *QE2* had completed 797 Atlantic crossings and 20 full World Cruises

## New Year Blowout

In the early morning of New Year's Day 2005 while on passage from San Juan to New York, *QE2* suffered a total loss of power as a result of loss of air supply to a damper in a 3.3kw transformer room. The emergency generators kicked in straight

## The 2004 Refit for Cruising

For the first time in many years *QE2*'s annual refit took place in spring rather than the traditional November/December period and the 21-day refit again took place at Bremerhaven. The main purpose of the refit was to adapt *QE2* for her future role of cruising from the UK. Consideration was given to enhancing and improving the air-conditioning for warmer climes; opening up the ship a little more to make use of the now more usable outdoor deck space; adapting the fresh-water tanks; and adapting the ship's holding capacity – especially as *QE2* would be calling at more ports where stringent regulations covering items such as discharge were being introduced.

The centrepiece of the enhancements was the remodelling of the Sun Deck area behind the funnel and the creation of the Funnel Bar. Work included the installation of a new awning 86m² (925 sq ft) in the form of a stretched canvas ceiling with teak frames, 200m² (2150 sq ft) of new re-sanded teak decking and a raised bandstand with a sound and light system. A new bar (with teak façade) and under-counter was built featuring two taps for draught beer and four bar stools. In addition a coffee machine, two refrigerators and a self-service soft ice-cream machine were installed. New furniture included 12 teak tables and chairs, new steamer chair cushions for the Fidus Loungers, a set of teak store cabinets and stainless steel bins. New deck signage was also added and the existing teak doors were re-sanded.

away and emergency services were on line immediately, and the New Year festivities continued in full swing in the Yacht Club and Casino. It took a little longer to restart a main generator as units 'Golf' and 'India' had leaked all the air to the bilge. Using one air compressor, starting air had to be made up to sufficient pressure to start 'Alpha', which came online again at 0310 hours. The ship was underway again at passage speed, 25 knots, with power reinstated throughout at 0352 hours.

On 16 February 2005 while *QE2* was in Fremantle, four locals, two men and women, broke through the perimeter fence at a car pound adjacent to *QE2*'s berth, stole a fork-lift truck and then gained entry to the ship via the bunker station door on Five Deck. The door was manned at the time by the engine-room rating of the watch and the shoreside operator of the sewage truck. However the four, who appeared to be drunk, overpowered the two and made it to Five Deck. The rating raised the alarm and the four were quickly apprehended by the security staff on board and escorted off the ship via the Two Deck gangway into the terminal by which time the police had arrived. After initial questioning, one male was arrested on the scene and placed in a secure vehicle while the other three were escorted to a local police station for tests and statements before being charged.

The 2005 World Cruise was something of a magical mystery tour for *QE2* passengers. Bad weather resulted in the cancellation of four ports – Kona, Philip Island, Exmouth and Keelung – and also delayed by one day the scheduled embarkation and disembarkation in Dubai.

The eventful 2005 World Cruise ended with even more headlines. During the night of 13/14 April, as *QE2* approached Southampton, three crew members went on a rampage through the ship.

*Flagship no more:* QE2 *passes* Queen Mary 2 *in Southampton in May 2004 just after the newer ship had been endowed with flagship status*

One of three tapestries on Boat Deck E Stairway depicting the ship's launch went missing and was presumed to have been thrown overboard; another of the tapestries was torn and damaged; blue paint was thrown from the Royal Promenade into the Grand Lounge below.

The men were handed to the police upon arrival in Southampton and subsequently bailed. The missing tapestry was eventually found hidden in ductwork above the penthouse suites. All three tapestries, designed by Helena Barynina Hernmarck, were sent to the British Museum and repaired at a cost of £14,500. They were returned to the ship on 15 October 2005.

Both *QE2* and *Queen Mary 2* met each other in Southampton on 16 April and this time it was the turn of *Queen Mary 2* to sail past *QE2*. The newer ship was taking *QE2's* American full World Cruise passengers back to New York.

---

'…while approximately 40 miles off the NW coast of Spain we came into contact with the decomposing body of a dead whale.' ***Captain Nick Bates***

---

On 17 April 2005 while en route to Madeira from Southampton *QE2* ran into the body of a decomposing whale. The ship's speed was reduced and the body fell away. Captain Nick Bates reported:

…while approximately 40 miles off the NW coast of Spain we came into contact with the decomposing body of a dead whale. The ship's speed was reduced to 6 knots and the carcass fell off the bow. I would estimate the whale to be in the region of 60 feet long, quite a reasonable size. No damage was sustained to the ship as far as I am aware.

The 36th anniversary of her maiden voyage departure was celebrated in Southampton on 2 May with a special birthday party.

On 6 June, while leaving Aalesund, one of the tugs assisting *QE2* aft capsized as *QE2* was proceeding forward. The tug lines were still connected to *QE2* but the tug righted itself very quickly.

During the night of 22/23 June 2005 a deck seaman was lost overboard as *QE2* was arriving in Lisbon. By the time she was safely alongside the ship had been thoroughly searched and no trace of him could be found. It was presumed the seaman had jumped overboard.

*QE2* undertook a special four-night cruise between 25 June and 29 June as part of the Trafalgar 200 commemorations marking the 200th anniversary of the famous sea battle. *QE2* took part in the Fleet Review by Her Majesty The Queen and HRH The Duke of Edinburgh of warships from around the world together with merchant vessels, tall ships and smaller craft.

There was an even more prestigious milestone for *QE2* on 4 September 2005 while she was anchored off Sydney, Nova Scotia. She completed 36 years, four months and two days in service, making her the longest-serving Cunard ship ever – taking the record from the *Scythia*, which served from 1921 to 1957.

## Medical Crises

On 1 December 2005, while *QE2* was en route from Port Stanley (Falkland Islands) to Rio de Janeiro, a passenger and then a crew member became ill, requiring transfer to a hospital ashore. The 53-year-old passenger, who had suffered a heart attack and cardiac arrest, was successfully resuscitated and the cardiac artery unblocked with drugs. The 49-year-old chef had lost about 3 litres (5 pints) of blood and owed his life to the transfusion protocol put in place. There was an overwhelming response to the appeal for blood. Arrangements were made with the Uruguayan authorities to transfer the patients. A helicopter transfer was successfully completed approximately 105 nautical miles off the port of Montevideo. Passengers were kept informed throughout and the ship continued en route to Rio where she arrived on schedule. Captain Nick Bates was

full of praise for the efforts of the authorities in making the arrangements.

For the first time since her Acceptance Trials in 1969, *QE2* spent Christmas in European waters. For the first time ever, passengers had paid for a European Christmas cruise, and New Year's Eve was spent in Madeira.

On Friday 10 March 2006 during an eventful World Cruise *QE2* made her maiden call at Shanghai where she was to remain overnight. *QE2's* scheduled 1800 hours departure on Saturday 11 March was subsequently delayed as the port was closed due to fog. In the end *QE2* departed the

*P&O's new* Arcadia *passes* QE2 *in Southampton in August 2005*

berth at 2130 hours, three hours late. During the transit of the river the weather conditions deteriorated badly and the wind increased to 50 knots. It was not possible to disembark the pilot and, after negotiations with the Chinese authorities, it was agreed that he would be carried to Hong Kong.

At about 2210 hours on 12 March, about 32 nautical miles south of Jinmen Dao on the coast of China, the ship rolled severely to starboard around 15 to 18 degrees. Wind conditions at the time were strong, Force 9–10 on the Beaufort scale, with seas of 6–8m (20–27ft). The cause was most probably a freak wave lifting the stern, causing the ship to swing to starboard. This was followed by another wave lifting the stern again and adding to the roll. Three passengers received head injuries while in the Casino but no broken bones were reported. Fifteen crew members also reported injuries.

Shortly after the roll senior officers walked the ship to reassure passengers and organise any assistance. A cabin-to-cabin check was undertaken to ensure all passengers were well. Captain Nick Bates made a broadcast about ten minutes after the event to reassure everyone that the ship was safe. There was no sign of serious concern from passengers, who continued to enjoy the ship's facilities as best they could. There was some damage to equipment in the shops, galleys and other public areas but despite that *QE2* arrived in Hong Kong just two hours later than scheduled.

On 3 April on the same World Cruise, while cruising after leaving Dubai, passengers reported seeing seven high-speed boats approaching *QE2* at

QE2 *in Oslo after her 2004 refit for cruising*

about 50 knots just after 1800 hours. Initially passengers who saw them thought they were suicide bombers intent on attacking *QE2* but Captain Bates thought they might be smugglers trying to take advantage of *QE2's* radar shadow. The ship's sonic weapon, a Long Range Acoustic Device (LRAD) was powered up and made ready for immediate use. The crew of the boats appeared to have masks over their faces, and waved as they went past. It was later discovered by the officers that the high-speed craft were part of an Iranian naval exercise. *QE2* briefed the Regional Security Officer in Egypt.

For security reasons the call at Aqaba on Monday 10 April was cancelled. *QE2* proceeded through the Suez Canal and called at Alexandria in Egypt a day earlier than scheduled on Wednesday 12 April.

## High Security in Egypt

While *QE2* was in Egypt, Cunard issued a statement saying that the company was aware of certain information concerning the security of *QE2* as she transited the Egyptian region and treated all such information very seriously. The UK, US and Egyptian security authorities were kept fully informed and the company placed the ship on a higher level of security as it passed through this area. In addition shoreside security was increased at the various ports of call. But the voyage proceeded without incident.

On 23 April both *QE2* and *Queen Mary 2* were in Southampton and, in a repeat of 1 May 2004, *QE2* sailed past *Queen Mary 2* in the early afternoon while heading for refit. *Queen Mary 2* played James Blunt's 'You're Beautiful' and Diana Ross's 'Forever Young' as *QE2* sailed past.

## The 2006 Refit

*QE2* entered the dry-dock on 24 April upon her arrival at the Lloyd Werft shipyard and her 16-day, $15 million refit began. A great deal of re-carpeting had been undertaken throughout 2005 while *QE2* was in service and that re-carpeting was completed during the refit. Most of the new carpeting was of exactly the same design as before. During the dry-docking, seating in the Queen's Room, Grand Lounge, Yacht Club, Golden Lion Pub was re-upholstered and six public toilets were refurbished. Re-plating work in the aluminium superstructure also took place. *QE2* arrived back in Southampton on 8 May and re-entered service with a 10-day Mediterranean cruise departing 9 May.

*QE2* made her first call at New Orleans on 27 November 2006, a welcome visitor in a city still striving to return to normality after the devastation of Hurricane Katrina in August. She was the longest passenger ship ever to visit the city.

As this record of *QE2's* life is being written, the ship is preparing to enter her 40th year – a year that promises to add yet more historic events, to break more records, to establish further 'firsts', and to generate even more adulation for what is already the most famous ship in the world.

*QE2* is preparing to set off on her 25th full World Cruise – a significant milestone in itself and far more than any other Cunarder has achieved. In September 2007 she will undertake a 'lap-of-honour' around the British Isles, calling at Newcastle – birthplace of *Mauretania* and *Carpathia* – for the first time. She will then visit Edinburgh, followed by her own birthplace on the Clyde on the 40th anniversary of her launch, and Liverpool, Cunard's ancestral home. Plans are being worked on right now in all these places to ensure *QE2* is afforded the welcome she deserves on such a significant anniversary. But we can be sure that even if no one planned anything, thousands would turn out at each port to greet her. *QE2* needs little help to be the centre of attention.

## A Must-do Experience

But as the ship reaches 40 – a greater age than most ships ever attain – our thoughts must turn to what her future can be; how long can she go on? The answer seems to be that she will go on for as long as travellers regard a voyage on *QE2* as a 'must-do' experience. *QE2's* hull is as good today as the day she left the Clyde for the first time; her diesel electric propulsion system is the most powerful plant on any merchant ship and continues to perform well, so the ship's heart is sound; and Cunard has ensured, by constant refurbishment, that *QE2* remains as comfortable and as inviting as any ship afloat.

Every age seems to produce a ship that grabs the affections of millions. In the early part of the 20th century it was the *Mauretania*, which was saluted by thousands in 1935 as she progressed up the East Coast to the breaker's yard. After that it was *Queen Mary*, the ship described as the 'nearest thing to a living being', which is still a huge attraction in Long Beach. For the last 40 years it has been *Queen Elizabeth 2*. We can safely predict that she will remain the maritime icon of the age for many years yet to come.

*QE2* was born into a world of uncertainty, built by an almost bankrupt shipyard for an almost bankrupt shipping company. Her future was predicted to be so short as to be nonexistent, and many deplored her departure from the style norms of her predecessors. But she has survived; more than that, she has triumphed against the odds.

Today *QE2* is as secure as she has ever been. She is owned by a company that is unequalled in the art of successfully operating ships; a company with enormous financial clout that has both the will and the means to maintain *QE2* to the standard she deserves.

She may be getting on in years now – but her future is brighter than it was in 1967. All those who love her have much to be grateful for and much to look forward to ■

*Following page: A royal meeting in Sydney Harbour. In February 2007* QE2 *on her 25th World Cruise meets* Queen Mary 2 *on her maiden World Cruise.*

# *Appendix 1*

## GENERAL INFORMATION

**KEEL LAID:** 4 July 1965
**LAUNCHED:** 20 September 1967 by Her Majesty Queen Elizabeth II
**BUILT BY:** John Brown and Co. (Clydebank) Ltd, Scotland; later Upper Clyde Shipbuilders
**COST:** £28,825,185

**MAIDEN VOYAGE:** 2 May 1969
Southampton to New York
**RE-ENGINED:** November 1986 – April 1987, by Lloyd Werft, Bremerhaven, Germany

**PORT OF REGISTRY:** Southampton, England
**SIGNAL LETTERS:** G.B.T.T.
**OFFICIAL NUMBER:** 336703

## VITAL STATISTICS

| | | |
|---|---|---|
| **TONNAGES:** | Gross: | 70,327 grt |
| | Net: | 37,182nt |
| | Deadweight: | 11,590dw |
| **LENGTHS:** | Overall: | 293.53m (963ft) |
| | Bridge to Stem: | 86m (282ft 2.5in) |
| | Bridge to Stern: | 220m (724ft 10in) |
| **BREADTH:** | 32.06m (105ft 2.5in) | |
| **DRAUGHT:** | 9.94m (32ft 7.5in) | |
| **HEIGHTS:** | Mast-head above Keel: | 61m (200ft 1.5in) |
| | Funnel above Keel: | 62.20m (204ft 1.5in) |
| | Masthead above Sea Level: | 51.05m (167ft 1in) |
| | Funnel: | 21.20m (69ft 6in) |
| | Bridge Height of Eye: | 29m (95ft) |

**PASSENGER CAPACITY:** 1777

**DECKS:** 13
**PASSENGER DECKS:** 12
**ELECTRIC CURRENT:** 110/115 volts and 240 volts AC
**LIFTS:** 13 Passenger
2 Car
8 Store
1 Engine Room

## TECHNICAL DATA

**Engines:**
Nine 9-cylinder 58/64 (580mm bore/640mm stroke) medium speed turbo-charged diesels, running at 400 rpm and connected to individual alternators generating 10.5 megawatts each at 10,000 volts. Built by MAN B & W Diesel GmbH, Augsburg, Germany, each engine weighs 220 tonnes.

**Motors:**
Two 400-tonne electric motors, one on each propeller shaft, rated at a maximum of 44 megawatts each at 144 rpm. Built by GEC, Rugby, England, the motors are over 9m (29ft) in diameter.
- They are the largest marine motors ever built.
- The diesel electric system produces 130,000hp, which is the most powerful propulsion plant of any merchant ship in the world.
- The 95MV total power output is enough to light a city the size of Southampton.
- QE2 is the fastest merchant ship in operation.

**Boilers:**
Nine waste-heat recovery gas boilers mounted on the engine exhaust uptakes, and two oil-fired boilers. These produce steam for fuel heating, domestic fresh water heating, heating of swimming pools and steam for the laundry equipment and kitchens. Built by Sunrod, Sweden.

**Propellers:**
Two outward-turning, controllable-pitch, of diameter 6.1m (19ft 8in). The propeller shafts are both 80m (262ft 6in) long. Built by Lips, Drunen, Netherlands.

**Bow Thrusters:**
Two Stone KaMeWa of 1,000hp per unit

**Steering Gear:**
Brown Bros 4 ram electro-hydraulic

**Stabilisers:**
Four Denny Brown; each fin projects from the ship's side by 3.65m (12ft) and is 1.85m (6ft) wide. They reduce rolling by 60%.

**Speed:**
**Maximum** 32.5 knots
**Service** 25 - 28.5 knots.
Service speed is achievable using only 7 of the 9 engines.

**Fuel Consumption:**
18.05 tonnes per hour, or 433 tonnes per day.
- The daily fuel consumption is equal to six of the ship's swimming pools.
- The ship's fuel oil tank capacity of 4,381.4 tonnes is sufficient for 10 days' sailing at 32.5 knots, equalling 7,800 nautical miles.
- One litre of fuel will move the ship 3.32m (11ft); with the previous steam turbine engines, one litre of fuel moved the ship 2.41m (8ft).

| Tank Capacities: | | |
|---|---|---|
| | **Fresh Water** | 1,852 tonnes |
| | **Laundry Water** | 489 tonnes |
| | **Diesel Oil** | 206.8 tonnes |
| | **Fuel Oil** | 4,381.4 tonnes |
| | **Lubricating Oil** | 335.7 tonnes |
| | **Ballast** | 4,533 tonnes |
| | **Feed Water** | 113.8 tonnes |

**Water Production / Consumption:**
- Four Serck vacuum flash evaporators, producing 250 tonnes each per day
- One reverse osmosis plant producing 450 tonnes
- Total production – 1,450 tonnes per day
- Consumption – about 1,000 tonnes per day; equivalent to 14 of the ship's swimming pools

**Anchors:**
- **Forward** two of 12.5 tonnes each, on 10cm (3.94in) diameter cable 330m (1,080ft) long.
- **Aft** one of 7.5 tonnes, on 7.62cm (3in) diameter cable 220m (720 ft) long.
- **Spare** Spare – one of 12.5 tonnes.

**Rudder Weight:** 80 tonnes

**Stopping Capability:**
- The ship can reduce speed from 32.5 knots full ahead to standstill in 3 minutes 39 seconds, in a distance of 0.75 nautical miles.
- The ship can go from standstill to full speed astern (19 knots) in 12 minutes.

## SAFETY INFORMATION

| | |
|---|---|
| **Lifeboats:** | 20; total capacity 2,244 persons |
| **Liferafts:** | 56; total capacity 1,400 persons |
| **Buoyant Apparatus:** | 5; total capacity 100 persons |
| **Lifejackets:** | 3,474 |
| **Lifebuoys:** | 30 |

**Safety Control Room**
At the heart of the ship is the Safety Control Room, which is manned 24 hours a day. From this room, there is a continuous watch on every part of the ship. In the centre of the room is a desk, carrying an illuminated master plan of QE2. Any particular area of the vessel can be presented, displaying all safety precautions available. The desk also carries direct communication links with the Bridge and Engine Control Room.

## EXTERIOR

**The Funnel**
This is the most recognisable feature of QE2, the funnel is 21m (69ft) high and is one of the most efficient and practical designs in any passenger liner.

**The Mast**
The mast structure performs the useful functions of clearing waste gases from the main kitchen, and carries the radar scanners, aerials and navigation lights.

## FOOD & BEVERAGE

**Consumption and Stores**

| | DAILY | ANNUALLY |
|---|---|---|
| Tea Bags | 2,500 bags | 912,500 bags |
| Coffee | 45kg (100lb) | 16.5 tonnes |
| Cooking oil | 227 litres (50 gallons) | 82,966 litres (18,250 gallons) |
| Eggs | 3,200 | 1,168,000 |
| Milk | 1046 litres (230 gallons) | 381,644 litres (83,950 gallons) |
| Butter | 159kg (350lb) | 58 tonnes |
| Breakfast cereal | 770 packets | 281,050 packets |
| Marmalade / jam | 553 portions | 201,050 portions |
| Bananas | 104kg (230lb) | 38 tonnes |
| Strawberries | 57kg (125lb) | 20 tonnes |
| Fruit juice | 2,910 litres | 1,061,967 litres (233,600 gallons) |
| Tomatoes | 55kg (120lb) | 20 tonnes |
| Smoked salmon | 30kg (66lb) | 11 tonnes |
| Caviar | 3kg (6.6lb) | 1 tonne |
| Lobster | 53kg (116lb) | 20 tonnes |
| Strip loin | 204kg (450lb) | 73 tonnes |
| Flour | 342kg (753lb) | 122 tonnes |
| Rice | 172kg (380lb) | 62 tonnes |
| Potatoes | 315kg (694lb) | 113 tonnes |
| Saffron | 1.5 packets | 547.5 packets |
| Beer | 2,400 bottles | 24,135 litres (5,309 gallons) |
| Spirits | 180 litres (40 gallons) | 65,700 litres (14,452 gallons) |
| Champagne | 200 bottles | 73,000 bottles |
| Wine | 370 bottles | 135,050 bottles |
| Soft drinks | 820 bottles | 299,300 bottles |
| Cigarettes | 1,000 packets | 365,000 packets |
| Cigars | 41 boxes | 12,425 boxes |
| Doilies | | Over 2 million |
| Napkins and Cocktail Stirrers | | Over 1 million each |
| Aluminium Foil | | 201km (125 miles) |
| Cling Film | | 277km (150 miles) |

- QE2 sends all its used cooking oil ashore for reconstituting into animal feed.
- The 277km (150 miles) of cling film used every year is enough to go around the QE2 nearly 731 times.
- Heineken and Becks together account for almost 50% of the beer consumed.
- Pound for pound, the most expensive food item on board is saffron (2.5 times the value of Beluga caviar).
- Enough fruit juice is used in one year to fill up QE2's swimming pools nearly 8 times.

**The kitchens and dining rooms have:**

| | |
|---|---|
| **glassware** | 51,000 items |
| **crockery/dishes** | 64,000 items |
| **cutlery** | 35,850 items |
| **kitchenware** | 7,921 items |
| **tableware** | 64,531 items (condiment sets, serving trays and a variety of other pieces in silver and stainless steel) |

## PUBLIC ROOMS AND PASSENGER FACILITIES

**Restaurants**

| NAME | DECK | CAPACITY |
|---|---|---|
| Queen's Grill | Boat | 231 |
| Princess Grill | Quarter | 100 |
| *Britannia* Grill | Quarter | 108 |
| *Caronia* Restaurant | Quarter | 554 |
| *Mauretania* Restaurant | Upper | 530 |
| The Lido | Quarter | 400 |
| Pavilion | One | 58 |

**Lounges**

| NAME | DECK | CAPACITY |
|---|---|---|
| Grand Lounge | Upper | 590 |
| Queen's Room | Quarter | 320 |
| Theatre/Cinema | Upper and Boat | 529 |
| Queen's Grill Lounge | Boat | 75 |
| Princess Grill Bar | One | 12 |
| Yacht Club | Upper | 208 |
| Chart Room | Quarter | 88 |
| Crystal Bar | Upper | 182 |
| Golden Lion | Upper | 135 |
| Midships Lobby | Two | 15 |

**Facilities**

| NAME | DECK | CAPACITY / NOTES |
|---|---|---|
| Casino | Upper | Featuring 106 slot machines; four Blackjack tables; two Roulette tables; two Caribbean Stud Poker tables; one mini Punto Blanco and one mini-dice. |
| Royal Promenade | Boat | Shops include: souvenirs, clothing, jewellery, perfumery. There is a formal wear rental facility and a branch of Harrods. A Cunard Collection Shop is located on One Deck. |
| Board Room | Boat | Can be arranged in a variety of seating styles: Conference 24 seats; Theatre 50 seats; Classroom 20 seats; Cocktail Party 60 people |
| Library and Bookshop | Quarter | 30. With 6,000 books, this is the largest library at sea (and the only one staffed by two full-time librarians). |
| Computer Learning Centre | Two | |

## HEALTH FACILITIES

**Six Deck - The Health Spa**
Facilities include separate saunas for men and women, a steam room, a whirlpool spa bath, an 'inhalation room' and a thalassotherapy pool. The latter is designed with strategically placed, high-powered jets to encourage relaxation, boost circulation and relieve aches and pains. The 'inhalation room' is an area where moist negatively ionised seawater or herbal mist is released into the air – this being ideal for the relief of asthma and sinusitis. A relaxation area, spacious changing rooms and lockers as well as three French hydrotherapy bath treatment rooms and seven further treatment rooms are also available. The latter are used for therapies including mud body masks, a variety of massages, and facial and soap massages.

**Seven Deck - Fitness Deck**
The Fitness Deck features a gymnasium and aerobic studio with 10 Life Fitness machines, rowers, stairmasters, 7 Cybex weight machines, life cycles, treadmills, graviton, running boards and dumb-bells. A shop selling fitness wear is also located here.

**Additional Sports Facilities**
- Two Swimming Pools (one outdoor, one indoor) – One Deck and Seven Decks
- Golf Driving – Boat Deck
- Table Tennis – Upper Deck
- Tennis Court – Boat Deck
- Shuffleboard – Boat Deck

## GENERAL

| NAME | DECK | CAPACITY / NOTES |
|---|---|---|
| Nursery | Sun | |
| Club 2000 | Quarter | For the 7 to 17 age range; features video arcade machines, board games and a dance floor for discos. |
| Kennels | Signal | Can accommodate 14 animals (dogs, cats and birds). |
| Hospital | Six | Fully equipped, with ward accommodation for 12 patients. Can deal with most medical cases. |

**Other Services**
- Butler service
- Florist
- Photo-lab (same-day service)
- Secretarial service
- Synagogue
- Television studio
- Hair and beauty salon

## PASSENGER ACCOMMODATION

| | |
|---|---|
| Total number of cabins: | 950 |
| Outside doubles | 634 |
| Outside singles | 37 |
| Inside doubles | 198 |
| Inside singles | 81 |
| Cabins equipped for disabled passengers | 4 |

## *Appendix 2*

### QE2 MASTERS
#### (With date assumed command)

**Commodore W E Warwick, CBE RD RNR** (23 December 1968)

**Captain G E Smith** (12 June 1969)

**Captain F J Storey, RD RNR** (18 October 1969)

**Captain J E Wolfenden, RD RNR** (8 May 1970)

**Captain W J Law, RD RNR** (19 June 1970)

**Captain M Hehir** (3 June 1971)

**Captain P Jackson** (6 August 1973)

**Captain R H Arnott, RD RNR** (22 May 1976)

**Captain L R W Portet, RD Cdr RNR** (13 April 1977)

**Commodore T D Ridley, RD Captain RNR** (26 August 1978)

**Captain A J Hutcheson, RD RNR** (13 March 1982)

**Captain R Wadsworth** (15 May 1983)

**Captain K H Stanley** (9 April 1984)

**Captain A C Bennell, RD RNR** (10 July 1987)

**Captain R A Woodall, RD RNR** (1 November 1987)

**Commodore J Burton-Hall, RD Cdr RNR** (7 March 1990)

**Captain R W Warwick, Lt Cdr RNR FNI** (26 July 1990)

**Captain L R Hasell** (12 April 1997)

**Captain P Wright** (22 August 1999)

**Captain R Heath** (29 August 2001)

**Captain I McNaught** (17 April 2003)

**Captain N Bates** (18 September 2004)

**Captain P Russell** (14 March 2005)

**Captain C Rynd** (18 July 2005)

**Captain D Perkins** (19 May 2006)

## *Appendix 3*

### FAMOUS FACES ON BOARD

Ever since Prince Charles became her first passenger almost 40 years ago, QE2 hosted more famous faces than any other ship in service.

**Members of Royal Families and the aristocracy who have travelled**

HM The Queen
HRH The Duke of Edinburgh
HRH The Prince of Wales
HRH The Prince Edward
Diana, Princess of Wales
The Emperor of Japan
King Hussein of Jordan
Princess Christine of the Netherlands
Prince Nikita Romanoff
The Sultan of Brunei
The Sultan of Selanghor
The Saudi Royal Family
Earl Mountbatten of Burma
Earl of Snowdon
Earl of Lichfield
Lord Montagu of Beaulieu
Lord Wedgwood

**Politicians, Diplomats and Churchmen who have travelled**

Lord Archer of Weston-super-Mare
President George W Bush
President Jimmy Carter
Edwina Currie
Sir Nicholas Fairbairn
H R Haldeman
Bob Hawke
Sir Rex Hunt
Dame Jill Knight
Lee Kuan Yew
Mayor John Lindsay
Graca Machel
President Nelson Mandela
Lord Mason of Barnsley
Shimon Peres
Dame Stella Rimington
The Most Revd Lord Runcie of Cuddesdon
Sir Cyril Smith
Lord Taylor of Warwick
Terry Waite

**Eminent people who have visited but not travelled**

HM Queen Elizabeth, The Queen Mother
HRH The Prince Andrew
HRH The Princess Royal
Lord Attenborough
Mrs Cherie Blair
Chief Mangosuthu Buthelezi
Chris de Burgh

Mrs Elizabeth Dole
Sir David Frost
Charles Haughey
Lady Ivar Mountbatten
Rt Hon John Prescott MP
Albert Reynolds
Earl and Countess Spencer
Baroness Thatcher

**Musicians who have travelled**

Larry Adler
Moira Anderson
Applejacks
Charles Aznavour
Count Basie
Dave Berry
David Bowie
John Briggs
Joe Brown
Petula Clark
The Cure
Vic Damone
Neil Diamond
Gracie Fields
Wayne Fontana
Gerry and the Pacemakers
George Harrison
Herman's Hermits
Edmund Hockridge
Mick Jagger

Elton John
Davy Jones
Jack Jones
Frankie Laine
Joe Loss
Patti Lupone
Dame Vera Lynn
Maureen McGovern
Harry Neilson
Yoko Ono
Oscar Peterson
Linda Ronstadt
Neil Sedaka
Carly Simon
Ringo Starr
Rod Stewart
Frankie Vaughan
Sarah Vaughan
Nancy Wilson

**Eminent journalists and authors who have travelled**

Fiona Armstrong
Dame Beryl Bainbridge
Lynne Barber
Carol Barnes
Alan Bleasdale
Jennie Bond
Craig Brown
Michael Brunson
Bill Bryson
Michael Buerk
Paul Burrell
Tom Clancy
Matthew Collins
Clive Cussler
Frank Delaney
Colin Dexter
Dick Francis
Sandy Gall
Hannah Hauxwell
Tim Heald
Richard Hendrick
Mary Higgins Clark
Brian Hitchen
Sir Bernard Ingham
Virginia Ironside
P D James
Paul Johnson
Sir Ludovic Kennedy

Roddy Llewellyn
Jackie and Sunny Mann
Brian Masters
Frank McCourt
Angus McGill
James Mitchener
Sheridan Morley
Flt Lt John Nichol
Sir David Nicholas
Pat O'Brien
Anna Pavord
Marje Proops
Claire Rayner
Celia Sandys
Selina Scott
Michael Shea
Mary Ann Sieghart
John Simpson
Peter Sissons
Sir Roy Strong
Carol Thatcher
Leslie Thomas
Jack Tinker
Hugo Vickers
Tony Warren
Nigel West
Roland White
Tennessee Williams

**Stars of stage and screen who have travelled**

Eamonn Andrews
Julie Andrews
Debbie Arnold
Michael Aspel
Peter Baldwin
Thelma Barlow
Roy Barraclough
Jeremy Beadle
Sean Bean
Isla Blair
Victor Borge
Jim Bowen
Tracy Brabin
Johnny Briggs
George Burns
Richard Burton
James Cagney
Beverly Callard
Jasper Carrott
Judith Chalmers
Glenn Close
Rosemary Conley
Judy Cornwell
Bill Cosby
Michael Crawford
Jimmy Cricket
Tim Curry
Tony Curtis
Jill Dando
Paul Daniels
Nigel Davenport
Liz Dawn
Les Dawson
Dame Judi Dench
Sue Eden
Douglas Fairbanks Jnr
Eddie Fisher
Bryan Forbes
Fiona Fullerton
Susan George
Hermione Gingold
Lillian Gish
Jilly Goolden
Peter Gordeno
Russell Grant
Hughie Green
Richard Griffiths
Tom O'Connor
Sid Owen
Patsy Palmer
Nicholas Parsons

John Peel
Dr Mark Porter
Robert Powell
Vincent Price
Charley Pride
Juliet Prowse
Esther Rantzen
Bertice Reading
Lyn Redgrave
Christopher Reeve
Debbie Reynolds
Gary Rhodes
Wendy Richards
Angela Rippon
Anton Rodgers
Ginger Rogers
Patricia Routledge
Jane Russell
Dr Ruth
Telly Savalas
Sir Jimmy Savile
Prunella Scales
George C Scott
Sir Harry Secombe
Larry Hagman
Stuart Hall
Rolf Harris
Lawrence Harvey
Dickie Henderson
Jim Henson
Sherrie Hewson
Geoff Hinsliff
Thora Hird
Bob Holness
Bob Hope
Frankie Howerd
Rock Hudson
Geoffrey Hughes
Lorraine Kelly
Kevin Kennedy
Robert Kilroy Silk
Eric Knowles
Barbara Knox
Kris Kristofferson
Sara Lancashire
Burt Lancaster
Roy Lancaster
Danny LaRue
Christopher Lee
Maureen Lipman
Moira Lister

Emily Lloyd
Deborah Lyttle
Barry Manilow
Dean Martin
Raymond Massey
Nichola McAuliffe
Leo McKern
Hayley Mills
Sir John Mills
Matthew Modine
Bob Monkhouse
Ken Morley
Bryan Mosley
David Neilson
Bob Newhart
Nanette Newman
Paul Newman
Barry Norman
Peter Sellers
Jack Smethurst
Delia Smith
Jon Snow
Robert Stack
Terence Stamp
Tommy Steele
Sharon Stone

Meryl Streep
Jimmy Tarbuck
Bill Tarmey
Chris Tarrant
Gillian Taylforth
Elizabeth Taylor
James Taylor
Shaw Taylor
Anthony Worrall Thompson
Christopher Timothy
John Travolta
Twiggy
Liv Ullman
Sir Peter Ustinov
Bill Waddington
Robert Wagner
Timothy West
Alan Whicker
Richard Whiteley
Desmond Wilcox
Simon Williams
Barbara Windsor
Ernie Wise
Natalie Wood
Helen Worth
Michael York

**Sports personalities who have travelled**

Eric Bristow
Frank Bruno
Sir Matt Busby
Jack Charlton
Brian Close
Sir Colin Cowdrey
Kenny Dalglish
Steve Davis
Keith Deller
Alan Hansen

Stephen Hendry
Denis Law
Cliff Lazarenko
David Platt
Peter Reid
Tessa Sanderson
Nobby Stiles
Daley Thompson
Murray Walker

**Astronauts who have travelled**

Buzz Aldrin

**_Titanic_ survivors who have travelled**

Milvina Dean

**Explorers who have travelled**

Colonel John Blashford-Snell
Sir Chris Bonington
Jean-Michel Cousteau
John Harrison
Sir Wally Herbert
Brian Jones
Dr Kathryn L Sullivan
Stephen Venables

**Philanthropists who have travelled**

J Paul Getty Jnr

# *Appendix 4*

## THE ROYAL CONNECTION

### 1967

| 14 July | **HRH The Duke of Edinburgh** toured the uncompleted liner and lunched with the Cunard chairman Sir Basil Smallpeice and John Brown chairman Lord Aberconway. |
| 20 September | *QE2* launched by **HM Queen Elizabeth II** in the presence of **HRH The Duke of Edinburgh** and **HRH Princess Margaret**. |

### 1968

| 20 February | **HRH Princess Margaret** opened the *QE2* Exhibition at the Design Centre in London. |
| 19 November | **HRH Prince Charles** sailed on board from the shipyard in Clydebank to dry-dock in Greenock. |

### 1969

| 1 May | **HM The Queen** and **HRH The Duke of Edinburgh** visited in Southampton continuing the tradition set by *Queen Mary* and *Queen Elizabeth*. |
| 16 May | While outward bound through Spithead on her second westbound voyage *QE2* passed through the assembled multi-national fleet of NATO, which **HM The Queen** was reviewing from the Royal Yacht *Britannia*. |
| 29 May | **HRH The Duke of Edinburgh** again visited and toured the ship in Southampton while presenting the 1969 Council of Industrial Design Awards. |

### 1970

| March | **HRH Princess Margaret** paid an informal visit in Barbados. Accompanied by Lord Snowdon and a party of 13, she toured all the public rooms, lunched in the Grill Room and enjoyed refreshments in the Captain's Cabin and Midships Bar. |

### 1970

| May | For *QE2's* tenth anniversary, **HM The Queen** sent a message of congratulations to *QE2's* captain. |

### 1982

| 11 June | *QE2* welcomed home in Southampton by **HM Queen Elizabeth The Queen Mother** on board Royal Yacht *Britannia*. |
| 2 December | **HM Queen Elizabeth The Queen Mother** lunched on board in Southampton and unveiled a Falklands Plaque. |

### 1986

| 3 May | **HM Queen Elizabeth The Queen Mother** lunched on board in Southampton to mark the 50th anniversary of *Queen Mary's* maiden voyage in 1936. |

### 1987

| 29 April | **HRH The Princess of Wales** attended a children's party on board, to mark the ship's successful re-engining. |

### 1988

| 14 December | **HM Queen Elizabeth The Queen Mother** lunched on board to celebrate the 50th anniversary of her launching *Queen Elizabeth* in 1938. |

### 1990

| 27 July | Royal review of Cunard and Royal Navy ships at Spithead by **HM The Queen** and **HRH The Duke of Edinburgh** on board Royal Yacht *Britannia*. The Queen and Duke of Edinburgh transferred to *QE2* by Royal Barge. |

### 1991

| 15 June | **HRH The Duke of Edinburgh** and **HRH Prince Edward** attended a Royal Ball on board in Southampton. |

### 1993

| 12 June | **HRH Prince Edward** lunched on board to celebrate the 40th anniversary of the Queen's accession. |

| 5 August | HM The Queen and HRH Prince Andrew visited Southampton to join the 175th anniversary of the British Sailor's Society. After the service Her Majesty boarded the Royal Yacht *Britannia* and, accompanied by *HMS York* and *Patricia*, she reviewed various units of the Merchant Fleet, including *QE2*. |

**1994**

| 4 June | HM The Queen and HRH The Duke of Edinburgh reviewed *QE2* from the Royal Yacht *Britannia* as part of the 50th Anniversary of D-Day Commemorations. |

Also on board *Britannia* for the review:

**HM The Queen Mother**
**HRH Princess Margaret**
**HM Princess Anne**
President (and Mrs) Bill Clinton
Prime Minister John Major
The King of Norway
Prince Bernard of the Netherlands
The Presidents of Poland, the Czech Republic and Slovakia
The Prime Ministers of Canada, Australia and New Zealand

| 17 December | HRH Prince Andrew was guest of honour at lunch on board in Southampton to mark *QE2's* return to service after her major refit. |

**1995**

| 17 July | HRH Princess Anne lunched on board in Edinburgh prior to *QE2* leading the Tall Ships out of the Firth of Forth. |

**1996**

| 28 September | HRH Prince Edward attended a Royal Ball on board in Southampton. |

**2004**

| 1 May | On the day that *QE2* handed over flagship status to *Queen Mary 2*, Buckingham Palace sent the following message: |

'Her Majesty and The Duke of Edinburgh remember with pleasure their many visits to the ship and send their best wishes to you for a memorable event.'

**2005**

| 28 July | HM The Queen and HRH The Duke of Edinburgh reviewed *QE2* from *HMS Endurance* as part of the Trafalgar 200 Celebrations off Spithead. |

# *Appendix 5*

## *QE2* WORLD CRUISES AND EXTENDED VOYAGES
### (1975–2007)

| YEAR | WORLD or EXTENDED | EMBARK – DISEMBARK | No OF DAYS | No OF PORTS | VIA |
|---|---|---|---|---|---|
| 1975 | World | SOU – SOU | 92 | 28 | Cape |
| 1976 | Extended | NYC – NYC | 39 | 14 | |
| 1977 | World | NYC – NYC | 81 | 21 | Cape |
| 1978 | Extended | NYC – NYC | 90 | 28 | |
| 1979 | World | NYC – NYC | 80 | 24 | Cape |
| 1980 | World | NYC – NYC | 80 | 27 | Suez |
| 1981 | World | NYC – NYC | 80 | 24 | Suez |
| 1982 | World | NYC – NYC | 80 | 27 | Cape |
| 1983 | Extended | NYC – NYC | 89 | 28 | |
| 1984 | World | NYC – NYC | 88 | 28 | Suez |
| 1985 | World | NYC – NYC | 95 | 34 | Cape |
| 1986 | World | NYC – NYC | 95 | 32 | Cape |
| 1987 | | | | | |
| 1988 | Extended | NYC – NYC | 107 | 38 | |
| 1989 | Extended | NYC – YOK | 74 | 27 | |
| 1990 | Extended | SOU – HON | 27 | 12 | |
| 1991 | World | NYC – NYC | 94 | 33 | Cape |
| 1992 | World | NYC – NYC | 100 | 38 | Suez |
| 1993 | 3 x Extended | NYC – NYC | 128 | 46 | |
| 1994 | World | NYC – NYC | 100 | 30 | Cape |
| 1995 | World | NYC – NYC | 102 | 38 | Suez |
| 1996 | World | NYC – NYC | 95 | 32 | Cape |
| 1997 | World | NYC – NYC | 103 | 37 | Suez |
| 1998 | World | NYC – NYC | 104 | 37 | Cape |
| 1999 | World | NYC – NYC | 104 | 38 | Suez |
| 2000 | World | NYC – NYC | 104 | 37 | Cape |
| 2001 | World | NYC – NYC | 104 | 33 | Suez |
| 2002 | World | NYC – NYC | 106 | 34 | Cape |
| 2003 | World | NYC – NYC | 107 | 36 | Cape |
| 2004 | World | NYC – NYC | 110 | 37 | Cape |
| 2005 | World | NYC – NYC | 102 | 39 | Suez |
| 2006 | World | SOU – SOU | 109 | 42 | Suez |
| 2007 | World | SOU – SOU | 108 | 40 | Cape |

*QE2* has undertaken more World Cruises and Extended Voyages than any other Cunarder.

**NOTES**

- **An Extended Voyage** is classed as a circle Pacific or circle South America cruise.

- **SOU (Southampton)**
  **NYC (New York)**
  **YOK (Yokohama)**
  **HON (Honolulu)**

- *QE2* **was being re-engined in 1987**; the Cunarders *Sagafjord* and *Vistafjord* stood in for her.

**STATISTICS (1975 – 2007)**

| Steamship | **12 voyages** |
| | 9 World Cruises (6 via Cape and 3 via Suez) |
| | 3 Extended |

| Motorship | **20 voyages** |
| | 16 World Cruises (9 via Cape and 7 via Suez) |
| | 4 Extended |

| TOTALS | 25 World Cruises (15 via Cape and 10 via Suez) |
| | 7 Extended |

# *Bibliography*

Arnott, Captain Robert H, *Captain of the Queen,* 1982

Hutchings, David, QE2 - *A Ship for All Seasons,* 2002

Johnston, Ian, *Ships for a Nation,* 2000

Maxtone-Graham, John, *Liners to the Sun,* 2000

Potter, Neil, and Frost, Jack, *The* Queen Elizabeth 2 - *The Authorised Story,* 1969

Queen Elizabeth 2 - *The Story of a Conversion,* Lloyd Werft, 1987

Smallpeice, Sir Basil, *Of Comets and Queens,* 1980

Thatcher, Carol, QE2 - *A Voyage of Discovery,* 1999

*The Sea,* Granta, 1998

Warwick, Captain Ronald W, QE2 - *Cunard's Flagship,* 1999

## Other sources

- Various national newspapers and the *Southern Daily Echo*
- The files of Dan Wallace, John Whitworth, Tom Kameen and Sir Basil Smallpeice
- Correspondence from Lord Aberconway and John Rannie to Cunard during the build
- Cunard publicity

## Reports

- Marine Accident Investigation Branch (MAIB) report of the investigation into the grounding of passenger vessel *Queen Elizabeth 2* on 7 August 1992 (published July 1993)
- United States Coastguard report into grounding (published May 1993)
- MAIB report of the investigation into flooding of aft engine room of passenger cruise ship *Queen Elizabeth 2,* 21/22 May 2002 (published March 2003)
- MAIB report on the investigation of the escape of steam and hot water on board *Queen Elizabeth 2* in the mid Atlantic resulting in one fatality, 23 June 2002 (published July 2003)

# Index

Page numbers in italics refer
to picture captions.

A&P shipyard 217, 219
Abbotsinch Airport 71
Aberconway, Lady 59
Aberconway, Lord 40, 60, 68, 71, 78, 101-2
Adeane, Sir Michael 77
Adler, Larry 20, 172
Adriaans, Pieter 226
*Akademik Keldysh* 227
*Alacrity*, HMS 196
*Alsatia* 63
Andrew, Prince 210, 211
Anne, Pricess 76-77, 214
*Antelope*, HMS 161
*Antilles* 117
*Antrim, HMS* 160
*Aquitania* 18, *19*, 22
Architectural Association 52
*Ardent, HMS* 160, 196
Arison, Micky 223, *224*
Arnott, Captain 79, 80, 124, 127, 128, *154*, 155, 170, 224
Associated Electrical Industries 55
Astaire, Fred *23*
*Atlantic Causeway* 160
*Atlantic Conveyor* 193, 196
Attenborough, Lord 222

Bainbridge, Dame Beryl 144
Bannenberg, John *49*, 52, 70
Barker, Captain 196
Basie, Count 113
Bates, Captain 240, 241, 242, 243
Bates, Colonel Denis 28
Bates, Philip 49
Bates, Sir Percy 16, 19, 28, 31
Bedford, Duke and Duchess of 143
Beloe, Elizabeth 53, *53*

*Benavon* 186
Benn, Tony 99, 100, 101, *101*, 102
Bennell, Captain 186
Benson, Charles 139
Benson, Sir Henry 67
*Berengaria* 18
Beswick, Lord 99
Bisset, Commodore Sir James 21
*Bittersweet* 198
Black, Misha 53
Blair, Cherie 222
Blohm & Voss 172, 194, 200, 207, 208
Blue Ensign *24*
Blue Riband 16, 21, 66
Board of Trade 42, 66-67, 69, 82, 92, 93, 105, 115
Bolton, Captain 192
Boothby, Lord 153
Bowie, David 113, *145*
*Britannia* 14, 15, *25*, 59, 192, 238
*Britannia* Grill 208
*Britannia* Restaurant 111, 112, 133, 151
*Britannia*, Royal Yacht 78, 113, 161, *162*, 193, *194*, 206
British & North American Royal Mail Steam Packet Co. 13, *15*
British Admiralty 14, 15, 16
British Ship Research Association 42, 43, 54, 64
Broackes, Nigel 122, 204
*Broadsword, HMS* 193
Brocklebank, Lady 52, 60
Brocklebank, Sir John 31, *31*, 34, 37, 40, 60
Buerk, Michael 183
bulbous bow *42, 43, 55*, 148
*Burra* 226
Burton-Hall, Captain 214, 224
Buzas, Stefan 53, *53*

Cammell Laird & Co. 33, 39
*Campania* 16
*Canberra* 157, 160, 161, *161*, 206
*Cap Trafalgar* 16
Cape Horn 22
*Carinthia* 63
*Carmania* 16, 51
Carnival Corporation 222, 223, 224
*Caronia* 31, 210, 224, 226, 228, 232
*Caronia* Restaurant 208, *209*, 225
*Carpathia* 12, *17*, 18, 244
Cary, Sir Michael 144
Chamberlain, Neville 20, 24
Chandos Committee 30
Chandos, Lord 30
Children's Room 111
*China 15*, 16
*Chubut* 160
Churchill, Sir Winston 12, 22, 76
Clements, Alan 204
Clinton, President 206
Club Lido 163, 169, 194
Clyde *8-9*, 19, 20, 21, 24, 40, 41, 63, 68, *70*, 71, 72, 79, 80, *81*, 87, 88, 90, 92, 95, 244
Coffee Shop 111, 133
Collins Line 17
*Columbia* Restaurant 111, 124, 133, 158, *187*, 194, 195, 205
Computer, Ferranti Argus 64
Concorde 150, 152, 170, 171, 182, 193, 236
Conover, Pamela 232, 236
*Cordella* 161
Coronation Street 216
Council of Industrial Design 49, 113
*Coventry, HMS* 161, 196
Craig Commodore 196
Craig, Robert 73

Crimean War 12, 16-17
Crosby/Fletcher/Forbes 53
Cunard Eagle Airways 31, *32*, 33
Cunard Line
finances of 22, 24, 33, 68
history of 12, *13*, 20
management decisions 23, 28, 30, 62, 98-99, 103
Cunard Steam-ship Co. *15*
Cunard, Samuel 12-14, *12*, 16, 192, 238
Cunninghame Graham, Admiral 71
Curtiss, Air Marshal 196

*Daily Mirror* 76
Daniels, Paul 214
Day, Frances 21
de Burgh, Chris 206
de Klerk, President 194
Dean, Milvina 220
Deedes, Lord 222
Depression 20, 24
Design Centre, London 49
Dickens, Charles 15
Dickson, Charles 126, 130
Dietrich, Marlene *23*
Dingemans, Rear Admiral 196
Dole, Elizabeth 222
Donaldson, Arthur 77
Double Room 111, 112, 133, *133*, 158, 175
Duffy, John *193*
*Dumbarton Castle* 160, 161
Dunlop, Commodore 196
Dunn, Geoffrey 53

EC Payter & Co. 132
Economist Intelligence Unit 45
Edinburgh, Duke of 63, *70*, 71, 78, 108, 113, 193, 195, 206, 236, 240
Edward, Prince 195, *195*, 204-5, *205*, 217

Elizabeth, HM The Queen Mother 21, 161, 164-5, 172-3, 186-7, *187*, 206, 210, 227, 232

Elizabeth II, Queen 22, 63, *70*, *74-75*, 77, 78, 108, *109*, 113, 193, *193*, 206, 210-11, 236, 240

Elizabeth, Princess 21, 210-11

emigration 17

*Endurance, HMS* 196

*Evening Press* 50

Fahye Design 194

Fairfield Shipbuilding 33, 39, 68

Falklands War 9, 12, 31, 157-61, 163, 172, 196, 232

*Farnella* 161

FBI 134

Ferranti Argus computer 64

Fieldhouse, Admiral 161

Fields, Gracie 113

film stars 22, *23*, 26

First World War 12, 18

Fleet Air Arm 71, *78*, *109*, 114

Forbes, Malcolm 183

*Fort Austin* 196

Foster Wheeler boilers 55

*France* 26, 110, 140, 143, 170

*Franconia* 52

Freund, Professor 134

Frost, Sir David 222, *223*

funnel design *44*, 46-48, *82*, 163, 166, 178

Gadaffi, President 137

Gardner, John 45-48, *46*, 49, 52, 53

Gardner, Sir George 100

Geddes Report 68

Geddes, Reay 68

George V, King 19, 20, 24

George VI, King 21

*George Washington, USS* 206

Gingold, Hermione 170

GIs 21, 22, 26

Gish, Lillian 143

Gloag, John 52

Gomez, Luis 122

Grace, Princess 127

Grand Lounge 175, 182, 193, 195, 243

Grant, Cary *23*

Greenpeace 222, *222*

Greig, R 139

grey catbird 223

*Grey Rover* 159

Grill Room 112, 116, 133

*Guam, USS* 206

Gulf War 195

Gurkha Rifles 159

Hadley, Captain 197

Hall, Henry 21, 76

Harland & Wolff 33, 39, 172

Harrier aircraft 182, 193, 236

Harris, Keith 182

Harrods 170, *170*

Hasell, Captain 220, 224

Haughey, Charles 192

Hawke, Bob 185

Heath, Captain 235, *235*, 236

Heaton, Tony 53, *53*

Hehir, Captain 122, 124, 142, 146, *146*, 224

Hepper, Anthony 82, 85, 93, 94, 100

Hercules aircraft 128-29, *129*

Heritage, Robert 112

Hicks, David 52, 53, *53*

*Highlander* 183

Hitler, Adolf 21

Hobhouse, John 30

Hockridge, Edmund 214

Hollywood 26

HongKong Land 204

Hope, Bob 206

House of Commons 28, 30, 99

House of Lords 99

Hunt, Sir Rex 232

Hurricane Gloria 171

Hurricane Katrina 243

Hurricane Luis 214-16, *217*, 219

Hutcheson, Captain 157

*Imperator* 18

Inchbald, Michael 52, 112

Inchgreen dry-dock 87

Ingham, Sir Bernard 235

*Intrepid, HMS* 196

IRA 9

Irvine, Alan 53

Jackson, Captain 138, *139*, 140, 158, 160, 161, 164, 196, 224, 232

James, Baroness (PD) 189

Jay, Douglas 68

*Jeremiah O'Brien* 206

John Brown & Co.

building of *QE2* 28, 33, 39, 44, 54-55, 59, 63, 68

building of *Queen Mary* 19, 24-25

Cunard contract 62

John Brown Engineering 70, 101, 122, 151, 166, 192

John McNeece Ltd 207, 208

Jones, Captain 19

*Journal of Commerce* 152

Juke Box 111, 133

*Junella* 161

Kameen Tom 40, 41, *41*, 42, 49, 53, 89

*Keeping Up Appearances* 205

Kelly, George 127

Kennedy, Alan 180, 182-83

Kennedy, Ludovic 143

*Kennedy, USS* 227

Kinsale 16

Knott, John 159

Koch, Ed 183

*Koshima* 226-27

Kvaerner 217, 218, 222

*Laconia* 18

*Lancastria* 63

Law, Captain 51, 127, *127*, 128

Leach, Admiral 161

Leach, Frank 100

*Leeds Castle, HMS* 161

Lennon, Dennis *48*, 52-53, 114, 163

Lever, Harold 67

Libyan government 9

Lido 211, 212, 220

Lindbergh, Charles 18, 22

Lindisi, Joseph 131

Lindley, Sir Arnold 98, 100, 102, 103, 104

Lindsay, Mayor John 110

Lips manufacturers 184, 186

Lloyd Werft shipyard 168, 171, 172, 180, 185, 194, 222, 225, 227, 243

Lloyds 38, 42, 44, 223

London Gallery 111, 133

Lookout *52*, 111, 133

*Lord Nelson* 214

LRAD 243

*Lusitania* 16, 18, 26

Lynn, Dame Vera 206

Lyon, Kenneth 146

Machel, Graca *221*, 222

Magrodome 163, 169, 192, 208, 209

Major, John 195, 206

*Manchester, HMS* 227

Mancroft, Lord 49, 108, 114, 122

Mandela, Nelson 9, *221*, 222

'Man Overboard' 116, 228, 240

Margaret, Princess 21, 49, *74-75*, 76-77, 116

Marples, Ernest 32, 37

Marr, Commodore 220

Mary, Queen 20, 24, 25

Matthews, Victor 123, 126, 138, 150, 159, 161, 163, 164
Mature, Victor *23*
*Mauretania* 18, *18*, 26, 33, 244
*Mauretania* Restaurant 175, 183, 194, 195, 208, 218
Maxtone-Graham, John 163
McGregor, Andrew 104
McKinsey & Co. 120, 150
McLaren, Michael 71
McNaught, Captain 238
MET Studio 207, 209, 218
Ministry of Defence 126, 134, 144, 229
Ministry of Labour 78
Ministry of Technology 99
Ministry of Transport 29, 37
*Modern Transport* 51
Molyneux, Malcolm 153
Monro, Jean 52
Moore, Major General 160, 196
Moorehead, Nancy 114
Mountbatten, Lord 113, 144
Muppets 235

National Physical Laboratory 42, 43, 46
National Research Devt Corp. 64
National Union of Seamen 134, 142, 196
Nemon, Oscar 108
*Newsweek* 153
Nightingale, Florence 16
Nimrod aircraft 128-29, *128*, 160, 228, 236
*Norland* 161, *161*
*Northella* 161
*Norway* 170, 229

*Oceanic* 17
*Of Comets and Queens* 67, 108

Olsen, John 206, 210, 212, 213
*Olympic* 51
*Oriana* 33, 213
Orient Lines 33
Orsini, Jean 122

Pametrada turbines 43, 95, 101-2
Panama Canal *38*, 39, 44, 54, 143, *152*, 154, *155*, 192
Parker, George *70*, 71, 84
Patton, Richard 131
Pattrick, Jo 53
Pearson, Mervyn *27*
Peck, Gregory *23*
Perez, George 123
*Pict* 161
Piercy, Lord 37
pilfering 79-80, 90
Pimentel, Larry 224
Pinching, Evelyn 52
Pinkney, Anthony 67
Pitt, Captain 196
Pollock, Admiral 127
Portet, Captain 182, 184
Prescott, John 195, 236
Prince of Wales 86-87, *86*, 206
Princess Grill 174, 194, 208
Princess of Wales 180-1, *180*, 206, 220
*Private Eye* 170
Project Lifestyle 206-9
Proops, Marjorie 144

*Q3* 26, 28, *28*, 36, 37, 42, 43, 50
*Q4* 28, 37, *37*, 38, 39, 40, 41, 42, 43, *43*, 44, 46, 48, 49, 50-51, 54-55, 58-59, 63
*Q4* Room 112, 158, 163
*Q5* 189
*QE2*
  breakdowns 93, 95, *98*, 120, 137-38, 159, 162, 166, 167, 180, 183, 185, 196, 230-31, 235-36, 238-39

building 8, 59, *59*, *61*, *65*, *66*
crew 134, 142, 182, 189, 195, 218, 228, 234, 239-40, 241
fitting and refitting 79, 80-82, *84*, 132-33 132, 133, 151, *151*, 157, 163, 171-9, 194, *199*, 200, 204, 206-9, 217, 218, 220, 225, 229, 239 243
launching *8-9*, 22, 63, 70-73, *70-75*
plots and crimes 122, 123, 126-31, 137, 144, 147, 239, 240
rescues 116, 117, 140-41, 193-94, 226
storms and accidents 114, 124-25, *125*, 142, 146, 153, 164, 171, 186, 197-99, 21, 205, 214-16, 217, *217*, 219, 223, 226, 234, 241, 242
trials 88, *89*, 90, 91, 92-93, *93*, 94-95
*QM2* 12, 63, 223, 228, 232, 235, 236, 238, *238*, 240, 243, *244*, *246-47*
*Queen Elizabeth* 8, 12, 21, 22, 24, 26, 28, *29*, 33-34, 36, 41, 45, 59, 71, 83, 115, 186, 187, 210, 220, 227, 228, 236
*Queen Mary* 8, 12, 16, 18, 19-25, *20*, *21*, *23-25*, 26, 28, 33-34, *35*, 36, 37, 41, 45, 52, 59, 71, 82, 115, 152, 172, 228, 232, 236, 244
Queen's Grill *132*, 133, 158, 163, 175, 183, 194, 220, 229
Queen's Room 53, 87, 110, 112, *113*, 155, 165, 175, 193, 195 205, 211, 225, 243
Queensberry, Lord 53

Rannie, John 59, 60, 74-75, 82, 84, 85, 86, 94, *94*, 185
Rantzen, Esther 174

Red Arrows 171, 206
Redgrave, Lynn 113
Reynolds, Albert 206
RIBA 52
*Richard Robbins* 183
Ridley, Captain 137, 153, *153*, 183, 224
Rippon, Angela 171
Roberts, Captain 96
Robertson, Purcell 128
Roosevelt, President 22
Rostron, Captain 18, *18*
Royal Mail 14
*Royal Viking Sun* 216
Rudnik, Oscar 134

Sadat, President *136*, 137
*Sagafjord* *168*, 171, 216
Salt, Rear Admiral 196
SAS/SBS 129, 136, 229
Savile, Sir Jimmy 113, 144, *145*
*Saxonia* 161
*Schamonchi* 199
Schreiber, Gaby *48*, 52
Scotland Yard 126
Scots Guards 159
*Scythia* 241
Sea King helicopters 158, *160*, 193, 214
*Sea Princess* 206
*Seawise University* 121
Second World War 12, 26, 165
Seligman, Geoffrey 67
Sellers, Peter 113, *145*
Senior, Ronald 77
*Servia* 17
SG Warburg 67
Sharkey, Gerry 123
Shearer, Moira 143
*Sheffield, HMS* 196
Shelvey, Barbara 134
Shipbuilding Credit Advisory Board 37
shipbuilding industry 33
*Sir Galahad* 196, 234

*Sir Percival* 196

Smallpeice, Sir Basil 49, 51, 60, 67, 71, 76-77, 86, *86*, 93, 94, *94*, 100, 101-2, 108, 110, 113, 114, 115, 144

Smith, Captain 188

Smith, Sir Cyril 169

Snowdon, Lord 113-14, 116

SNP 77

*Spirit of Newport* 199

Spotwood, Air Chief Marshal 127

Stanley, Keith 224

Starks, John 40, 42, 72, 95

Starr, Ringo 113, *145*

Steiners of London 200-1

*Stephanie* 140

Stewart, Rod 113, *145*

Stokowski, Leopold 127

strikes 64, 78, 82-83, 84-85, 168, 174

Suez Canal 154, 195, 243

suites 151, 176, 204, 218, 225, 229, 240

*Sunday Times* of Ceylon 148

Sutherland, Dame Joan 185

Swan Hunter & Wigham Richardson 33

*Syllogic* 226

*Sylvania* 54

Tabb, Haslehurst 53

Tables of the World 151, 158, 163, 175

Taylor, Elizabeth *23*

TBT protest 222, *222*

Thatcher, Margaret 196, 232, 234, *234*

*The Times* 14, 52

Theatre 111, 113, 133, 158, 229

Thew Engineering 184

Thomas, Leslie 142

Thompson, Norman 126

*Titanic* 12, 18, 220, 227

Tobin, Commodore 196

Tonseth, Erik 223

Trafalgar House Investments 122, 132, 150, 180. 185, 186, 189, 195, 204, 212, 217

*Typhoon* 161

*U20* 16

U-boats 16, 21

Upper Clyde Shipbuilders 70, 82, 94, 95, 98, 100, 101, 102, 103, 104-5

*United States* 28, 44, 66

United States Lines 28

US Coast Guard 198-99, 200, 212, 227

Venzal, Nelson 234

Vickers/Swan Hunter consortium 34, 36, 37, 38

Vickers-Armstrong 33

*Viking Queen* 199

Villasis, Edgar 234

*Vistafjord* 193, 206, 224

Vosper-Thorneycroft 95, 132, 140, 144, 151, 184

Wagner, Robert 124

Wallace, Dan 40, *41*, 42, 45, 49, 51, 53, 60, 78-79, 80-82, 84-85, 86, 88, 89, 99, 100

Warwick, Captain Ronald 63, 193, 194, 214, 215, 216, 224, 227, 229, *231*, 235, 238

Warwick, Captain William 49, 63, *63*, 77, 86, *86*, 104, 113, 114, *114*, 115, 116, 193, 224

Weedon, Bert 126

Welsh Guards 159

*West Gamma* 194

Weston, Simon 234

Whicker, Alan 143, 165

White Star Line 17, 20

Whitworth, John 41, 84, 87, 89, 90, 99, 100

Wilcox, Desmond 174

Williams, Captain Robert 129-31

Williams, Tennessee *23*

Willing, Archdeacon 220

Wilson, Brigadier 160

Wilson, Harold 60, 64

Wood, JN 30

Wood, Natalie 124

Woodall, Captain 143, 192, 193, 197, 224

Woodroffe, Captain 16

World Trade Center *148*, 229, 232

Wright, Captain 226

Yacht Club 211, 229, 236, 239, 243

*Zosmarr* 116

## *Picture Credits*

Simon & Schuster UK Ltd would like to thank the following for their kind permission to use their photographs.

Cunard Line
Michael Gallagher
Glyn Genin
Greenpeace, p.222
*The Herald*, Glasgow, pp.74–75
www.istockphoto.com, pp. 35, 38, 128, 129
Anders Johannessen
Steve Matthews, Waterside Photographic
National Union of Seamen (National Union of Rail, Maritime and Transport Workers), p.134
Albert Novelli
Rex Features, pp. 101, 136, 137, 145 (all)
University of Liverpool, *Architectural Review* Archives
University of Liverpool, Cunard Archives

**Thanks also to**
David L Williams for permission to use the image he commissioned of *Q3* by Mervyn Pearson, p.27.
The University of Liverpool.